*A Publication of the Horace Mann–Lincoln Institute
of School Experimentation
Teachers College, Columbia University*

LEARNING
TO WORK
IN GROUPS

A Program Guide for Educational Leaders

BY

MATTHEW B. MILES

ASSOCIATE PROFESSOR OF EDUCATION
TEACHERS COLLEGE, COLUMBIA UNIVERSITY

TEACHERS COLLEGE PRESS

TEACHERS COLLEGE, COLUMBIA UNIVERSITY

NEW YORK

Eighth Printing 1971

FOREWORD

In the midst of every educational endeavor is the problem of making theory and practice mutually consistent. Anyone who dares to attempt influencing the actual work of others must be prepared to risk failure— that is, to risk being accused of being practical at the expense of theoretical consistency, or theoretically consistent at the expense of realistically conceived practice.

In *Learning to Work in Groups,* Mr. Miles has taken the risk. His attempt is to talk directly to the person who would act, but to talk in such a way as to deepen the theory out of which the talk arises. In so doing, he confronts the theory-practice problem directly, courageously, and (I think) successfully.

Like the other publications of the Horace Mann-Lincoln Institute of School Experimentation, to which Mr. Miles alludes in his Preface, this book is addressed to the practitioner in the school—and in other institutions—who seeks to improve his own work. The concept "training" infuses the book, but training is something one does to one's self. In this case, the purpose of this self-training is to alter one's point of view toward work in groups. In this, its proper sense, the concept is coterminous with the idea of education itself. Unlike the term "education," however, training is in no sense a euphemism. It speaks directly, even bluntly, of the responsibility that teaching entails; it demands of us that we openly intend to improve our way of working.

This is a serious book, about a serious subject. It will be of value to a great many people: in the school, to the principal, counselor, supervisor, superintendent, teacher; in industry, to the manager, the personnel development man, the industrial relations officer; in social agencies, to the field consultant, the administrative officer, the volunteer leader; in government, to the staff officer, the administrator. In short, what is said here about getting work done in school holds for most of the social enterprises through which the work of the world is done.

ARTHUR W. FOSHAY
Executive Officer, Horace Mann-Lincoln
Institute of School Experimentation

AUTHOR'S PREFACE

Some Convictions

THESE are exciting times. Adam said that, too; what makes the statement more than a commonplace today need not really be documented. Not the least exciting feature of today's America is a vigorous public concern with what is happening in the schools—a concern which evokes genuine inquiry as well as the impassioned advocacy of panaceas. What must we do to be saved? Fortunately, this book is not an answer to that question. What, then?

The school is, after all, a social situation. The child does not learn under a bell jar, but in the midst of a group of other learners. To help the child learn, adults involve themselves in more groups—staff meetings, interviews with parents, committees, school board hearings. The conviction follows that better education depends, in a very central way, on everyone's skills of cooperative effort. It depends on many other things too. This book is only to insist that learning to work in groups is important, and to show that something can be done about it.

Do these convictions leave us with Whyte's "organization man"—the anxious, passive member of a "groupthink" enterprise—and with Riesman's "other-directed" person who takes all his cues for action from outside himself? [1] What about self-reliance, autonomy, creative integrity of the person as a separate, not a corporate being?

One can only assert firmly and unendingly that integrity is a social, as well as a personal matter. Man fulfills himself in the process of confronting

---

[1] As in D. Riesman, *Individualism reconsidered* (Free Press, 1954); and *The lonely crowd* (Yale University Press, 1950). W. H. Whyte has most recently discussed these problems in *The organization man* (Simon and Schuster, 1956).

vii

others—from the family onward. And man in today's world does most of his work with others in group situations. The great challenge of today is that we discover more social arrangements in which joint achievement and personal integrity are not opposed, but mutually contributory. The negative aspects of "groupthink"—conformity, manipulation, passivity, mediocrity—are real. But we must cope with them, rather than attempt a retreat to a mythical groupless existence. More of us must know more about groups—and be able to act intelligently on our knowledge—if our associations with others are to cherish and deepen individual differences rather than suffocate them, are to achieve great things instead of dissolving in twaddle.

All this is nowhere truer than in our schools, and this book is written in the belief that teaching school personnel more about the skills of working together is a high-priority need. By now, American educators are well past the uncritical golden days when every educational problem was thought to be rapidly soluble by means of "the group process," and buzz groups abounded. It is not widely realized, however, how far the early evangelistic, cultist, technique-centered aspects of "group dynamics" have been replaced by a sober and steadily growing concern with the nature and functioning of small groups. Social scientists and practitioners from all fields are helping to make training in increased group effectiveness more and more a part of the American scene. The methods and procedures discussed in this book are being used extensively today in industrial executive development and supervisory training programs, in religious education, in the training of youth leaders, in the in-service education of professional staff in large voluntary health organizations, in crew performance improvement in the armed services, in the preparation of community workers, and in the preparation of medical and nursing personnel.

This book is an attempt to bring together what is now known about the practical problems of helping people learn better group behavior, and to apply this knowledge to the special and important case of American public education.

Acknowledgments

At the Horace Mann–Lincoln Institute of School Experimentation, Teachers College, staff members have been concerned for some years with the problem to which this book is addressed. We experimented with many different types of group learning experiences with local school people, and wrote about our adventures.[2] Some of us have also been associated with the intensive three-week summer sessions at the National Training Laboratory in Group Development at Bethel, Maine. For my part, the Bethel experience was a graphic demonstration of how the method of science can infuse and guide the exciting process of learning better group behavior. My work there has given great impetus to the production of this book.

The book began six years ago at a Horace Mann–Lincoln Institute staff conference. Staff members who wrote and/or criticized some early portions of the book (which were based on transcripts from the conference) included Stephen M. Corey (then Executive Officer of the Institute), Dale C. Draper, Arthur W. Foshay, Paul M. Halverson, Richard E. Lawrence, A. Harry Passow, and myself.

The first version of the manuscript was set aside for three years; it seemed more and more clear as Institute research and training experiences accumulated that major additions and changes were in order. I am deeply grateful for the encouragement and substantive help of my friends, Stephen M. Corey and A. Harry Passow; the ritual of prefaces leaves their help only inadequately acknowledged.

The Horace Mann–Lincoln Institute in Teachers College provides a unique and unusually challenging work environment. Arthur W. Foshay as present Executive Officer has steadily provided warm support and intellectual stimulation of a high order.

[2] S. M. Corey and P. M. Halverson, "The educational leader's ideas about his interpersonal relations," *Bulletin, National Association of Secondary School Principals*, 36:57–63, 1952.

S. M. Corey, P. M. Halverson, and E. Lowe, *Teachers prepare for discussion group leadership* (Teachers College Bureau of Publications, 1953).

R. C. Doll, A. H. Passow, and S. M. Corey, *Organizing for curriculum improvement* (Teachers College Bureau of Publications, 1953).

G. N. Mackenzie, S. M. Corey, and associates, *Instructional leadership* (Teachers College Bureau of Publications, 1954).

T. C. Clark and M. B. Miles, "Human relations training for school administrators," *Journal of Social Issues,* 10, 2:25–39, 1954.

A. H. Passow, M. B. Miles, S. M. Corey, and D. C. Draper, *Training curriculum leaders for cooperative research* (Teachers College Bureau of Publications, 1955).

M. B. Miles and A. H. Passow, "Training in the skills needed for in-service education programs," in *Fifty-sixth Yearbook,* National Society for the Study of Education (University of Chicago Press, 1957), pp. 339–67.

M. B. Miles and S. M. Corey, "The first cooperative curriculum research institute," in *Research for Curriculum Improvement,* 1957 Yearbook, Association for Supervision and Curriculum Development (The Association, 1957), Appendix B, pp. 305–48.

M. B. Miles, "The Leadership Training Project," in *Progress Report,* Horace Mann–Lincoln Institute of School Experimentation, Teachers College, Columbia University, 1958.

The entire book has been considerably revised and enriched because of the comments of many people. Several Institute and College staff members read and criticized the manuscript. These included Max R. Brunstetter, Hamden L. Forkner, Jr., Miriam L. Goldberg, Francine Lang, Harold J. McNally, Franklin W. Neff, Abraham Shumsky, and Goodwin Watson.

Many public school personnel reviewed the manuscript in detail, as did persons in the field of human relations training. For their comments, I am indebted to Rowannetta S. Allen (and colleagues), Prudence L. Bostwick, George W. Brown, Paul C. Buchanan, John R. Cochran, Robert B. Crook, Elaine Davidson, Elizabeth R. Dilks, Ronald C. Doll, Nicholas G. Econopouly, Jean D. Grambs, Eric Groezinger, Anne S. Hoppock, Hulda F. Knowles, Malcolm S. Knowles, Robert E. Krebs, George K. Levinger, Robert A. Luke, Cecil Martindale, Richard J. McDonald, Esther Milnes, Glyn A. Morris, Donald Nylen, George M. Sharp, Robert W. Scott, Irving R. Weschler, Edith G. Wilson, and Norman H. Wilson.

Human relations training in the last decade has been a fascinating process of social invention. Without the dedication and creativity of dozens of different persons—in public schools, in the National Training Laboratories, and elsewhere—the book would simply not have been possible. I cannot credit the anonymous inventors of all the procedures described in this book, but I must acknowledge my indebtedness—personal, professional, and intellectual—to Kenneth D. Benne, Warren G. Bennis, Leland P. Bradford, Irving Knickerbocker, and Herbert A. Thelen.

During the various stages of preparation of the book, Yvonne J. Jackson, Ruth E. Teitelbaum, and John Padula were especially helpful in turning interminable piles of marked-up copy into presentable manuscript.

Betty Miles' detailed editorial comments on the last two versions of the manuscript were made with patience and great skill. She supplied more day-to-day assistance than I had any right to expect.

M.B.M.

January, 1959

CONTENTS

LEARNING TO WORK
IN GROUPS

A Program Guide for Educational Leaders

CHAPTER I

THE NATURE OF THIS BOOK

We are well into the second decade of intensive scientific study of small group behavior. Most school people appear to believe that getting things done through groups—of children, teachers, parents, administrators, supervisors—is not just a good idea but a natural, essential part of the educational enterprise. Yet group work, instead of being a productive and psychologically satisfying experience, is often unrewarding, puzzling, and frustrating. Why should this be?

The Problem

There is considerable evidence that the problem is one of *skill,* broadly conceived; we really do not know how to work well with others. For most adults of today, the abilities required to work effectively as a leader or member of a cooperative group do not come naturally, perhaps because our traditional educational system has generally ignored or discouraged shared effort. Many adults have a pessimistic picture of what can be done through groups. ("A camel is an animal that looks as though it were put together by a committee." "Committees keep minutes and waste hours.") And in spite of much experimentation in the classroom, many teachers are puzzled about how to make sure that group work really aids learning.

In short, we are faced with the need for much re-education. Adults working with the schools need help with their understandings of and skills in group work if their shared efforts—in curriculum committees, staff meetings, parent-teacher conferences, in-service groups, and most especially in the classroom—are to accomplish desired goals in healthy ways. This is not to suggest that school people are incompetent at working together, or that everything can or should be done through group effort. It is simply to say that time spent on the improvement of group processes in schools is a good investment. What would happen in any school system, for example, if the effectiveness of the groups in it—committees, classes, staffs, school boards—were increased by even 25 per cent?

Better group behavior can be learned. It must be.

Audience

This book describes some practical steps for improving the quality of group work in schools. It was written for the interested person who is in a position to help others do a better job in groups. Such help requires, in the author's experience, a reasonably systematic program rather than hit-or-miss attempts. So the book is aimed at persons who are in a position to start and carry out training programs designed to improve group processes in schools.[1] These persons are principals, classroom teachers, curriculum directors, supervisors, superintendents, guidance counselors, chairmen of study groups, state department consultants, workshop directors, and teachers in colleges and universities.

Definitions

What is "training"? To many people the word has connotations of rote or mechanical learning, but it is used here to mean a systematically-planned approach to learning better group behavior, with certain important features. The conception of training used in this book is described in detail in Chapter III.

A "program" is a planned combination of training sessions taking place over a period of time. The types of possible programs for improving group processes may range widely: a series of afternoon meetings on "Improving Committee Work"; a year-long study group on leadership

---

[1] As indicated in the Preface, the ideas and procedures described here are currently being used in many fields outside public education. Although the examples in the book are taken from school settings, persons from other areas will have little difficulty in using in their own training programs, the approaches suggested.

methods; a one-day fall teachers' institute before the beginning of school; the regular use of "process observers" in staff meetings; a series of orientation sessions for prospective officers of classes or student organizations; a university extension course in group dynamics; a week-end workshop for committee chairmen in a school study council; a biweekly professional meeting of central office staff where problems of group work are analyzed; regular evaluative discussions with an eighth grade core class of how their committee work went and how it might be improved; an adult education class which serves as a "leadership clinic"; community film forums dealing with problems of effective group work.

By "group" is meant several persons working in a face-to-face setting on a task that requires their cooperation. For example: a study group dealing with reading retardation; a subcommittee of a school staff looking at merit rating; a kindergarten class and teacher planning a trip to the airport; a central curriculum council deciding on textbook recommendations; a PTA group analyzing the recreation opportunities in the community; a committee in a social studies class reporting on what they found about primary elections; a school board plowing through its agenda; a teachers' association meeting on a new salary schedule; an interested group of teachers doing action research on the teaching of spelling.

Finally, what are "group processes"? The idea of process is an abstract one; it implies some structure changing over a period of time. All that is meant here are the actual, concrete behaviors in the group—*how* things are happening, rather than *what* is being talked about. Whether the members of a group are discussing merit rating, textbooks, or the difference between jet and piston engines, certain processes—basic to all groups—are taking place.

For example, the goal or task of the group must be agreed on; this is a process which takes time. Members must exchange ideas understandably through the process of communication. A process of systematic problem solving and decision making must take place, or the group discussion will waste time. Group members must develop reasonably harmonious relationships with each other through the processes of getting acquainted and developing mutual support. Group processes are thus going on all the time, *not* just when the leader decides to "use the group process."

The skilled person can help carry on such processes effectively in all the groups of which he is a member or leader. If, through a training program, he has improved his skills in aiding group problem-solving, he can apply these skills whether the other group members are kindergarteners or adults.

This book, then, is designed to help people put on training programs which will improve group processes in schools. This is a broad area of interest, and some narrowing and focusing is in order.

The Limits of the Book

Small-group focus

The book's concern is with the improvement of the quality of work in small face-to-face groups of people working on school problems. The primary interest is in *group*-relevant matters. Relatively less attention is given to matters such as teachers' inner pictures of themselves, the authority conflicts in the school organization, or public relations in the community. This focus stems from the assumption that the small group—including, of course, the class—is the place where most of the work of the school gets done. Personality factors and organizational and community functioning are important, but for purposes of this book these factors are discussed only as they help or hinder what happens in groups.[2]

Task orientation

The book is designed to help people improve the work of task-oriented groups, groups with a job to get done. Informal groups (for example, the faculty lounge bull sessions, family groups, social gatherings, and classroom cliques) are important to the school, but the focus here is on the working group with specific goals or tasks about which the members want to—or are required to—make decisions and take action. (The classroom is a group with a rather general task—causing all members to learn certain things. A class, or subgroups of it, may also focus on more specific tasks, such as planning a trip or practicing spelling words.)

[2] For a discussion of the group as an arena for forces of many different kinds, see M. B. Miles, "Human relations in cooperative research," in *Research for curriculum improvement*, 1957 Yearbook, Association for Supervision and Curriculum Development, Chap. VIII, pp. 187–226.

Process emphasis

The emphasis in this book is primarily on ways of solving problems, processes, procedures—how people behave in groups—rather than on the content of specific problems. Group process skills are in effect the fundamentals with which the book is concerned. As participants in a training program improve their understanding of group processes, they can help the groups with which they work in the classroom and on the job accomplish the tasks they were formed to accomplish. Away from training, group processes are the basic means to work accomplishment and personal satisfaction, but are not usually examined or discussed. During the kind of training program discussed here, however, group processes are in central focus.

This focus on group processes during training aids learning. By analogy, an apprentice carpenter who is having difficulty with nailing needs to take time out to focus on hammering processes, to improve his skill. No one is suggesting that as he builds his next house he must analyze his hammering every minute. But without a process emphasis during his training, and occasional glances at process while he works, his hammering skill will simply not be sufficient to build a house that will stand up.

Program emphasis

The training approach discussed here emphasizes a sequence of training meetings scheduled for a given length of time. This emphasis does not rule out self-development and study activities, but simply indicates the belief that a worthwhile goal requires careful programming if it is to be reached in any satisfactory way. Such programming—whether for a four-day workshop, a series of Thursday evening meetings, or a one-day staff institute—implies thorough assessment of training problems, the production of many different training activities, and thoughtful evaluation. (See Chapters IV and VI for more on this.)

Comprehensive recruitment

The programs focused on in this book are aimed at training *all* persons to help with shared group effort, whether they happen to be appointed leaders or not.[3] Why this approach is taken is discussed further in Chapter II, "Effective Group Behavior."

Multiple training goals

The book does not deal with quick-answer "gimmicks," technique-centered training, or advice on "how to handle people." Rather, factors important for effective group work are discussed. These include attitudes, feelings, sensitivities, understandings, and behaviors. People and groups are complicated; any program which ignores this fact will fail in what is essentially a re-educative task. This "whole-person" approach to learn-ing is elaborated further in Chapter III.

Problem focus

The focus is on immediate problems which people face in trying to work in groups with others, rather than on bodies of systematic theory or organized knowledge as such. Good training is impossible without at-tention to theory; the approach here is only that immediately-perceived *problems* of real people in specific situations should serve as the organizing principle.

[3] The majority of the examples given in the book deal with adult groups, but specific procedures which can be easily and directly used in the classroom and in co-curricular groups are also presented.

The training activities described can be used to aid classroom group work in subject matter fields (for example, social studies, English), or as direct teaching when effective work with others is the subject matter (as in homeroom guidance and some core classes).

Some experience with adolescent training groups suggests that nearly any procedure in the book can be used with high school students, if the teacher is willing to make adaptations to fit the needs of the classroom situation.

For an extremely comprehensive and practical treatment of group work with secondary school and college students, see R. Strang, *Group work in education* (Harper, 1958). Also, G. Morris, *Practical guidance methods for principals and teachers* (Harper, 1952) is recom-mended as a fascinating and concrete account of how one principal carried on informal train-ing with high school students (as well as staff) over a period of several years; see especially pp. 103–25, 27–64.

N. Flanders, with a group of classroom teachers, has written *Teaching with groups* (Burgess, 1954). An experimental viewpoint is taken, like that presented in Chapter II of the present book. And see also L. E. Hock's pamphlet, *Using committees in the classroom* (Rine-hart, 1958), for specific suggestions as well as general principles.

For material on helping younger children work more effectively in groups, see A. Miel, *Cooperative procedures in learning* (Teachers College Bureau of Publications, 1952), espe-cially pp. 302–417; and R. Cunningham, *Understanding group behavior of boys and girls* (Teachers College Bureau of Publications, 1951), pp. 272–92.

Middle-range experiences

The book is aimed between two extremes. The activities described are exciting and valuable for people who have experienced them. They focus primarily on improving the group skills of people in a concrete way.

As such, the learning activities move much beyond a didactic, intellectual, traditional-classroom approach. On the other hand, they also fall far short of the type of therapeutic experience that results in deep insight and drastic personal change. People reading this book will naturally differ in the range of learning experiences they feel capable of guiding, and the author's intent is to respect these differences.

Non-prescriptive approach

The book is not a manual. It does not give step-by-step directions for setting up and running training activities. Rather, many different activities are suggested in outline form. The reader will have to adapt them, thinking of the training group he is working with and of his own skill as a trainer. Given this specific planning, it is likely that the materials will be used effectively rather than applied without purpose or plan.[4] Suggestions for planning are made in Chapters IV, VI, and VII.

All in all, this book does not assume the reader to be a person with years of social-psychological study and experience, and makes no attempt to convert him into such a person. But it is expected that most readers of this book, with practice and self-evaluation, can learn to do a good deal to help people do a better job in groups.

How to Read This Book

This book is not short and simple, because effective training takes considerable care and thought, and because an attempt has been made to bring together a comprehensive set of materials. Too, there is no straightforward logical sequence of explanation that can be used to provide a framework for the entire book.

[4] For an indication of the importance of careful planning, see N. R. F. Maier, A. Solem, and A. Maier, *Supervisory and executive development: a manual for role playing* (Wiley, 1957). The authors walk the prospective trainer and group through twenty role-played cases.

A look at the general structure of the book may help the reader find his way about in it. Chapters II and III, just following this one, deal with basic principles and ideas underlying the remainder of the book. Chapter II explores the nature of effective group behavior, to state clearly what it is that training is aiming for. Chapter III explains what training for better group behavior is like, and describes the process of learning which members of a training group go through. (The Preface, incidentally, contains some more general ideas about the importance of small groups and the need for training.)

The person who wants more concrete examples beyond the short case study given in Chapter III may wish to skip directly to Chapter V. Chapter V contains over a hundred different training activities, described clearly enough to be used as sources for planning.

Chapter IV deals with planning. It explains how to get a training program under way in a local school situation, and shows six different ways to run an opening session. Next, problems that usually come up as a program continues through to its end are discussed, with suggestions for planners.

After the spate of training activities in Chapter V, Chapter VI examines in some detail how to go about planning a training activity (either by adapting those in Chapter V or by making up brand new ones), and explains how to use role playing, films, and tape recording most effectively.

The reader may be wondering who is to guide the multifold activities of a training program. Chapter VII explains the role of the trainer, who helps the group members plan, carry out, and evaluate training activities. It also discusses what effective trainers do, what background abilities they need, and how the reader can study and improve his own performance as a trainer.

Chapter VIII describes how to evaluate the effectiveness of training programs in order to aid with immediate and long-term planning. Many evaluation instruments are suggested.

There are two appendices. Appendix A reviews twenty-nine different published accounts of training sessions, which give an additional feeling for the way training activities proceed. Appendix B is a selected set of materials which a school system conducting a training program of the sort described here might well purchase as a resource library.

Just how the reader proceeds through the book will depend on his background in this approach to training, his interests, and his preferred style of reading expository material. He is encouraged to skip around with the help of the description above and the table of contents, and (if he owns the book) to take an active, scribbling-in-the-margins approach. At several points during Chapter IV on planning and Chapter V on the actual activities, space is provided for jotting down work notes and reactions.

To aid clarity and extend the book's usefulness, several kinds of reader aids have been incorporated in the text:

Cross references. Since the material is complicated, and everything relates to everything else, many references are made to other parts of the book. The reader who finds these irritating or distractive can ignore them without peril.

Footnotes. A book of this length cannot possibly encompass all that is useful in carrying on training. The many footnotes tell the reader where he can find supplementary material to solve a particular problem being discussed at that point in the text.

Many readers find footnotes distractive, and prefer to have them bunched at the end of chapters or in an appendix. The author's decision was to include them in the text at the point where they are needed most. The text can be read sensibly without them.

Indexes. The training activities of Chapter V are in a sense the heart of the book, and so they are specially indexed by problem dealt with, and by type of activity (pp. 100 and 175–76, respectively). The general index has also been constructed to be as helpful as possible in the rapid location of material.

Some special comments are in order on the problem of jargon. One public school person who read the manuscript said, "Clean up that language!" There are two main types of jargon in the book, in addition to the special words ordinarily used by educators. One is social science language ("deviance," "communication," "power structure"). The other is training jargon ("audience sectors," "process observer," "setting up the scene," "alter ego"). Either sort of special language can be mystifying, angering, or simply confusing.

The author's policy on jargon (where he has been aware that a given term *was* jargon) was either to (1) take it out when a more familiar term would do, or (2) leave it in, with explanation, when no usual term was accurate. Many jargon terms from the social sciences and the field of training have a delightful precision, and are far clearer to the reader— when he understands them—than clumsy circumlocutions or attempts to use "plain language." And jargon defined, after all, is no longer jargon.

This chapter has characterized the book as focusing on the improve-ment of group processes in schools, through explicitly-set-up training programs. The book's audience is made up of educational leaders—persons who would like to plan, carry out, and evaluate such programs. In this first chapter, many suggestions have been made to aid the reader in using the book; with this the author relaxes his hold on the reader's elbow considerably, and invites him to proceed. The next chapter discusses the nature of effective group behavior.

CHAPTER II

EFFECTIVE GROUP BEHAVIOR

What makes for unresolved conflict, tension, apathy, and wasted effort in groups? What makes for warmth, realistic solutions, support, and better learning? In short, what can be done to help people minimize the negative, frustrating features of group work, and build up the satisfying, productive aspects of cooperative endeavor?

The answer depends, basically, on one's underlying ideas about group behavior, leadership, and membership. This chapter, after presenting illustrative anecdotes, will discuss briefly a conception of effective group behavior, and its implications for selecting and training leaders and members of groups. The chapter closes with some thoughts on training outcomes—what the effective group member needs to know.

Problems in Group Behavior

During the preparation of this book, several hundred school personnel agreed to describe incidents that had occurred in working groups. They reported events with unfavorable, ineffective outcomes, and events that seemed to turn out successfully. The range of problems was wide; the variety of ways school people saw and described the problems was wider.

Ineffective group work

Here are samples of negative incidents. Some dealt with leader behavior:

"The five industrial arts teachers of our school met in conference with the assistant principal at his request. He read a list of prepared statements and asked for any statements or questions. Since there were none, the meeting was ended." (Teacher of industrial arts)

"A meeting to discuss articulation between junior and senior high school. No conclusions reached. Meeting had little direction or goal. Leader made topics too open and broad." (Guidance counselor, adult education director)

"This year the cheerleaders have become completely disorganized and disinterested. They don't follow county rules, and argue constantly among themselves. Their adviser isn't present at practice and often not at games. Without leadership a group can't function. After her experiences last year she didn't have them elect a captain; hence they have no one to guide or lead them at any time. At present they have become the problem of the athletic director and the administration." (Physical education teacher)

Other incidents focused on ineffective individual behavior and its impact on group work:

"A meeting of the Adult Education Committee of our School Study Council. Had a wide variety of interests present and several dogmatic individuals. Topic for discussion met with resistance that resulted in committee failing to agree on area of joint effort. Ultimate result was suggestion that committee disband." (Research assistant, school study council)

"In a study group concerned with educational philosophy, the discussion turned to the meaning of the reconstructionist viewpoint. This is an abstract concept and many people were groping. The discussion leader had been selected from the group a week before, and seemed to have little philosophical training, but at least took the attitude that we were searching together. One of the members of the group did have philosophical background and could have been of great assistance. However, he took a condescending attitude toward those who were obviously having difficulty, yet at the same time appeared to have a desire to set himself up as a source of information and authority. This tended to stifle expression, and the pervading atmosphere was tense." (English and social studies teacher)

Some persons chose to describe ineffective group situations where it seemed that neither leader nor members were to blame—faulty group procedures, disabling conflicts, and misunderstandings blocked productivity:

"Evaluation committee—to evaluate our junior high school. Staff had no choice in the matter, and most of the teachers are critical of whole evaluation process. Progress is very slow, because members of the committee spend a great deal of time ridiculing or criticizing the evaluation forms." (Mathematics teacher)

"I attended Student Council meetings where the topic for discussion was hall conduct. A committee was formed to study the problem and has not as yet developed into a constructive attempt to aid the apparent problem." (High school principal)

"The event: a meeting of a Board of Education with a teacher of retarded children. The Board, for reasons of school building capacity and enrollment, moved the class to another school building. The teacher had already submitted her resignation in protest.

The result: the meeting opened with the Board hoping to retain the excellent services of the teacher by discussing all the problems related. The teacher hoped to get the Board to change the decision. Neither happened." (Assistant superintendent)

"The executive board of our PTA is largely made up of members from a certain section within our school boundaries. This group has formed what might be termed a clique and controls all activities. Teachers who are on the board, and parent members from other localities, are very dissatisfied with the setup. It just isn't the democratic approach at all. At the last meeting anyone who offered a constructive suggestion—outside this group—received very little encouragement, in fact was practically ignored. One could almost feel an undercurrent of discontent from these 'left out' people and faculty members." (Teaching assistant principal)

Effective group work

The incidents above focused on the ineffective, frustrating aspects of school groups. Below are samples of successful incidents. Again, some of them dealt with leadership:

"The staff meetings conducted by our school principal generally have favorable outcomes. In forming school policies where there can be a choice, he is open to all suggestions from all teachers and the will of the majority is then followed." (First grade teacher)

"A meeting with the custodial personnel of the several school building units to clarify certain questions relating to the Board's proposed salary plan for the next school year. It developed that many, and probably most, objections to the plan were the result of a misunderstanding. A solution was worked out rapidly." (Assistant superintendent)

Other incidents emphasized constructive individual behavior and ways in which group experiences enhanced personal growth:

"A study group on reading decided to meet in the home of one of the participants for the last session. During this session we gained greater personal regard for and understanding of all members, and the one member who tended to mislead the discussion into personal channels came through and volunteered to write up the minutes of our work, and did a superior job. I believe the group assisted this individual." (Social studies teacher)

"In a university class for in-service credit, I participated in a group of eight adults. The topics discussed concerned the role of community and family life in relation to the school, and were very pertinent to my personal experiences. Because of my participation I have been able to widen my scope of understanding of others, and also to understand myself better." (Audiologist)

"Working with salary committee of local teachers' association in preparing salary request to be presented to the Board of Education. Much research material was needed; each member of the group assumed responsibility for a certain part of the material. At subsequent meetings all facts were presented and thoroughly discussed. Result was a reasonable and adequate proposal—well received by Board." (Mathematics teacher)

And some descriptions were taken from situations where satisfying, productive group problem-solving was going on:

"Discussion with fourth grade class concerning difficulties involved in boys and girls playing games on playground during lunch period. Children were able themselves to formulate suggestions for improving the situation. I realize that the problem was not completely solved at this point, but heated accusations were modified into constructive suggestions with only two rules —take turns speaking and do not mention names." (Substitute elementary teacher)

"A guidance symposium was held by interested mathematics teachers and guidance counselors. They discussed causes of pupil failure and faults in channeling pupils properly. The meeting was initiated by me because people were interested and because two teachers in particular were pursuing the matter with active interest. The meeting familiarized the group with school problems and suggested courses of future action." (Chairman, mathematics department)

"We were choosing possible themes for the Yearbook, and a small committee (5 youngsters) met with me. We sat down and listed the possible themes and how they could be illustrated, etc. Without any prohibitions, the committee came to the conclusion, after carefully weighing all the pros and cons for each theme, that one that would make them feel foolish or embarrassed in years to come ought not to be chosen, even if the immediate appeal might be strong." (Teacher and art supervisor)

"I am a Room Mother chairman for my local PTA. My committee and I attempted with considerable thought and research to try to strengthen the existing rapport between the Home Room Mothers and their teachers. The teachers met together and pooled ideas of help they could use, sending a representative to our main meeting. The general feeling following our meeting was one of increased warmth and understanding on both sides, and a sense of unity of purpose in the welfare of the children." (Housewife)

"At our recent teachers' meeting we were beginning to run into difficulty over having 'recess or not' during this bad cold snap. Older grade teachers said, 'Yes we should,' younger grades, 'No.' A few were against the teacher being out at all. Fortunately, all was resolved when our fourth grade teacher suggested we work it out by groups; 1st and 2nd grade teachers meet and decide, 3rd and 4th, 5th and 6th. As a result we all had recess, but of various lengths, depending on grade level and teachers' dispositions toward the cold." (Second grade teacher)

These examples suggest the wide range of group situations with which school people are involved. They also underline the complexity of effective work with groups, and the joys, upsets, depressions, and gains which people feel when they work with others. The reader can doubtless supply many more incidents from his own experiences in groups. The basic question remains: How can we improve the quality of group problem-solving and learning in schools? The length of this book should suggest that there is no easy or simple answer. In a real sense, attempts to help people learn better ways of working together begin with clarifying one's conception of leadership and group behavior. The next section explores this topic.

How Leadership Works

This chapter focuses on effective group behavior rather than on "leadership" as such. This focus is consistent with the belief that leadership cannot be understood without reference to an immediate, specific group situation. An outline of research on leadership may illuminate this view

Some different approaches

People have widely varying beliefs and feelings about leadership ("Leaders are too bossy," "A leader who doesn't know what he wants is weak," "The leader must keep a distance between himself and his followers," "Leaders are born, not made," "Leadership is intangibles," "Leadership is vested in the group"). Research, too, has reflected these feelings.

One approach to understanding leadership, which received most emphasis between the two World Wars, assumes that leadership is a matter of personal *traits* (such as initiative, neatness, courage, warmth, intelligence). These traits are thought to make for leadership in most or all situations. It is also assumed that different persons by reason of heredity—and some learning—possess these traits to a greater or lesser degree. Thus they are more or less likely to be leaders.

This approach has not proved very useful for predicting leadership behavior. One survey of 20 experimental studies [1] found that only 5 per cent of the traits examined (adaptability, aggressiveness, ambition, ascendance, etc.) were common to four or more studies. Initiative and intelligence appeared most frequently. Another investigator who examined the evidence for 29 traits appearing in 124 studies found that while IQ, scholarliness, dependability, social participation, and socio-economic status were found to bear some relation to leadership,

> ". . . the evidence suggests that leadership is a relationship that exists between persons in a social situation, and that persons who are leaders in one situation may not necessarily be leaders in other situations." [2]

This finding lends weight to the idea that leadership is largely a *situational* matter; that who is (or becomes) a leader depends mainly on the demands of the job at hand. Another review of 74 studies of military leadership emerged with this conclusion:

> "Leadership is specific to the particular situation under investigation. Who becomes the leader of a particular group engaging in a particular activity and what the leadership characteristics are in the given case are a function of the specific situation . . . [there are] wide variations in the characteristics of individuals who become leaders in similar situations and even greater

---

[1] C. Bird, *Social psychology* (Appleton-Century, 1940). One study of trait names (G. W. Allport and H. S. Odbert, "Trait-names: a psycho-lexical study," *Psychological Monographs*, No. 211, 1936) located 17,000 of them; any person would be above average on many traits.

[2] R. M. Stogdill, "Personal factors associated with leadership: a survey of the literature," *Journal of Psychology*, 25:37–71, 1948.

divergence in leadership behavior in different situations. . . . The only common factor appeared to be that leaders in a particular field need and tend to possess superior general or technical competence or knowledge in that area. General intelligence does not seem to be the answer . . ." [3]

Both the trait and the situational approaches have values, but leave much to be desired. They imply in a sense that it's what you are rather than what you can learn to do that counts. This is extremely discouraging to the would-be leader. Assuming that he believes his IQ is high enough for him to qualify as a "leader," he must either improve his "initiative" and other traits by sheer will power, or spend his time studying up on the vast technical knowledge required in all the possible situations where he contemplates leading. These assumptions about leadership may well add to the tension of today's executives—in and out of school systems.

One way out of this dilemma lies in the view that the leader is a person seen by the group members he is working with as helping them fulfill their needs. Stogdill suggests:

"It is primarily by virtue of participating in group activities and demonstrating his capacity for expediting the work of the group that a person becomes endowed with leadership status." [4]

and Knickerbocker in a thoughtful synthesis proposes that:

". . . leadership exists when a leader is perceived by a group as controlling means for the satisfaction of their needs. Following him may be seen either as a means to increased need satisfaction or as a means to prevent decreased need satisfaction." [5]

This viewpoint implies a functional approach to leadership, and emphasizes what the leader actually *does,* rather than what he is or what he knows. In the functional view, any and all members of the group may perform specific leadership acts or *functions,* such as stating a goal, summarizing, encouraging others to speak. These functions must be taken care of—supplied by someone—if the group is to reach its objectives. [6]

Group objectives are of two broad types: (1) getting the job or group

---

[3] W. O. Jenkins, "A review of leadership studies with particular reference to military problems," *Psychological Bulletin,* 44:54–79, 1947.

[4] Stogdill, *op. cit.*

[5] I. Knickerbocker, "Leadership: a conception and some implications," *Journal of Social Issues,* 4, 3:23–40, 1948.

[6] The word "function" will sound like jargon to many readers. It is purposely used here as a reminder that the leadership act is one *required by the group.* Doodling or clearing one's throat might be acts of a leader, but they almost certainly would not be leadership functions.

task done; (2) keeping the group maintained in good working order. Both these types of objectives or group needs are present, for example, in a committee meeting discussing reading problems in the primary grades. To meet these needs, the designated chairman may serve as a leader by *initiating* a creative approach to the problem, a new teacher by *asking for clarification* of the goal of the meeting, and another committee member by *giving friendly support* to a blocking, complaining member. Since these acts aid the group in moving toward effective, personally satisfying accomplishment of goals shared by all group members, they are leadership functions, even if they last only a moment. Thus the importance of leadership rather than *the* leader. The essential thing is that functions be supplied when they are needed—not that any particular person supply them.

Note that this functional approach also includes the highly-controlling leader usually labeled "autocratic." The autocrat supplies nearly all the task-relevant functions, but tends to ignore or frustrate the personal needs of group members. Such a leader is followed because not to do so would mean the loss of certain satisfactions—or punishment of some sort. The approach also includes a full range of other styles of leadership:

Bargaining, where a horse-trading approach involving rewards and punishments is central. The focus tends to be on the leader's agreeing to meet members' personal needs if they in turn will work on the official group task.

Paternalism, where the leader supplies nearly all the functions—benevolently—and does not permit members to perform leadership acts.

Laissez-faire inaction, where the leader supplies no functions, and does nothing to help members supply them.

Cooperative problem-solving, where the demands of the problem and the needs of persons are both central, and anyone who sees a missing function is expected to supply it.

As the reader considers these styles of leadership and thinks of group situations he is in, he may well begin judging their relative goodness or badness. Labels are not usually helpful, however. To damn a staff meeting as "paternalistic" is to ignore the fact that paternalism (for some groups, at some times, working on some tasks) may be very effective. Effective in terms of what? Here are some criteria for judging leadership acts:

Augmentation: Does the leadership act *augment* or facilitate group members' positive search for need-satisfaction? Or does it accentuate the negative—threaten people with punishment or loss of present satisfactions if they do not perform as desired by the leader?

Effectiveness and efficiency: Does the leadership act aid the group to do its job rapidly and well (effectiveness), besides improving internal working relationships (efficiency)? Or does it tend to evoke a group product of poor quality and feelings of low morale and antagonism?

Learning: Following the leadership act, have other group members grown— either in knowledge of the subject matter they are working on, or in ability to contribute effectively to working groups? Or do they remain at their previous level of knowledge and skill?

Taking a functional approach, and applying criteria like these, can free us from labeling leadership and leaders as "democratic" or "authoritarian." The focus is on the real consequences of specific leadership acts performed by individuals in a specific situation.[7]

One additional comment is in order: The functional approach does not get bogged down (as other theories tend to) on the issue of the appointed leader versus the emergent leader. Both the official leader and the group member who happens to come up with the right function at the right time are doing the same thing: supplying functions needed by the group. The appointed leader who does not do so will become leader in name only, even though he may retain his authority until he retires twenty years hence. Most groups do have appointed leaders as a kind of "safety net" or guarantee that *someone* will fill needed functions, but the approach taken here assumes that the appointed leader and members alike may exert leadership.

Leadership functions

It may be useful to look at some leadership functions in more detail. Benne and Sheats [8] have described a series of functions, such as "information-giving," "harmonizing," and the like. As indicated above, these can be divided into two broad categories: group *task* functions, concerned with aiding direct accomplishment of group goals, and group *building and maintenance* functions, concerned with improving and maintaining work-

[7] For more material on leadership, see the clear overview by M. G. Ross and C. E. Hendry, *New understandings of leadership* (Association Press, 1957).

[8] K. D. Benne and P. Sheats, "Functional roles of group members," *Journal of Social Issues*, 4, 2:41–49, 1948. See also *Adult Leadership*, 1, 8:2–23, "Spotlight on member roles," January 1953.

ing relationships. Typical task functions are "opinion-seeking" and "orienting." Typical maintenance functions are "encouraging" and "standard-setting." [9]

A working categorization of the many different roles described by Benne and Sheats has been suggested by Gibb and Gibb.[10] They indicate five broad categories of leadership functions:

Initiating: keeping the group action moving, or getting it going. (ex: suggesting action step, pointing out goal, proposing procedure, clarifying)

Regulating: influencing the direction and tempo of the group's work. (ex: summarizing, pointing out time limits, restating goal)

Informing: bringing information or opinion to the group.

Supporting: creating emotional climate which holds group together, makes it easy for members to contribute to work on the task. (ex: harmonizing, relieving tension, voicing group feeling, encouraging)

Evaluating: helping group to evaluate its decisions, goals, or procedures. (ex: testing for consensus, noting group process)

A group needs all five of these types of functions if it is to survive and get the job done. At the beginning of a group's work, initiating functions are much needed. Later, as solutions are proposed, informing and regulating functions may assume much more importance. Supporting and evaluating functions are needed all the way along, but especially as the group moves toward final decisions. Group work will be effective, then, to the degree that needed group functions are supplied by members at the time they are needed.[11]

Leadership functions may be handled almost completely by one person, or these functions may be supplied by many different group members. When needed functions are missing, group progress is slow and uneven. If members do not sense or cannot supply what is needed, they may fall back on meeting their own needs at the expense of others' (ex: by fighting,

[9] The authors also discuss negative individual behavior, such as "aggressor," "playboy," and the like, which are devoted to meeting one's own needs *at the expense* of other people's need-meeting. The maintenance function of "encouraging," on the other hand, meets the encourager's own needs to be warm to others while simultaneously helping the group. Or the function of "criticizing" may at the same time satisfy a person's needs for preciseness and aggression toward others *and* the need of the group to produce a good solution to a problem.

[10] J. R. Gibb and L. M. Gibb, *Applied group dynamics* (National Training Laboratories, 1955).

[11] For a training exercise designed to help group members understand group task and maintenance functions as they work out in action, see Chapter V, pp. 130–31.

talking endlessly, withdrawing, or burying everything in sweetness and light).

Although most people usually have preferences for providing one or another function most frequently [12] (some are inveterate summarizers, some characteristically support others, etc.), the typical person usually has a fairly wide repertoire of functions, or he could not relate effectively to others. In a real sense, training as described in this book can aid the individual in developing a wider repertoire—but more important, it can help him be surer about *why* and *when* to supply a particular function.

Some Implications

A functional view of leadership and group behavior has some clear consequences for one's beliefs about how people learn to be more effective in groups—either as members or as leaders. That is, this view tends to lead to the belief that leadership is learnable, and is shared by many group members, instead of being only a matter of one person's behavior. Too, the functional view encourages strong attention to the leader's skills in diagnosing group process problems as a basis for supplying needed functions. These implications are outlined more fully below.

Leadership can be learned

First of all, this view of leadership implies quite clearly that leadership behaviors can be improved, are not fixed by heredity or childhood experience. Learning "initiative" or "intelligence" is difficult or even impossible. But learning, for example, to summarize at the right point the contributions of others in a group is quite possible and is certainly easier than mastering most of the content of a particular field, as in the situational approach. The functional view leads, then, to an emphasis on training, on growth of persons. A trait-centered approach—since traits are relatively fixed—tends to encourage attempts at better *selection* of leaders, which is a difficult task at best.

---

[12] Proponents of a functional approach to leadership have been accused of ignoring the personality determinants of group behavior. Personality is clearly very important in determining whether Jack will summarize, encourage, fight others, or walk out of the room—but the demands of the group situation are probably equally important. Both must be considered. Many people have a tendency to *over*-personalize and blame others, and forget about the group-level situation.

Leadership is a shared matter

This approach to leadership explicitly indicates that all members of a group may supply leadership; that it is less a case of *a* leader and his followers, and more a case of persons contributing, with different amounts of effectiveness, to the operations of a working group. The whole range of leadership functions needed by a group suggests that no one person can do the job alone. Whether these functions are handled by one person or widely distributed through the group, however, the emphasis is on the fact that the functions are needed: without needed functions, the group will fail in its task and the members will feel frustrated. Thus leadership training is important for everyone; it is for this reason that this chapter's title is "Effective Group Behavior" rather than "Effective Leadership." Much practical experience suggests that while supplying training to appointed leaders in a situation (for example, principals in a school system, discussion leaders in a one-day conference, committee chairman in a PTA) is helpful, supplying training experiences that improve *everyone's* abilities to contribute to working groups is substantially more valuable.

Process skills are essential

This view of leadership indicates that careful attention must be paid to the process or procedural aspects of group behavior. Noticing *what* is said is not enough. The effective group member must also be aware of *how* things are said, by *whom, when,* and *what function* they serve in *what group context*. From this point of view, learning to be a better contributor to groups is more a matter of acquiring essential process skills than intensively studying the content or topics to be discussed. Knowledge of content is essential, but it is not sufficient for effective group work.

Diagnostic skill is basic

Finally, the view of leadership and group behavior outlined above implies that a fundamental process skill is that of diagnosing group difficulties and sensing needed, missing functions. A doctor must learn through his training to look at symptoms, form a diagnosis, and prescribe treatment. Just so, group members must learn to notice group difficulties, form a careful diagnosis of what is blocking productivity, and take appropriate action in light of their diagnosis. A diagnostic focus emphasizes growth in the learner's ability to examine group situations thoughtfully and accurately. No medical school would teach a doctor to prescribe the same medicine for every ailment, and no effective program for learning about group behavior can focus on panaceas or gimmicks which promise to solve all group problems. This diagnostic point of view is explored more fully in the next section.

The Outcomes of Training

In light of the discussion of leadership so far, it may be useful to outline some general outcomes of effective training for better group behavior. What do individuals characteristically bring to a training program in the way of needs?

People coming to training usually list a wide variety of specific problems and gripes:

"How do you handle the person who talks all the time?"
"What can be done about apathy?"
"I don't know what to do when there is a clash of personalities."
"What is the best way to start off a meeting?"
"How about the person who goes off on tangents constantly?"
"How do you avoid making mediocre decisions in groups?"

On one level, such problems as "handling a person who goes off on tangents" can be worked with by discussing why people do this and proposing techniques for "handling" such a situation. This, at its worst, is the "gimmick" approach, which implies that X problem can always be resolved by the application of Y technique, and that training consists of supplying the learner with as large a bagful of Y's as possible.

On the second level, however, such a problem can be looked at as an example of a missing but needed group task function. In this case, possibly, no one has clarified the group goal, so that going off on irrelevant tangents is a natural response. On this level, the specific training problem is put in the broader context of group operation, rather than being permitted to remain on the technique level. In training, more observation and analysis of group behavior is implied, and the promise of short and easy answers cannot be made as lightly.

On the third level, we can turn to the *learner himself,* and to training problems or needs like the following:

Sensitivity. Can I *notice* that person X always seems to be going off on tangents? Do I notice how the rest of the group members react? Are there some people whose comments never seem irrelevant, bcause the group immediately picks up on their suggestions even though they are quite different from what has been the topic of discussion? How *confident* am I of what I notice? Do I have blind spots—are there things others do that I never seem to notice? Or do I notice certain things *especially*—such as going off on a tangent—because they bother me personally in some way, or have other special significance for me?

Diagnostic ability. Do I understand *why* person X seems to be getting off on tangents? Is it a case of the group's goal not being clear? Or is it that person X would like to be the center of things? Or is it that the group does not really care to work on this particular topic and would rather be doing something else? What functions are missing and why? Am I focusing on the really relevant and crucial functions?

Action skill.[13] Can I actually step in and help the group by bringing in the needed function effectively? If I have (1) noticed that person X goes off on tangents; (2) decided that the probable trouble is that the group is not actively involved in the topic at hand and will permit or even encourage divergence, then there is still the problem of (3) *action.* What can I do or say to help the group do a better job at this point? How well can I do it? What will be the consequences?

Training needs stated at this third level imply some general outcomes. Members of a training group are learning to take a diagnostic, experimental approach to the improvement of group life, whether the specific group setting is the classroom, a faculty meeting, a committee, a workshop, or a parent-teacher conference. The outcomes are: more accurate hearing and seeing in groups; more insightful ways of deciding what's causing group difficulties; better ways of taking action to supply the group with what is needed.

Groups are so very complex that an effective member must do all of this fairly routinely and without much thought. Otherwise our groups would everlastingly be caught up in involuted analyses of who did what to whom, and group tasks would never get done. A good group member,

---

[13] This discussion assumes that the person (*a*) is free to take some kind of helping or corrective action; (*b*) **wants to do so.**

then, operates habitually much of the time—he notes missing functions and supplies them almost automatically. Most of his energy, as it should, goes into thinking about the content of the discussion and contributing his ideas. Good groups don't get into serious difficulties often—people can "navigate" well.

But when difficulties loom, a good group member must be able to pay more attention to process events, to notice accurately what is going on, to think out and try corrective behaviors experimentally, to see what action will bring the group out of its crisis or trouble. So people need both "normal" and "emergency" skills in order to do a good job in groups. They need, too, it should be said, the sensitivity and good sense to know when the situation demands painstaking diagnosis, and when it doesn't.

Incidentally, the assertion is *not* being made that good groups have no conflict. In fact, a group without conflict may be in serious difficulty; points of view are being masked and inhibited, and good solutions cannot be worked out. It is important for group members to learn to distinguish between disagreement which disables a group and disagreement which is to be encouraged, because it enriches problem-solving and productivity.[14]

It should be apparent that a diagnostic conception of training needs implies a thorough, essentially educative approach to training. New understandings, attitudes, and skills are required. The desire for prescriptions on "how to handle the guy who goes off on tangents" must be replaced by *experiencing, thinking through,* and *trying out* leadership (membership) acts in a situation that is as real as possible.[15] In short, we can only help people to take a diagnostic, experimental approach in working groups if the training program itself is diagnostic and experimental and allows the learner to gain insight into the causes and effects of his own behavior in groups.[16]

[14] One research study found that effective aircrews were more able to tolerate disagreement than were ineffective ones. (E. P. Torrance, "Perception of group functioning as a predictor of group performance," *Journal of Social Psychology,* 42:271–82, 1955.)

[15] What do learning experiences of this sort look like? The reader may wish to refer to Chapter V, pp. 131–33, 148–49, for activities aimed at improving member sensitivity to feelings of others, and to pp. 149–51, for an exercise in how to diagnose and predict what will happen next in a group.

[16] This general formulation owes much to thinking done at the National Training Laboratory in Group Development, and to L. P. Bradford's work in particular. See National Training Laboratories, *Explorations in human relations training, an assessment of experience 1947–53* (National Education Association, 1953).

The experimental approach to leadership acts is also explored thoroughly in H. A. Thelen, *Dynamics of groups at work* (University of Chicago Press, 1954).

Summary Comment

The examples and leadership research reviewed in the paragraphs above point to a conception of leadership which is indistinguishable from the idea of "effective group behavior." In this view, groups need certain specific task-relevant and group maintenance-relevant functions, if effective joint effort is to ensue. One or all members may fill these functions, and the central question of training then becomes: How can we become more skillful at supplying the appropriate group functions at the right time? [17]

All this implies that an active, concrete, experimental approach to training for better group behavior is essential. In the next chapter we turn to discussion of the training process itself.

[17] The reader with background in social psychology will realize that this approach is deceptively simple. Many other factors are at work in groups besides the presence or absence of appropriate group functions (ex: group goal-setting, cohesiveness, decision-making methods, the influence of outside authority relationships). Ultimately, however, any training program must focus on the actual, specific behavior of persons in a group situation, and so the functional approach is taken here. Broader knowledge of group factors like those above certainly enriches diagnosis and can lead to improved action. In the training activities of Chapter V, frequent reference is made to available written material. The reader who wishes to extend his general knowledge about small groups will find profitable:

K. D. Benne and G. Levit, "The nature of groups; helping groups improve their operation," *Review of Educational Research*, 33:289–308, 1953.

L. P. Bradford and others, "The dynamics of work groups," *Adult Leadership*, 2, 7:8–27, 1953.

D. Cartwright and A. Zander, *Group dynamics* (Row, Peterson, 1953); see especially introductory chapters 1, 7, 11, 22, 28, 36.

M. Horwitz, "The conceptual status of group dynamics," *Review of Educational Research*, 33:309–28, 1953.

CHAPTER III

THE TRAINING PROCESS

Assuming that one wants to help others learn more about effective group behavior, what can be done? How can people become more sensitive to the forces at work in group situations, clearer on what group functions are missing, better able to supply a summary or an encouraging comment at the right time?

Learnings of this order are not easily achieved. They require special learning conditions, of an intensive, concrete, focused nature. Such conditions have been labeled "training" in this book, and are described in some detail in this chapter.* An actual training activity in a school setting is used to illustrate the ideas presented. Here are two pieces of advice for the reader: (1) try to suspend for a while any negative reactions you may have to the word "training"; (2) test the ideas vigorously against your own picture of how teaching and learning proceed.

This chapter is written primarily from the point of view of the learner as he proceeds through a training program. For comments on the role of the trainer, the person who aids in the learning process, see Chapter VII.

Can Better Group Behavior Be Learned?

Some people believe that an individual's behavior in groups can be changed quickly and easily. Many others believe that alteration in the way a person works with others is almost impossible. Practical experiences with training suggest that a realistic view, not surprisingly, lies somewhere in between.

* Parts of this chapter are based on material originally prepared by Stephen M. Corey.

It is true that learning better group behavior is an example of complex, comprehensive learning, involving new understandings, attitudes, skills. Since adults learn some of their ways of working with other people quite early in life, we are faced with the need for much unlearning, and re-education in new ways of seeing, hearing, and acting in groups. Everyone experiences normal resistance to change, and it could be argued that bringing about real personal change, especially in adults, is a near-hopeless undertaking from the start.

But, on the other hand, new knowledge about how people learn in group situations suggests that much more change is possible than many of us are inclined to think.[1] Quite clear changes can take place in the way people see group situations (including their view of their own role), and in the way they act, as a consequence of training experiences.[2] But all is not magic, and in thinking about training we need to plan for learning conditions that will evoke realistic and feasible changes in people, avoiding prejudgments of a pessimistic or optimistic nature. What do such learning conditions look like?

An Illustrative Training Activity

As a basis for later discussion of the nature of training, it may be helpful to look at a particular training activity. By "training activity" is meant an organized group experience intended to develop one or several skills. An example of such an activity, drawn from work with public school personnel, is discussed in the following paragraphs.[3]

[1] Lewin, for example, compared group discussion and decision with lectures as a way to bring about change in behavior. Group discussion and decision was several times more effective than lecturing, and was more effective, even, than individual interviews. The people involved were mothers, and the behavior change involved serving new items of food—sweetbreads or cod liver oil—to infants or the family as a whole. See K. Lewin, "Studies in group decision," in Group dynamics, D. Cartwright and A. Zander, eds. (Row, Peterson, 1953), Chap. 21. Recent research checking and extending these findings in the area of health education has been done by B. W. Bond, and described carefully in Group discussion-decision (Minnesota Department of Health, 1956). See also note 1, p. 57.

[2] For research evidence on this point, see: R. Lippitt, Training in community relations (Harper, 1949), pp. 172–212.

National Training Laboratory in Group Development, Explorations in human relations training: an assessment of experience 1947–53 (National Education Association, 1953), pp. 66–68.

R. Lippitt, J. Watson, D. Kallen, and S. Zipf, Evaluation of a human relations laboratory program. National Training Laboratories Monograph No. 3 (New York University Press, 1959).

[3] Adapted from S. M. Corey, P. M. Halverson, and E. Lowe, Teachers prepare for discussion group leadership (Teachers College Bureau of Publications, 1953). See also R. C. Doll,

A curriculum revision committee, the Reading Group, working in a suburban school system, arranged a half-day Reading Conference of the entire professional staff of 208 persons. The conference was designed to explain and help improve the school's reading program. The plan included time for small groups to identify problems in the teaching of reading which were common throughout the system. Such groups would, of course, need capable discussion leadership.

Twelve group chairmen were selected by peer nominations. Most of them indicated that they felt somewhat insecure in approaching group discussion leadership. Accordingly, a training session was set up for the chairmen with the help of outside consultants. A subcommittee prepared a tape recording showing episodes that might occur during the work of a "typical group" during the Reading Conference. The episodes were vivid and unfinished, and illustrated eight common problems faced by discussion leaders, such as "starting the meeting," "handling conflict," and the like.

A full day was set aside for the training session. After an introduction, the episodes were played back, one by one. At first, the group chairmen discussed with growing interest the problem raised and how well or poorly the chairman (on the tape) handled it. Then, with the help of trainers, they began actually trying out—through role playing—ways of coping with the problem. Careful analysis of the role playing followed, and generalizations about effective behavior were made (for example, "In a conflict, always admit there is a problem. Focus the group's attention on the need for facts"). This discussing, practicing, analyzing, and generalizing process went on all day. It ended with summary statements from members on how they planned to work with their groups at the actual Reading Conference.

During the activity, and at the end of the day, the chairmen wrote down their evaluations of the training. Then after the Reading Conference, they filled out another questionnaire, as did the teachers who attended as group members. Eighty-five per cent of the teachers, checking a rating scale, thought the group discussions were "very adequate" or "quite adequate." The chairmen rated their own training experience as "very valuable," an increase over the rating they made at the time of the training. They said, for example, "It gave me not only concrete ideas, but took away

---

P. M. Halverson, R. E. Lawrence, and E. Lowe, "An experiment in training teachers for discussion group leadership," *Educational Leadership,* 10:112–17, November 1952.

my fears," and "I have new insights into some of the problems every leader meets." They suggested new episodes for taping, such as "The supervisor who took over" and "The group offering no agenda items." The outside consultants were impressed with the intense interest shown by the chairmen, and with their enthusiasm in commenting on the practical helpfulness of the training.

If we examine this training activity, some important themes can be distinguished. They are listed here and will be discussed more fully in the next section.

1. The chairmen were concerned with the improvement of particular, focused *skills,* such as handling conflict effectively.

2. To do this, the chairmen had to learn as thinking, feeling, acting *whole persons.*

   That is, as they listened to the tapes, discussed them, and tried out new ways of coping with a conflict situation, they *understood* conflict more clearly, they experienced the *feelings* that go with conflict (such as helplessness, anger, rejection), and they took concrete *action* to reduce conflict.

3. Such actions could be *practiced*—tried out repeatedly, analyzed, and learned from.

4. The session was psychologically *safe.*

   The meeting was, in a sense, "not for keeps." It took place out of the usual stream of work in this school system. The chairmen could feel free to admit inadequacy, to explore, and to try out ways of meeting conflict situations that they might never have dared to try out in an actual group meeting on the job.

5. The training group was set up for the explicit purpose of bringing about *change* in its members—more effective chairmanship behavior, greater confidence.

6. The change desired was in the *social* selves of the chairmen.

   No analysis was made of persons' lifelong deep inner feelings (for example, anxieties about expressing hostility and being rejected by others). The focus was on the level of here-and-now behavior: how do you act most effectively when you are the chairman and people begin arguing with each other angrily? The chairmen did express and analyze their feelings of insecurity and anger, as mentioned above, but always in terms of the demands of the immediate situation and their roles as chairmen.

A training activity, then, is a group experience with features like the six listed above. It is a planned way to *practice* and *improve* what one is doing or needs to do in the future. In this sense, a training activity is analogous to scrimmage in football. What the team learns from scrimmage enables it to play the actual game better. And a scrimmage has the advantage that it can be started and stopped at will, criticized, explained, and made to serve the general purpose of training—improvement in skills. When the chips are down—in a football game or in a reading committee— then the real and crucial test of training comes: Do people function better, or not?

Chapter V contains a large number of training activities. They can be used in training programs to help people improve their own skills of working with groups. The reader may wish to browse in that chapter for more examples before proceeding to the general discussion of training below.

The Nature of Training

Any training aims at change in the person. The point of view taken here is that training for better group behavior represents re-education in the fullest sense.[4] Why, then, use the word "training"? To many people, it connotes a reward-and-punishment approach to the rote learning of narrow, mechanical tasks. In such a process, the learner may be quite unaware of the trainer's purposes in putting him through the activity. "Training seals," "training in using a comptometer," "toilet training," and "physical training," all carry some of these negative overtones. Even "pre-flight training" and "vocational training" seem to imply narrow, restricted learning activities.

Currently, however, the word "training" is coming to have wider connotations, as in the phrase "human relations training."[5] These connotations may have been evident in the list of six important features of training given just above. Here it may be useful to discuss these features in some detail.[6]

---

[4] For a provocative and relevant discussion, see "Can leadership training be liberal education?" *Adult Leadership*, 2, 2:1, June 1953.

[5] See National Training Laboratory in Group Development, *op. cit.*

[6] This discussion is adapted from M. B. Miles and A. H. Passow, "Training in the skills needed for in-service education programs," in *Fifty-sixth Yearbook*, National Society for the Study of Education (University of Chicago Press, 1957), pp. 341–42.

Skill emphasis

Training implies a focused concern with *skills*—the tools a person needs to bring his actions into line with his intentions. A skillful person can act so that the consequences of his behavior in a group fit his intentions. Skillfulness is thus a complex integration of sensitivity, diagnostic ability, and action, as they were outlined in Chapter II.

Skill in this sense is an amoral concept. It is possible to have skillful gangsters or skillful rumor-spreaders or skillful blockers of group decision. Even the skills of the 3 R's are basically amoral.[7] But once a person or a group has made the decision that a goal is to be desired, then matters of "how to" become uppermost. This book is based on the premise that improving group work is an important goal. Unless the reader shares this belief, there is little point in his reading further about the means to this goal. Here is a statement worth underlining: The person who, basically, does not *want* to help the group he is in do a better job will emerge from a training activity with a few empty, mechanical techniques at best. "He knows the words, but not the music," as one supervisor remarked.

The skills focused on in this book, then, are *helping* skills—the abilities necessary to aid effective, satisfying work in groups. Examples of such skills, which can be learned and improved on in a training group, are:

> Setting up an agenda with a group.
> Helping group members work through a conflict.
> Testing for the presence of consensus in a group at a given point.
> Giving support to a new member.
> Assisting a group to clarify where it is in a problem-solving sequence.
> Increasing other members' willingness to express frank feelings.

Such skills as these are not motor skills, like those which the operator of a punch press has, nor are they conditioned responses or rote learning skills, like a dog's tricks. They are complex—but focused—integrations of understanding, attitudes, and behavior.

[7] W. French, in *Behavioral goals of general education in high school* (Russell Sage Foundation, 1957), makes this point neatly with a quotation from John Ruskin:

"Education does not mean teaching people to know what they do not know. It means teaching them to behave as they do not behave. . . . It is not teaching the youth of England the shapes of letters and the tricks of numbers; and then leaving them to turn their arithmetic to roguery, and their literature to lust. It is, on the contrary, training them into the perfect exercise and kingly continence of their bodies and souls."

This leads again to the question: Is training concerned with teaching people "gimmicks"? The discussion in Chapter II (pp. 22-25) should make it very clear that while the hope for simple techniques and magic panaceas is a natural one, effective training must be broadly based. Although training does deal with specific problems in group behavior, recipes and prescriptions cannot be substituted for the learner's ability to help groups diagnose their own difficulties and grow.

Whole-person learning

This unfortunate term seems the easiest label with which to remind the reader that the process of learning to perfect particular skills in group behavior is not narrow. It requires thinking, feeling, choosing, and acting-out. Traditionally, education has been concerned often with solely verbal learning, less often with growth in the expression of feeling, and (some would say) least often of all with what people actually *do*. Ideas, values, principles, attitudes, feelings, and concrete behaviors are involved in whole-person learning, and good training for improved group work includes them all.

Guided practice

Training also implies practice—repeated performance of particular skills, with explicit, immediate information on the results of a particular try. If we are to train the whole person, then the whole person must think, feel, *act*—and then learn immediately how well he has done. Learning to talk more effectively about human relations, as by discussion of cases or "principles of leadership," is not enough. The person needs to experiment with his own behavior, learn what the consequences are, and try again. Someone has called this "trial-and-success" learning.

Psychological safety

Finally, training implies a situation which is at least partially protected and psychologically safe. Why is this?

Once again, skills in group behavior cannot be pulled together into a list and presented serially to learners as one would train seals successively in flipper-clapping, ball-balancing, and horn-tooting. Rather, the learner needs to experiment and explore, try things out for himself, learn from doing, until he can behave appropriately. He must learn that human relations problems are not caused solely by the behavior of other people, that his own actions are a part of any problem situation, and that he may, on occasion, not be perfect.

Such learning requires a "not-for-keeps" setting, because the learner must be free to be creative, to think provisionally, to make missteps, and to try out new ways of behaving without fear of the usual painful consequences of failure.[8] When the usual constraints on the individual are temporarily lifted, the results can be dramatic. Methods like role playing, "brainstorming," [9] and client-centered therapy [10] seem to free the individual to be more creative and productive than he usually is. During role playing, for example, when the individual is spontaneously acting the part of another person, he is safe from criticism by himself or others, because he is "just pretending." And yet the "not-for-keeps" behavior is real—real enough to make for personal learning.[11] Under these circumstances, a three-step process can be said to take place:

1. The learner enters a safe situation and, in a sense, "unfreezes," or relaxes, his usual set ways of behaving.

2. In the unfrozen, fluid state he creatively explores and tries out new behaviors.

3. He refreezes, or makes firm, the new behaviors as he moves back to the usual demands of the job situation.

Most of us stay frozen most of the time, and training's biggest contribution is in making a temporary thaw not only possible, but safe and desirable.

[8] Many kinds of "low risk" situations are used when a person or group is trying to learn something new. Scrimmage in football, the pilot plant in industry, laboratory experiments, and the dry run in teaching the operation of military weapons are examples.

[9] A method used in industry and advertising: members of a group suspend judgment and list solutions to a common problem as rapidly and non-critically as possible. As many as 100 novel solutions may appear in a few minutes; they are later winnowed down for feasibility. See A. F. Osborn, *Applied imagination* (Scribner, 1953).

[10] See C. R. Rogers, *Client-centered therapy* (Houghton Mifflin, 1951), esp. pp. 19–64. In this process the counselor attempts to understand the client as he appears to himself, to see through the client's eyes, without attempting to control, advise, or punish the client in any way, and to communicate this understanding to the client.

[11] This generalization is based primarily on practical experience in training. For a skeptical and thoughtful review, see J. Mann, "Experimental evaluations of role playing," *Psychological Bulletin*, 53:227–34, 1956.

How Does a Training Group Differ from Other Groups?

For a variety of reasons, which will be discussed later, training for better group behavior takes place best in a *training group*. Such groups differ in certain respects from work groups, from classroom groups, and from psychotherapy groups. A description of these differences may help to clarify the nature of training further.

Focus on member change

A training group differs most centrally from a *work group* on the job in placing less emphasis on the accomplishment of a specific external task and more emphasis on improvement of its members' skills. For example, a work group that had great difficulty in reaching decisions would be a flop on the job. When a training group has decision-making difficulties, however, they are grist for the mill. The members can analyze the difficulties, try again, and learn from the experience. This is the essential nature of the laboratory approach.

Since a training group's objective is *change* in its members' ways of doing things, their procedures, their practices, most training groups do not also try to accomplish "work" tasks. Their work, in effect, is to cause themselves to learn to be better group participants. Since a training group does *not* have to make up new curriculum guides, agree on playground policy, or clarify bond issue proposals, the members are freer to experiment and learn about group behavior. This idea is often puzzling to people who have not attended training groups. "What on earth do you talk about?" The answer—it is perhaps a maddeningly vague one—is that a training group talks about any and all group process problems that appear in the course of its work. (For illustrations, see Chapter V, pp. 101–23.)

Most training groups, then, have a limited life span. They remain together for a specified period of time. It is assumed that their members, as they move back to their work groups, will keep on behaving in the new, more effective ways they have learned in the training group.[12]

[12] Some recent experiences with training groups which were actually job groups suggest that good learning is possible, but rather difficult unless added freedom to experiment is built in. This can be done by meeting for longer periods of time than usual (1–2 days), working in a physically isolated setting, encouraging informal dress, etc.

Focus on the here-and-now

How does a training group differ from the usual *classroom group?* Both are concerned with changes in their members' behavior, yet these changes are of somewhat different sorts.

In a classroom, the content discussed and the skills learned are ordinarily drawn from the surrounding culture. Thus children are to learn to read, to write, to handle numbers, to be familiar with certain facts and generalizations essential to adequate functioning in the adult world. Most of this content is externally given, originating outside the classroom in time and space. The teacher's task, in a sense, is to help the child relate his here-and-now experience to this body of content.

In a training group, on the other hand, the here-and-now is the major source of content. What is discussed originates almost completely within the group. The members of a training group are actively motivated to discuss group process difficulties of a sort which a teacher may well choose to ignore, handle without mentioning, punish, or only analyze wearily in the teachers' room with friends. In some classrooms (for example, core classes, homerooms), a large fraction of time may be spent in discussing here-and-now behavior and nearly all teachers encourage such discussion occasionally (as in evaluation of committee work). But it is unusual to see a class situation where almost exclusive attention is paid to the analysis of what is happening between people, right now, as a means to learning. This is as it should be. The classroom group is not primarily a training group.

Focus on the social self

It may be asked, finally, what the difference is between a training group and a *group for psychotherapy.* Both groups are concerned with changes in their members' behavior, and both use here-and-now content.

Although all positive change in people has therapeutic aspects, there are some important differences between training and therapy. In a therapy group, the participants are patients. They are ill. Illness implies that something in the person has gone wrong, that the person is troubled or suffering and needs cure.

In a training group, on the other hand, the members are healthy, are not suffering, but do have dissatisfactions about their own *skills.* They would like to be able to do something better, to cope with everyday problems in an improved manner.

Finally, in a training group, as the distinctions above imply, there is less emphasis on a person's inner workings and much more emphasis on his "outer workings"—the way he relates to people. A training group is usually less concerned with the inner reasons for *why* someone does something, and more concerned with *how* he does it, what the impact is on others, and how he can improve what he does to become more skillful.

A member of a training group may discover for himself how his inner problems are hindering his effectiveness with other people, but the training group is not the place for him to work out all the intricacies of these problems. It is the place for him to gain more insight into his social self—to see how his behaviors impinge on others. This distinction cannot, of course, be sharply made, but the emphasis is as stated.

In summary, then, a training group is a group designed to help its members make constructive changes in their social selves, by means of analysis of here-and-now experiences.[13, 14] The remainder of this book is devoted to explaining specifically how training works, and what must be done if it is to be successful.

It might be added here, incidentally, that the relatively impersonal account above probably communicates little of the specific sense of excitement and involvement that is a part of most training group sessions. The reader who has not attended a training group may get some of this sense by examining the activities in Chapter V, or some of the accounts of training groups mentioned in Appendix A.

How People Learn through Training

Given the background comments above on the nature of training, it may be helpful to present here a description of the process of learning better group behavior. What is the experience of a person like, as he grows and learns during one or several training activities? On the following page is a general outline of the psychological steps in the training process, expressed in graphic form.

[13] Some of the distinctions made above are explored in H. Lerner and H. C. Kelman, eds., "Group methods in psychotherapy, social work and adult education," *Journal of Social Issues*, 8, 2, 1952, entire issue.

[14] See also the discussion of group "norms" or standards for behavior in the training group, which appears in Chapter VII, pp. 207–09.

STEPS IN THE TRAINING PROCESS

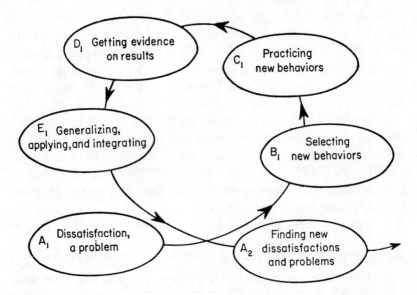

The process of learning is here shown as cyclical. After going from step A_1 through step E_1, the learner returns to step A_2, which is then followed by B_2, C_2, and so on. Over a period of time, the learning cycle would be repeated many times:

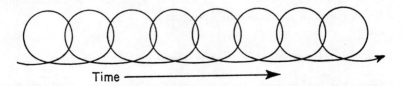

Time ⟶

If training is effective, this spiral moves, over time, in the direction of better and better behavior in groups.

It should immediately be said that learning is more than a rational process. At each of the stages above, the person faces emotional problems and stresses, since what is involved is change—*change in me*. For this reason, learning during training is not the neat, stepwise progression implied; but it is useful to look at a simplified model as a means of understanding the living, exciting process of learning more clearly. Here again the reader is invited to turn to his own model of learning for comparison.

The ideas presented below have roots in more general conceptions of learning (compare John Dewey's treatment in *How we think,* for example), but are focused on the special case of learning to work more effectively in groups.

Below, each of several stages in learning is discussed in turn, and the basic feelings involved are explored. The problem of training, in effect, is to provide conditions to help this learning process go forward effectively.

Dissatisfaction, a problem

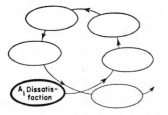

Why *would* a person want to change and learn? Before there is likely to be much significant improvement in a person's group behavior, the person himself must first, believe that effective group work is an important matter for him; and second, be dissatisfied to some extent with his own attitudes, understandings, and behaviors as participant in working groups. Initially, this may be a vague, unfocused feeling of discomfort, but as learning proceeds, it becomes more defined ("How can I explain my ideas more clearly to others?"). The learner must, in effect, come to feel some more or less specific *inadequacy* in relation to his own role in groups, or learning cannot go forward. This inadequacy is a relative matter; even a very capable group participant may wish to improve what he does, even though he feels his behavior is fairly effective already.

Immediately, emotional problems are involved; frequently the natural desire is to protect the self by believing that all human relations problems are somehow due to the inadequacies of others. And old fears of punishment and failure are at work; so it is hard for the individual to feel —let alone openly express—inadequacy. If all this is so, how do feelings of dissatisfaction and perceived inadequacy come to increase before and during a training program?

If an "outsider," such as a consultant, a supervisor, or a status leader, points out some of the person's limitations to him, the person's dissatisfaction with his own group behavior may increase. This is psychologically hazardous—and usually doesn't work. If the outsider is seen as having power over the individual, what often results is resentment, covering-up of real dissatisfactions and inadequacies, and various types of attempts "to please the boss."

Another source of desire for change is a situational difficulty in the person's work in the school. A sensitive person is constantly made aware, in one way or another, of the successes and failures of his work. ("Why are the committee members so apathetic?" "Did I handle the situation all right when Mary kept going off on a tangent?" "Why don't the principals carry through on decisions they seemed to agree to?") Most school people want strongly to do better what they are already doing, and this is a basic source of creative dissatisfaction.

Finally, if the person has become dissatisfied enough with his own behavior to enter a training activity (which he hopes will reduce the dissatisfaction), additional desires for change may appear. In a supportive training group, he may learn that "I'm not the hot-shot I thought I was," as one principal ruefully remarked. He may be able to shift from blaming others to looking at what he himself is contributing to make group work ineffective. Until such a shift can be made—and it is difficult—he may feel frustrated or angry that he is not getting the answers he had hoped for.

Practical experience in training programs suggests this generalization: When the primary motivation for improvement comes from an individual's concern about what "outsiders" want him to do, the changes in his behavior are apt to be confused, transitory, un-integrated, and irrelevant to the real demands of the job. When the primary motivation for improvement comes from the strong desires of the person—aided by "insiders" who are members of the same training group—to improve his own ways of working with others, then the changes in his behavior can become increasingly systematic, permanent, integrated, and job-related.

Even when there is intrinsic motivation for changing, however, there are still emotional problems of resistance, loss of status, and fear of failure. An atmosphere must be developed in which people can safely talk about the tensions, dissatisfactions, and difficulties they personally are experiencing. Such expressions serve as a basis for training. But dissatisfaction with one's effectiveness in work is not likely to be voiced in an atmosphere that involves hazards of threat, punishment, or criticism. It is important to use off-the-job meetings, role playing, and other methods to increase psychological safety.

Selecting new behaviors

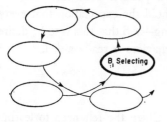

Given dissatisfaction and the willingness to attend a training activity to reduce that dissatisfaction, there is a next important step.

The person in training must become aware of, and consider trying out, new actions which promise to help him solve the problem(s) he faces in his work with groups. That is, the learner needs to think creatively of different practices that might reduce his dissatisfactions with his present behavior. ("Maybe I don't have to hold the reins so tightly when I am the chairman," or "Perhaps I should try to listen more carefully instead of thinking of what I'm going to say next.")

These pictures in the mind, or models of better behavior in groups, stem from many different sources. They may come from books or materials on group work, from the observed behavior of other members of the group (including, quite frequently, the trainer), and from the comments and suggestions of other associates.

In effect, the learner is now framing an action hypothesis which might read: "*If* I try this new behavior (for example, 'Shut up in meetings for a change'), *then* some desirable consequences will result ('Other people will take more responsibility and be less apathetic')." [15]

At first, people do not usually consider a very wide range of different behavioral possibilities. In early meetings of training groups, members may not think of ideas much more challenging than "talking more" and "talking less." This restriction on possibilities for changed behavior is not just happenstance. Most people have specialized in certain ways of behaving for so long (being the aggressive deflater, the smooth harmonizer, the non-listener) that freely and frankly considering the idea that one could behave differently is quite difficult. And the idea that problems in groups are really *someone else's* fault is a very durable one. For these reasons, the

---

[15] For an interesting discussion of how "If-then" relationships can be formed, see A. W. Foshay, "Action research as imaginative hindsight," *Educational Research Bulletin*, 34:169-71, October 12, 1955. Foshay suggests that the "then" term can be found by considering a problem (such as inadequate faculty meetings) and trying to answer the question: "What would be happening if the problem were actually solved?" The "if" term can be developed by answering the question, "How did it happen that the problem was solved?"

creative non-judging atmosphere of the good training group is important. It can help to widen the range of new possible behaviors from which to select. Too, if the group members hold the expectation that everyone is in the process of changing and learning—and that this is to be desired— then visualizing new and improved behaviors is really aided.

Practicing new behaviors

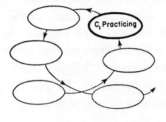

Given the felt need to learn, and some new ideas about what might work, the person must have numerous opportunities to practice, with reasonable safety, some of the behaviors that he and others consider to be promising. This practice can be thought of as a provisional try, taking place under circumstances that involve a minimum of threat and risk. In effective training programs, considerable energy usually goes into the planning of methods that permit behavioral experimentation with little risk. (See Chapter V.) Role playing, for example, can be used to practice skills and behaviors under semi-real conditions before they are tried out in job situations.

Role playing is not the only way to practice new behavior. In a training group where people have supported each other through initial phases of frustration and hesitancy in admitting inadequacy, a person who has been extremely vigorous and articulate, even interruptive, may decide to keep quiet for a meeting to "see how the other half feels." Or someone who wants chairmanship skills may volunteer to serve as chairman while the next agenda item is discussed.

In a good training program, group members also carry on considerable experimentation on the job. Successful experience with new behaviors in the training group gives them courage to try out these new behaviors in their work situations. Intense discussions of "how it worked" follow. And when concrete and realistic job problems are brought into the training group, there is considerable promise for improved job functioning.

During this tryout stage of learning, the primary emotional need is for *support*. The individual has, in effect, unfrozen some of his old ideas about the way to work with people, wants to try out some new ones, but is unsure what the consequences of The New Departure are likely to be.

He is defenseless and awkward at this point. If others in the training group accept and admit their own uncertainty as they try out changes, this can supply much support to all.

Getting evidence on results

The person who is experimenting with his behavior in a training situation must be able to get *evidence* as to the effectiveness of what he does. Learning by doing is not enough. The learner must, in addition, see the actual effect of his new behavior on others. What happened when, ever so gently, he invited non-participant Jane to comment? If in spite of all his attempted tact Jane says she felt put on the spot, then this information is important evidence for the learner to have as a basis for generalizing and applying his learnings further.

One of the limitations most of us struggle under on the job is our inability to get honest appraisals of our impact on others. We have to rely on fleeting facial expressions and official protestations, and we do not learn how we're doing in groups very often, or very accurately.

In the language of training, the term for a report to the learner of how his behavior is affecting others is "feedback." This technical term comes originally from the field of automation (ex: thermostat gives feedback to a furnace on how well the furnace is doing at heating the house), but seems clearly applicable to training as well. To be most helpful for learning, feedback must: (1) be clear and undistorted; (2) come from a trusted, non-threatening source; (3) follow as closely as possible the behavior to which it is a reaction. With quick, accurate, trusted evidence, the learner can proceed to correct his behavior effectively.

Much of the power of human relations training seems to stem from building in regular feedback procedures as a part of the training setup. Evaluation at the end of meetings, analysis of role playing, use of a process observer who reports what he sees to the group, playback of tape recordings—all these can serve as a mirror, and give the learner more and better information about "what behavior leads to what" than he has ever had before. And it's exciting.

Generalizing, applying, and integrating

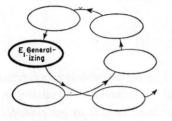

Now that the learner knows what works (or perhaps more frequently, what doesn't work), he must tie this new knowledge into his picture of himself, relate it to his job situation, and in general make it part of the way he sees group life. Concrete action implications need to be drawn ("Do not call on anyone unless he clearly wants to get into the discussion and can't"). The learner needs to see links between the training experience and his job situation ("Here in the training group, we found we had all these hidden feelings about the decision to meet Thursday night, and that's why we didn't carry it out. I think that same kind of thing may account for the poor attendance at my grade level meetings. What can I do about that?").

During this stage, careful, sober thinking is needed—but even here the person needs support and positive emotional reinforcement from other learners in the group, as he considers new learnings that are hard for him to accept, deep down. Otherwise the learnings stay at the "talk" level and never really become a part of his normal ways of behaving.

Finding new dissatisfactions and problems

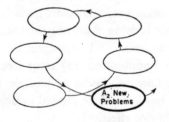

Finally, the learner almost inevitably emerges from a process like that described above with *new* dissatisfactions and problems, in addition to new insights and ways of behaving. ("All right, apathy may mean that the goal of the group is not clear to some people, but what can you do to make it clear, then?" or "Bringing out the gripes did seem to clear the air in this group, but I'm not sure I'd know how to encourage it—or whether I would want to—in the principals' meeting.")

New ways of behaving lead to new problems (which might never have occurred under the old ways of behaving), and the training cycle continues. In other words, after the feedback of evidence which helps him see the consequences of his own group behavior, the individual realizes that his behavior is still inadequate, or is inadequate in some new respect. He then repeats the process of getting creative ideas regarding further change, trying them out in both contrived and real situations, seeing what works, and generalizing about the results. It is through steady repetitions of this experimental learning process that he becomes more sensitive to what is going on in groups, has clearer diagnostic ideas as to what is needed and why, and can act more effectively.

Getting this conception of learning built into the person is even more important than his learning specific skills of "handling conflict," "stimulating participation," or whatever. If the learner has *learned how to grow and learn,* how to take an experimental approach to the problems of group life he encounters, then he will grow and learn on the job.

The Training Group As a Place to Learn

It may serve as a useful review of the process of learning better group behavior if the special usefulness of the training group, as such, is discussed. The training group has been repeatedly mentioned above, and the question might be raised: "Why can't an interested person improve his behavior in groups independently?"

Clearly, much individual reflection, analysis, and experimentation may be necessary before a person comes to the realization, as did one teacher, that "*I* am really the only person whose behavior I can do much of anything about." Experience with many different training programs, however, suggests that individual growth and learning about group behavior takes place best in a group setting. There seem to be reasons for this.

Shared support

In the first place, change in one's own group-relevant behavior, like any change, inevitably involves risk. If behavior changes are attempted by members of a group, the support they can give each other is extremely helpful. The training group is a collection of persons all dissatisfied to some degree with their group behavior. All are trying to get help in improving this behavior, and are willing to be vulnerable, in a sense—open to learning. This makes for shared support within the training group.

There is often the sense of having "lived together a lot in a short time," as one person said, with a resultant feeling of warmth.

Furthermore, in a successful training group, standards or norms are developed which encourage and support experimental change.[16] These norms can be quite strong; they are discussed more fully in Chapter VII.

After the training group has disbanded and members are attempting innovations on the job, each individual also receives support—and sometimes concrete help—from the fact that colleagues are trying similar things as they go about their work. Often recollection of what went on in the training group seems to serve as a kind of "conscience" for the member, continuing to encourage him at difficult points. Attitudes or values learned in the training group often have considerable carry-over, for this reason.

Added resources

Training goes well in a group setting because different individuals can provide widely varied resources for intelligent behavior change by any particular learner. Many different ideas about job innovations can emerge. Ingenious procedures for learning can be devised more quickly. There is a greater possibility of penetrating, mistake-correcting analysis. In addition, because of group support, each person can hear and respond to group suggestions about his behavior which he might ignore if they were the suggestions of an outside expert or status figure.

The group as laboratory

A third reason for the effectiveness of the group situation is that it provides a learning laboratory which helps the individual observe himself in relation to others. Not only can he see the effect that his behavior has on other people, but he can get frank, objective statements from them— their reports of the effects of his behavior. The group provides the individual with a testing ground where he can experiment with promising new behaviors. In a real sense, trying to study and improve one's own group functioning without being in a group is something like trying to learn to swim without going into the water.

[16] D. Cartwright has identified some very useful ideas which help explain why groups are so powerful in bringing about change in their members. See "Achieving change in people: some applications of group dynamics theory," *Human Relations*, 4:381–92, 1951.

Immediacy

Another advantage of the group situation is its immediacy. New behaviors are practiced *where* they are needed (in the group) and *when* they are needed (just following feelings of difficulty or dissatisfaction). Learnings are not postponed to another place or time, but are worked on here and now.

Realistic success

Finally, the group situation helps insure that learning goes on within realistic limits. (This, of course, assumes that the group makes its own decisions instead of having them made for it by the trainer.) Group members are not likely to attempt new behaviors that look extremely difficult. But the group can and does support innovations that are both challenging and feasible. During training, positive success experiences with new behaviors are essential—otherwise they will never be tried out on the job.

Summary Comment

This chapter has dealt with the general nature of training for better group behavior as viewed in this book. Such training involves the whole person, under "safe" conditions, in the practice and improvement of skills Learning is presented as a cyclical process of an experimental, diagnostic nature, taking place in a supportive group situation.

What is involved in setting up a program for such training? The next chapter deals with this question in some detail.

CHAPTER IV

PLANNING FOR TRAINING

Training, like any learning experience, requires careful planning. This chapter contains suggestions for getting answers to questions which planners usually face as they organize for, start, move through, and complete a training program.

Three aspects of getting started are discussed: (1) assessing the local situation, (2) planning for the program as a whole, and (3) planning for the first training session. These are presented in this order because realistic planning for the initial session is most likely to result from a careful assessment of local conditions and a thoughtful look at the broad outline of the total program. Occasionally, work pages are inserted in the text, so the reader can apply to his own situation the ideas that are suggested.

The need for planning does not disappear after training is under way. The last two sections of this chapter deal with the problems of maintaining a continuing training program, and planning for termination of the training program, carry-over into job situations, and follow-up.

Assessing the Local Situation

Initiation

Most training programs can be traced back to one person's initiating action. Some one person begins a conversation with: "Wasn't that a terrible meeting?" or "Well, we had a good day today. Why can't more of our sessions be like that?" or "There must be something we could do to get better decisions out of the committee in less time." The conversation continues, and weeks or months later, a training program will have been carried out.

Such an initiating person (here called "initiator," for convenience) often assumes a central role in getting planning under way. He may or may not carry a central role in planning or conducting training activities when a program materializes. That is, successful training requires more than an initial push. Thoughtful, imaginative planning ahead of time is essential. What does this process of planning look like?

The need for assessing

Ordinarily, much assessment—informal stocktaking—has to go on in a school system before the decision is made to start formal planning for a training program. The need for, and appropriateness of, some systematic training effort must be looked at carefully. Training must rest on more than the passing enthusiasms of a few. Too, without careful assessment, program planners may lose sight of the fact that training is a *means* to solving system-wide problems, not an end in itself, and that there are many other useful means available (such as administrative, policy, or personnel changes).

Further, if a training program is decided on, it will involve the time and effort of many people with already heavy responsibilities. This is a major reason for a careful diagnosis of the situation. A program hurriedly installed without adequate assessment is more likely than not to drag, blow up, or collapse.

Who assesses?

This discussion assumes that some person, the initiator, begins diagnosing the existing situation informally. Experience with training programs suggests that the sooner such diagnosis can be spread to a few others, the better. These other "assessors" involved in the stocktaking and diagnosis may be friends, people whom the initiator thinks may be similarly concerned, individuals who are unusually sensitive to how things are going in the system, or key administrators whose reactions are important to the success of planning for a training program. Later these informally-contacted assessors may well form the nucleus of the official planning committee, should the decision be to go ahead. At this preliminary stage, however, the approach should be informal. "Start small and easy," one curriculum worker said.

Assessing own motivations

A major and early step, especially for the initiator, is that of examining one's own motivations for taking the initiative in the first place. This is not said as a moralistic injunction. It is simply a warning that if the initiator and other assessors are not realistic about what they stand to gain (or are seeking to avoid losing) from a training program, they are likely to get tied up in ineffective relationships with others in the system. Initiators have to be trusted and accepted, or any training program they help develop will be shallow, or resisted thoroughly. If, at some covert level, a supervisor is advocating a training program for principals because it "will teach them a thing or two," or because it will ingratiate him with the superintendent, or because he enjoys manipulating and controlling people, *this will become apparent* to participants, and constructive learning is less likely to take place. So if you are an initiator, look within first.

Not all motivations to provide training for others are unlovely. Looking within can also help initiators and assessors to be thoroughly aware of real personal motivations of a constructive nature—the satisfactions of helping others grow and learn; of sharing the process of becoming a more adequate group member oneself; of creating a school climate that is human and self-fulfilling; of stimulating improvement in the school's program; of realizing oneself more fully as a professional person.

Assessing the state of the system

Given some self-awareness on the part of assessors, a next step involves looking at the state of affairs in the immediate system being considered. The word "system" has been used above several times in its usual sense of "school system." In a more general sense "system" implies any group or organization with interdependent parts functioning to accomplish a common task. For our purposes, then, examples of systems would be an elementary school staff, a school system, a classroom, the senior class, a state organization of supervisors, a high school. Several questions need to be asked thoughtfully, and answered with as good evidence as possible. (During this process, incidentally, it is very easy for assessors to forget that "we're in the system too." Assessors, and those who do the actual program planning later on, must be sensitive to where they fit, how other occupants of the system see them; otherwise assessment and planning may be quite unrealistic.) The first question follows.

Question No. 1: *What indications are there that groups are functioning poorly in the system, and that people are concerned about this?*

Evidence of poor group functioning may take a variety of forms. In meetings or informal settings, members of a working group may express dissatisfaction with the kind and amount of progress being made. Individuals may frankly describe situations where skills are lacking:

"We start at 3:30, then sit and wait until we adjourn at 4:30. Only two or three participate in any discussion and the rest just withdraw. It's just putting in time."

"Remember that hassle we got into over playground duty? It seems to me that we have more arguments in staff meetings than we used to. Maybe that's good, but there's a lot of time wasted."

"I couldn't get them to look at the whole problem. Someone would say something and off the group would go."

"They would make decision after decision but never translate these into action assignments. I tried several times to point this out but never got the idea across."

"I heard some of the area chairmen are complaining about the old-timers being antagonistic in the study groups."

"The same kids seem to be elected as committee chairmen each time we start a new project. They do a good job, but I think some of the rest of us ought to get in on the act."

Behind each of these statements is an indication of a need—some more clearly recognized than others—for better skills in group work. The quality of the evidence varies from hearsay to direct experience. If assessors keep an informal record of group problems and needed skills— both expressed and implied—it will provide much better evidence of training need than the vague expression by an initiator that "we really ought to improve our group work."

Even where spontaneous expressions of need are not frequent, assessors can sometimes open up discussions of needed improvements in group functioning at the time when difficulties occur. Frankness is enhanced when the assessor includes his own behavior as part of the problem. For instance:

> "We sure got bogged down during the last half hour. I wonder why we slowed up so markedly after the way we were going earlier? Is there anything that I as chairman could have done to keep us moving? Do you have similar problems when you chair meetings?"

> "We had a real impasse there, and I wasn't sure how we'd get out of it, but we did. Maybe because we're a small group. The thing that bothers me is that disagreements in the all-staff meeting never get worked out, just smoothed over."

> "As we listened to the reports from committees, I had the feeling that most of the rest of the class were not very much interested. At least I felt that way. Did you?"

> "Sometimes I get sick of meetings; I think we waste an awful lot of time in them around here. What do you think?"

Involving other group members in informal assessment helps to get better evidence about group problems—and also may sensitize people to needs that were dormant, vague, or only hesitantly voiced before.

[The facing work sheet can be used to guide preliminary checking on the existence of needs for improving group work.]

Assessing has its dangers. It is tempting to look at personality characteristics of individuals rather than at *needed skills*. ("Old McWilliams could sure use some mellowing, but you'd never get him to come to any session on leadership—he knows it all.") If assessing is nothing more than gossiping or snooping, real learning about better group behavior is unlikely. Another danger is that assessors may try to manipulate others into saying that needs for skill exist when, in fact, the situation is entirely adequate. These dangers can be avoided if assessors begin with a thoughtful examination of their own inadequacies in groups, and then proceed to an objective open assessment of how well others are doing. A thorough assessment demands evidence from all parts of the system—official leaders, members, disgruntled minorities, ex-chairmen, and eager beavers.

Assessors should focus most heavily on group problems as people see them—and avoid the temptation to make "wise" diagnoses like "The principals' meeting is really very poor, but they don't seem to recognize it." If the meeting *is* poor, the principals almost certainly do recognize it, but forces are at work that keep frank feelings submerged in the meeting

"What indications are there that groups are functioning poorly in the system, and that people are concerned about this?"

System being assessed ....

1. Examples of poor group functioning, reported second-hand:

2. Examples of poor group functioning, actually seen:

3. Examples of actual expressed concern about poor group functioning:

4. Where in the system (name specific groups or individuals) might further informal assessment be done?

5. Are there other persons who might aid in assessing the system?

itself. For example, politeness, concern with what the superintendent thinks, or fear that one's views are not shared by others may all have this effect.

Of course, many group members in the system may have low-level expectations for the quality of meetings, but one function of a training program—and the assessing phase itself—is to start with expressed needs and move on, helping people to upgrade their standards for what a good group can be like.

In general, it is a rare school system that does not have a good-sized reservoir of need—expressed and unexpressed—for improvement in group work. One of the most frequent comments the author encounters in discussions with school people about training is, "We could sure use some of that in our system."

Assuming that a clear state of need has been identified in the system, a second question must be asked and answered.

Question No. 2: *How can the need for better group operation be met most effectively?*

Training is a *means* to meet a need, a solution to an existing problem. If a careful assessment of a school situation is made, it is possible that other solutions besides a training program may be appropriate. For example, if principals' meetings seem continually unproductive, there are many possible means of improvement:

> Clarifying the role of the principal in relation to the supervisor.
> Changing the methods of setting up the agenda.
> Having separate elementary and secondary meetings.
> Having some meetings without the superintendent.
> Serving coffee.
> Changing the in-service program, which the principals happen to resent.
> Providing for a workshop in reading (general criticism of which has made many principals feel attacked and insecure).
> Providing a program to improve the principals' group skills.

All of these ways of improvement have training overtones. Which solutions are chosen should depend on the results of the assessment, not on someone's attempt to sell the idea of a specific training program to others. Quite clearly, some group problems can be solved through training as such, and others must be coped with by policy changes, new administrative procedures, or personnel shifts. The assessors should engage

"How can the need for better group operation be met most effectively?"

System ....

1. What do the major problems or needs for improvement in group work in the system seem to be? (See Work Sheet No. 1)

2. How might these needs be met most effectively?
   (In first listing, do not try to criticize ideas. List as many as possible.)

3. Go back over the list in item 2 and place "T" by those that might form part of a training program, and "O" by those that would require other action.

4. Do the "T"'s seem to add up to the desirability of further exploration of a training program?

5. Can action be initiated immediately on some of the "O"'s?

in careful, informed guessing as to which (if any) needs can be met by direct training, and which by other means.

(Doing something to start on the "other means," incidentally, is extremely important, although this will not be discussed further here. If group problems exist because of administrative and policy difficulties, then attempts to provide training may actually result in increased frustration, until the over-all situation is improved.)

Assuming that assessors feel needs exist which a training program would help to meet, then another question appears:

Question No. 3: *What is the state of readiness for a training program in the system?*

The reader is reminded of the extremely elastic definition of "program" given in Chapter I. A program may simply be, for example, an informal study group of area chairmen who meet to discuss the chairing problems they face. Much useful training can go on in informal, "let's try it out and see" kinds of sessions. The more extensive and formalized the program, the greater the need for thorough assessing and planning.

Whether the approach is formal or informal, a successful program is most likely to develop when the need for an explicit training experience is recognized by potential participants and not by the initiator or assessors alone. People in the system will naturally vary in their feelings about the need for a "program," and 100 per cent readiness is usually unnecessary at the start—given a good, stimulating opening session. But readiness is important. If people see the possibilities for growth through an organized program, they are less likely to feel that the project is being pushed by the initiator, and are more likely to be actively interested as the program materializes.

While assessors are getting evidence on group problems (as in Work Sheet No. 1), they can also pick up indications of readiness to enter a training program. Individuals in the system may suggest areas of needed help, and go on to specify means for getting the help:

"When Joan's in the group, the rest of the committee can't get a word in edgewise. How do I get her to talk less without losing her good ideas, and still get the rest of the group in? I'd like to sit down and talk with the other chairmen about the way they handle people like her."

"The trouble is we only have an hour to work in. You *cannot* get them to stay any longer. I wish I knew what to do to move things along faster and

keep people on the beam. You know, Bob saw a film on discussion leadership in his course in supervision. Could we get it to show here?"

"When we work in committees, I think we waste an awful lot of time arguing without getting anywhere. A lot of other kids feel the same way. Could
we discuss that in class Monday?"

"In the grade level meetings, when I bring in a new idea, they seem to
reject it as my pet project. As supervisor, how do you handle that problem?"

Statements like these suggest some readiness on the part of individuals
to find a way of improving their group skills. This may mean, at the
time, nothing more than a desire to talk about such problems.

Beyond gathering evidence like that above, it may be useful for the
assessors to look quite systematically at what factors in the situation may
hinder getting a training program under way or may help. For example:

Hindrances

People are reluctant to admit their inadequacies.
Old in-service program created some bad feelings.
Many people think they know the answers anyway.
Can we get people to stay after school?
Undesirability of some teachers coming and not others.
Board might not want to vote extra funds for this (if needed).
Vagueness as to what the program would include.

Helps

Many teachers feel pretty free to experiment and try new things.
Superintendent thinks something like this would be a good idea.
Washington County tried study groups on this last year and could tell us
about it.
In-service program built around concrete needs would be welcomed.
Program would be new for many—interesting.
Informality in program would bring in more people.

Such a listing can help assessors get a better idea of the state of readiness in
the system, and may also show ways of increasing readiness.[1]

[1] For illustration of a useful graphic method of analyzing helping and hindering forces,
see "Improving the processes of leadership training," *Adult Leadership*, 2:2, June 1953 (esp.
pp. 15–16). Notice that readiness can be increased by strengthening the helps or by working
to reduce the hindrances. The latter method usually results in easier, more relaxed change.
For a more detailed treatment of the graphic method, called "force field analysis," see K.
Lewin, "Group decision and social change," in E. E. Maccoby, T. M. Newcomb, and E. L.
Hartley, eds., *Readings in social psychology* (Holt, 1958), pp. 197–211. Also, D. H. Jenkins
has written "Force field analysis applied to a school situation," in K. D. Benne and B.
Muntyan, *Human relations in curriculum change* (Dryden, 1951), pp. 44–52.

WORK SHEET FOR QUESTION No. 3

'What is the state of readiness for a training program in the system?"

System ....

1. Examples or incidents that illustrate readiness or lack of it:

2. What factors are likely to *hinder* getting a training program under way?

3. What factors are likely to *help* a training program get under way?

Experience suggests that some of the crucial factors in readiness for training (given the existence of felt need) are the history of previous in-service programs, the attitudes of key figures, everyone's willingness to experiment, and (at least in beginning form) the concept that learning comes best by doing.

In general, this section has stressed the importance of assessing the state of the system quite carefully. Such assessment could easily become too elaborate. The thing to remember is this: Training is richer when it starts with real needs and problems about group work. Most of us leap to conclusions about people's needs, and this section says, "Look before you leap." Given some careful looking, a next step is involved.

Where might we start?

At this point—and a formal decision to begin official planning has not yet been made—the assessing group must look at some promising first steps for the proposed but still hypothetical program. Many kinds of questions may be explored:

> Who has to *decide* whether a program can be started or not?
> If they aren't in this group, how do we involve them?
> How formal a program are we thinking of?
> Who are the people we hope would come?
> What size program is reasonable to start with?
> What do we think people would learn from such a program?

As "official" planning becomes imminent, assessors should also look at their own roles:

> Do I/we want to continue with active planning?
> What do other people in the system think of our working on this?
> Who else should be involved?
> If an official planning group is formed, who should chair it?
> Do we need to involve an outside consultant at this point?
> Are there members of our own staff with experience and skill in carrying on training?

Answering questions like these may take time, especially if the system considered is an entire school system. In smaller systems, such as a school staff or a classroom, many of these questions can be asked and answered relatively quickly, or in fact may never come up at all.

Active Planning for the Program

The decision to proceed

At some more or less hazy point in time, given sufficient evidence of need and readiness, a decision is made to move ahead on an official basis. Informal assessment is to be replaced by active planning. An authorized planning group is identified, a chairman is named, and program plans are expected to emerge. Such a group will have to shuttle back and forth between key figures, ask for information, study needs further, revise plans, and so on. Basically, this group has responsibility for action.

Considerable formal detail will be given in this discussion. Readers with informal, small-scale programs in mind will of course understand that assessment and planning can go forward much more rapidly, loosely, and spontaneously than is suggested. (This is especially true of training in a classroom setting.) However, anything requiring extra expenditures of funds, involving many persons, or extending over a considerable length of time should be assessed and planned for much as outlined in this chapter. Informally and rapidly set-up training activities do involve all the steps suggested in the section on "Necessary decisions" (pp. 61–71), but some of them take thirty seconds to complete instead of thirty days.

In general, far too little time is usually budgeted for assessment and planning. One rule of thumb is: "It takes at least a day to plan a day."

Who plans?

The make-up of the planning group will vary according to the setting and the type of program envisioned. Typically, it might include interested persons from a list like this:

The initiator.

Some or all assessors.

Key authority persons (principals, superintendent, board member) who must approve decisions involving money or commitment of persons.

Outside consultants (if any) who will be actively involved in the program as trainers, speakers, etc.

Representatives of different kinds of people who will be in the program (elementary and secondary teachers, area chairmen, curriculum workers, etc.).

Persons with special skills or interests in the area of group behavior, who may serve as trainers in the program.

This list looks formidable, and planning committee size should probably not get much over 8 or 10. Usually any one person will fill several of the descriptions above (for example, a teacher who was an assessor, and also represents area chairmen). In the classroom, a planning committee (if used) would simply include the teacher and several interested students.

Who decides?

As planning for the program goes forward, many different kinds of decisions must be made—about policy, about administrative matters about the technical aspects of training. These decisions must be fitted into the regular decision-making machinery of the larger system, or the custodian will never appear at 8:00 to let in people for the opening session.

When decisions about training are shared by the total group of participants, they are most likely to be realistic and carried through effectively. But before the total group has come together, the members of the planning group—using the best evidence they can get—usually have to make many explicit decisions (see below). Even during training, many administrative or technical decisions cannot be made by the total group of participants. The planning committee, a subcommittee, the chairman, or the person(s) serving as trainers must sometimes decide.

Whoever decides, the important thing is that their responsibility be *clear*. Planning group, chairman, or trainers should not pretend to share decisions which they really don't want to share. It's far better to indicate clearly what has been decided, and free people to work on things they can do something about.

Here again, looking within is a good idea. Many more decisions can be effectively shared with people than we sometimes think. And even "minor" decisions often carry importance. For example, in one training program the decision on meeting place proved to be very difficult to make, since it involved a conflict between smokers and non-smokers and their different needs.

Bigger, more formal programs place more decision-making responsibility on planning groups. When the program is less of a "production" (as with a weekly study group or a class), planning decisions can usually be made by all participants on a shared basis.

Time is as precious in schools as it is anywhere else. The reader can only be assured that ample time spent in planning a training program will prove to be an economy in the long run.

Necessary decisions

Below are listed nine areas of decision which most planning groups have to face. For each area are given typical needed decisions, followed by general comments from the author's experience.[2] The order is not fixed;

---

[2] This is not the place for detailed discussion of the problems of conference and workshop planning. The reader who wishes to extend his skills in this area is referred to several entire issues of *Adult Leadership,* December 1952, May 1953, June 1954, and most especially to the concise, practical, and thorough treatment in R. Beckhard, *How to plan and conduct workshops and conferences* (Association Press, 1956).

ordinarily many of the areas have to be dealt with at each successive meeting of the planning group. The reader who is actively engaged in planning may wish to use the questions under each area as a checklist to be sure important decisions are not being overlooked.

1. *Purposes*

What do we hope, realistically, that the program will accomplish—on a long-range and short-range basis?

How may it fit into other in-service efforts?

What difficulties in the system is this program set up to help resolve?

What will people *do* differently as a result of coming?

What should we name the proposed training activity?

Comment: Dealing with this area early is important, so that everyone is working toward the same general goal. General purposes are often only dimly seen at first, however, and continued clarification is necessary. Talking at the behavioral level ("What would a person do?") helps. The question of the name of the activity is usually not a superficial one, since it reflects purpose, and makes a difference in recruiting.

2. *Costs*

Will this involve any extra dollar expenditure, or are the costs in terms of donated time and energy?

Where will funds come from—the school system? the participants?

Who is responsible for money matters?

Comment: Often decisions in this area cannot be made firmly until other decisions (for example, who will come and when, duration of the program, use of outside consultant help) have been reached. But financial limits on the group's work need to be made very clear at the outset. The major cost items are usually fees for outside consultants (if any are used), and salaries for substitutes (if teachers are to be released from their regular duties). Items like materials and coffee are minor.

Charging a nominal participation fee, incidentally, sometimes has the effect of increasing respect for the training program.

3. *Who will take part*

What kinds of roles (teacher, principal, guidance worker) will be represented?

Which particular persons?

Will they come voluntarily, or as part of their regular job duties?

Are all participants to come from the same working group (ex: an elementary school staff), or from many different levels and parts of the over-all organization?

Are non-professional personnel included? Parents? Citizens at large?

Will participants come mainly for their own benefit, or are we hoping that they will in turn train others?

Will participants come as isolated individuals, or as "teams"—people who already work together on the job?

What procedures will we use for recruiting?

How to select if we have more than we can handle?

Comment: Given the ideas presented in Chapter III about training, the single most important criterion for attendance is almost surely *interest*. In-service credit toward salary increments should certainly be given if the school system feels it is justified, but this should not be the method of attracting potential participants to the program.

Research indicates that people who come to a training program as team members are more productive—their learnings are supported and reinforced on the job.[3] The attitudes of system leaders are also very important in terms of carry-through—a teacher with new and exciting ideas about improving staff meetings is headed for frustration and failure if her principal doesn't understand. Implication: maybe the principal should attend the training program too.

Whether or not top administrators should come depends on the length and intensiveness of the program. Short programs may not allow time and perspective for working out long-standing problems of superior-subordinate relationships that may have been impeding group work. However, support and understanding of the program from top administrators are essential, and they may well be invited to attend, either as participants or in a special capacity, such as speaking in a general session of a large workshop.

If the program is limited to all the members of one working group (such as a curriculum committee, all the principals, a class, or a building staff), there is likely to be considerable interest and carry-through. It is possible, though, that some members may at first have low interest. If the existing homogeneous groups are not particularly supportive, a heterogenous group cutting across many parts of the system sometimes

[3] For evidence, see R. Lippitt, *Training in community relations* (Harper, 1949), pp. 172–212.

frees participants to be more frank and less defensive about their job problems and inadequacies.[4]

If the demand is likely to exceed the number that can be handled, then naturally an explicit list of selection criteria should be made, otherwise those who don't get in will have a legitimate reason to complain. Recruiting and selecting must be done in such a manner that prospective attenders have a clear idea what the program may involve (time, purposes, how preset or how exploratory the approach will be, and so on).

4. Time arrangements

How many sessions will there be; how long will they be?

Will the sessions be held on school time, off, part on and part off?

Will the sessions be held serially (every so often) or in one intensive block (as in a one-day teachers' institute)?

What times of day are reasonable for starting and stopping?

Comment: Serial meetings spread out over weeks or months allow for more on-the-job tryout and application, but involvement may drop. An intensive experience may help people really unfreeze and change more thoroughly, but get them in for more frustration when they move back to the job. A combination of intensive, spaced meetings may be the answer (for example, three 2-day sessions spread over the year).

Usually, single meetings to help people learn better group behavior are not profitable if they are shorter than an hour and a half or so. By contrast, in workshops taking two or three days, experience has shown that people can and will work from 9 to 9 and then talk informally until midnight, *if* change of pace, subgrouping, good use of breaks, and recreation are built in. Continuing training programs are usually built around one or more training groups. Such groups should usually have at least eight hours of total meeting time.

For adults, the question of whose time the session should be held on is important. Teachers can and will work after school hours, but if a school system cares about improving behavior in school groups, then experience suggests that school time should be used for a substantial part of the program.

Sometimes arrangements can be worked out for individual participants and the school system to share costs. Sometimes inexpensive arrangements

---

[4] This matter is discussed more fully in "Designing the training group," *Training group leaders* (Adult Education Association, 1956), pp. 28–32.

can be worked out for releasing teachers (for example, using regular in-service days, covering classes during free periods, doubling small classes, using teacher aides). But such arrangements usually cause more inconvenience to the classrooms and teachers involved than does the use of substitutes. Professional advancement of school personnel, basically, must involve investment by the school system. Time is money.

5. *Physical arrangements*

Where should the sessions be held: at a school, the central office, someone's home, in a hotel or conference center away from distractions?

What room arrangements will be needed? Furniture?

What audio-visual equipment will be used?

Can coffee be served during breaks? Are meals possible? Smoking?

Who is responsible for setting up and checking equipment arrangements?

Comment: Getting a location out of the stream of work in the school seems to be important, even when students are involved. Schools using camps or conference houses for extended meetings have found that such facilities encourage hard work and the kind of creative thinking that is difficult when phone calls and minor crises are ever-present. Isolated settings also mean that people will eat and live together, which provides added support and informal learning. Caution: avoid over-primitive or unstaffed settings which may interfere with work (members have to leave the group to peel the potatoes for supper, etc.)

Movable tables and chairs, chalkboards, and electric outlets seem to be the minimum essentials in meeting rooms. Newsprint pads (or other large sheets of paper) on an easel are helpful to keep intact ideas which might otherwise be erased. One room should be large enough to seat all the participants comfortably, and if there are more than fifteen people or so, additional rooms will be needed for work in small groups. The single most useful piece of audio-visual equipment (after chalkboards or newsprint) is a tape recorder. It can be used to aid training in a wide variety of ways (see index to Chapter V, pp. 175–76, and Chapter VI, pp. 198–202).

If people can drink coffee, smoke, and eat together, it helps training a great deal. Meeting "creature comforts" with others seems to intensify feelings of warmth and support. Food, especially, has been called "the great socializer." Eating together during a workshop often gives people the chance to relate to each other in a non-work-centered way, to reduce tensions, and to verify learnings that may have been only tentative or dimly-seen before. Conversely, poor accommodations and food can hurt the program. Careful attention to detail here during planning is important.

6. *Content*
Given our general purposes, what specific problems will be worked on in the program?
How can we be sure that this is what people really want? really *need*?
How can we determine new areas of needed content as the program continues?

Comment: Although people experienced in training for better group behavior can often predict the general types of problems that participants will bring to a training program, it is impossible to know all the specifics ahead of time. Usually, participant needs must be carefully assessed before the first session. Simple, open-end questionnaires are usually best. Here is one the author has used frequently.

PLANNING FOR LEARNING

The concerns and needs for change you describe below can be of much help in planning our sessions together. The more free and direct you can be in expressing yourself, the more meaningful the sessions can be.

"Groups" as used below can mean staff meetings, committees, workshops, classes you teach, or groups in the community.

1. Things I would like to *understand* better about the groups I work in:

2. Things I would like to learn how to *do* better in groups:

3. *Feelings* I have in groups which I would like to change or improve:

The responses to this instrument are usually quite vivid and concrete; summarized, they can guide content planning. A report of results may well form part of the first session. Here, for example, is a partial record of the learnings desired by twenty-seven teachers, principals, and guidance workers planning to attend a three-day workshop on group behavior. Figures show number of persons mentioning each topic.

1. Things I would like to *understand* better about the groups I work in:

8—General knowledge of group work ("what makes a group tick," "factors making for constructive accomplishment").

6—Reasons for disruptive individual behavior ("why people get set ideas and won't change," "the dominator").

5—Nature of effective problem solving ("how groups define and work through problems").

3—Causes for poor group work ("what makes for lack of communication," "why groups peter out").

2—Use of time ("why groups waste time on side issues, take so long to get together").

2—Leader role ("how democratic the leader can be without being ineffectual").

6—Other single comments (ex: "how to foster an atmosphere of security and freedom to participate," "why people listen to one person and not another").

4—Blank, no response.

2. Things I would like to learn how to *do* better in groups:

6—Aid groups in problem solving ("how to move discussion along," "channel discussion toward goal," "avoid going off on tangents").

5—Be a better leader or chairman.

4—Improve own participation pattern ("offer my opinion instead of keeping silent," "learn to cooperate instead of competing with others").

3—Improve communication skills ("get my points expressed and accepted in a group," "how to organize what I say better").

3—Handle own impatience ("how to be more tolerant of slow progress," "listen carefully and critically instead of rushing on").

3—Work more effectively in teaching situation ("handling myself in personality clashes with students," "making classes more interesting").

2—Aid others' participation ("help shy members get in").

6—Other single comments (ex: "getting along better with adults," "how to interpret group consensus").

1—Blank, no response.

3. *Feelings* I have in groups which I would like to change or improve:

5—Under-participation, shyness ("feel timid, and that my ideas are not worthwhile").

5—Over-participation ("I talk too much, am always a leader—would rather be a resource person").

4—Impatience ("I am quite intolerant when a group does not work at the speed I would like," "react negatively to aggressive persons and have no patience with them").

4—Negative reactions to frustration ("I tend to withdraw or be angry when things do not go my way").

3—Inadequacy ("I have a fear of being thought stupid in group situations").

10—Other single comments (ex: "I find it difficult to work in new or strange group situations," "the urge to clobber the self-elected leader," "the way I hurt others with my wit and vocabulary").

1—Blank, no response.

Note several things here. First, the content focuses on the understandings, skills, and feelings people have in relation to group *processes*. That is, people are not asked for, and do not give, reactions about bond issues, language arts guides, or report cards as such. The questionnaire asks for process problems which the person encounters in many different group situations.

Second, the range is wide. Training activities must be planned, for example, in which both under- and over-participator can pursue their needs. No single training need is shared by everyone.

Third, the questions are put in an order which encourages more and more personal expressions of need. The responses to question 3 tend to be more diverse and individual than those to questions 1 and 2. It is usually helpful, for planners and learners alike, to know that "I'm not the only person who feels this way (inadequate, impatient, insecure) in groups."

Other methods can be used to plan content. These include: observing self and others working in on-the-job groups; interviewing people who are planning to attend the program; and holding a pre-meeting of participants to make a census of problems in group behavior. If the training program is longer than a single session, the methods above, plus post-meeting reaction sheets (see Chapter V) filled out by members, can be used to identify new problems which participants would like to work on as the program continues.

7. *Procedures*

What kinds of meetings are required: general sessions, work groups, practice sessions, interviews?

How big should different kinds of subgroupings be, and how should they be composed?

Where can specific methods be best used—open discussion, role playing, listening to tapes, observation, lecture, films, process analysis?

How much should procedures be planned ahead, and how much "played by ear"?

What materials should be used?

Comment: Good training actively involves the learner in the process of restructuring his ideas, attitudes, and overt behavior. Such learning requires procedures that carry more impact than rambling discussion or didactic lectures. So an important aspect of the trainer's role is methodological—helping the planning group, and later the training group, set up and carry out exciting procedures for learning. Many school people have tended to use outside consultants in this area of planning. However, most school systems do have on their staffs persons with interest and skill in procedural planning. And beyond this, creative, ingenious procedural planning can be learned. The reader is referred to the wide range of training activities discussed in Chapter V, and to Chapter VII on the role of the trainer.[5]

A great deal of material has appeared in the last decade on various aspects of group behavior, and planners may wish to consider making books, articles, evaluation and observation instruments, and the like available for study by participants. An annotated list of materials suitable for purchase by a school system is given in Appendix B.

8. *Special roles*

What particular jobs are needed to carry out training as planned? Trainer(s)? Administrator? Group chairmen? Process observers? Recorders? Resource people? Evaluators?

Will doing these jobs require any special briefing or training?

Do we need outside consultant help, or are our own local resources adequate?

---

[5] See also Beckhard, *op. cit.*, and the readable little book by M. and H. Knowles, *How to develop better leaders* (Association Press, 1955) for many helpful ideas, not only on procedural planning, but on the whole range of problems of training which are discussed in the present book.

Comment: In a training program of any size or duration, it is a good idea to have different people in training and administrative roles. The trainer(s) can concentrate on helping people learn most effectively, and the administrator can be free to manage arrangements of all kinds to ensure that the program will go forward smoothly. (In the case of classroom training, the teacher usually performs both functions.)

Briefing for special roles like those of chairman, recorder, observer, and resource person should not be left to chance, casual conversation, or printed directions. Discussion is needed, and practice (i.e., training) is desirable.

The problems of working with outside consultants have been discussed thoroughly elsewhere.[6] Perhaps it is enough to say here that such people should be in on the planning as early as possible, and the nature of the desired help worked out explicitly. While this book has as a basic purpose the strengthening of local resources for training, the possibility of using outside resources should not be overlooked. In Chapter VII, where the trainer role is discussed, sources of consultant help are mentioned (see pp. 218–19).

9. Evaluation

How can we find out whether the training program accomplishes what we hope it will?

What information is needed before, during, and after the training program?

What information can be fed back immediately to steer continuous planning during the program, and what is more long-range in its implications?

Who is responsible for evaluation?

Comment: Much can be done to get useful information about existing skills and needs for improvement before training starts, about learnings and dissatisfactions during the program, and about consequences on the job afterward. Long-range results are always important, particularly if special funds have been spent. Chapter VIII discusses the problems of evaluating training in some detail; here it is sufficient to say that decisions about evaluation, to be effective, must be reached well ahead of the start of the program, or the information available to planners will be frus-

---

[6] See, for example, "Workshop on consultation" (5 articles), Adult Leadership, 3, 10, April 1955; and A. Miel, "How to use experts and consultants," and L. P. Bradford, "Training consultants and groups to work together," in Benne and Muntyan, op. cit., pp. 208–16.

tratingly incomplete. For example, it is necessary to get assessment of how skillful the participants are *before* the program starts, if changes in skill caused by the program are to be measured at all.

A final comment

Above, some typical areas of decision for planners have been listed and commented on. Once again, the amount of detail may create visions of Enormous Programs in the reader's mind. It should be made clear that many, if not most, good programs can begin and operate quite informally, without the need for elaborate arrangements of subcommittees, agendas, and decisions. For example, in a situation where a staff has decided to build in self-training as a regular part of its meetings, many of the planning decisions above (who will take part, where, when) have already been made, and the group can move right into setting up learning experiences for itself. Or, a teacher and class may move spontaneously into a discussion aimed at correcting difficulties in committee work, and then begin practicing specific group skills.[7] Careful planning *is* essential, but how formally and explicitly it is done will depend on the resources and demands of the immediate situation.

Planning the First Session

If the planners have reached some agreement on questions in each of the decision areas suggested above, they will probably have emerged with an over-all design for the training program. Problems of who, when, where, how, and to what end will have been struggled with, and resolved into a coherent action plan. Now the group is faced with setting up an opening session of some kind.

What should a first session accomplish?

The specific objectives of an opening session will naturally vary according to what is to follow (one more meeting? three days of work? a year of weekly study meetings?). But some general purposes for any first session can be identified.

[7] In M. and H. Knowles, *op. cit.*, there is an informal, concrete illustration of how "group self-training" can get started with a minimum of fuss (pp. 17–24).

1. *The session should clarify the nature of the training program.* Initially this means getting acquainted with the other people in the group (members, trainers, and any outsiders involved). Members need also to know some history (how does it happen that we are here tonight?). Beyond this, different individual expectancies may need to be stated and discussed. Proposed training approaches should be demonstrated, or at least explained. Plans for research and evaluation should be described. Over-all purposes need to be discussed and clarified. People should understand their commitment for attending further sessions. (Sometimes it is valuable to have a first session as a kind of "taste," after which individuals decide whether or not to continue as regular participants.) In general, as a result of the opening session, participants should know what to expect.

2. *The session should focus and intensify member needs.* Members usually enter a training program with general, vague dissatisfactions. A first session should not only sharpen and help define problems and needs, but also intensify and deepen dissatisfaction and the desire for change. The first session should be a sensitizing one; it should raise more questions than it answers, should move members into a searching, questioning position. The comments in Chapter III about dissatisfaction in the training process apply here.

3. *The session should help members see training as a means to meeting their needs.* Even if participants' feelings of need do increase and the program is clearly understood, learning is unlikely unless people come to believe that the program will, in fact, be of help. Hearing oral statements about future meetings in the training program is a start on this, but it is much more desirable for the group members to get right down to work on important problems in a training-centered way. That is, instead of making promises like "We will analyze what goes on in group situations," it is a good idea at the first session to help participants start analyzing and learning, right here, right now. If people can have an initial work experience together that is successful and exciting, they are much more likely to see the proposed program as a potentially useful path to reducing the dissatisfactions they feel. Concrete experiences, such as discussing a role-playing scene, also help to clarify the nature of the proposed program. Furthermore, starting out with work helps members get warmly acquainted with others, and to make the pleasing discovery that "I'm not the only one who has problems in groups."

4. *The session should provide a springboard to future sessions.* Members should leave the session with clear ideas of what is likely to happen next, and with active motivation to continue. If all the members are to carry on some kind of interim activity (such as observing group functions in a committee meeting) before the next session begins, so much the better. And clear evidence should be gathered on needs and concerns—either at the first session or during the interim—to help with the making of plans for the next session, as well as to maintain genuine member involvement and anticipation.

Some sample first-session plans

What might a first session of a training program look like? In the belief that concrete illustrations may be more helpful than general suggestions on "how to plan," six sample plans are presented here. All of them illustrate the four general purposes suggested above. They are quite diverse. There are surely many effective ways to start a program not mentioned here.

Any planning group considering a first session should (1) identify clearly the *specific* outcomes desired; (2) move to procedural planning, drawing on ideas like those given below. Form follows function! This dictum comes from architecture, but is just as relevant to training. Planners who start first with procedures (role playing, buzz groups, or whatever) without being clear about desired outcomes are bound for trouble.

The completeness of detail given below may, once again, give an impression of formality. Any of the designs can be easily expanded, contracted, abridged, or combined with other methods not mentioned here. The time intervals suggested are only to aid concreteness. Points in the design where easy expansion or contraction can take place are indicated. All the designs assume that someone is taking a "trainer" role, with explicit responsibility for guiding learning, and some comments are made about appropriate trainer behavior in each design.

Since so much depends on what types of people come to a training program, what their needs are, and what type of program is to follow the first session, it is impossible to specify a "good" opening session that could do for all occasions. For each session plan below, an illustrative program setting is suggested. Comments follow each plan.

First session: Plan I

Time: 2 hours.
Setting: A weekly study group on leadership problems, size 10–15.

Minutes		Activity
Total	Each	
0	10	General orientation: history of planning, general purposes, explanation of procedure for this session.
10	10	Brief introductions.
20	5	Summary of needs and interests obtained by pre-questionnaire (duplicated, or written on chalkboard):
		6—How to help everyone in the group participate.
		4—Getting more work done in groups (how to organize, stay on beam).
		3—Reacting to criticism when you are the leader.
		2—Dealing with problem members (dominator, people who block the group). (Etc.)
25	25	Discussion of needs, clarification, priority-setting.
50	10	Evaluation of where we are, how well we're doing.
60	15	Coffee break.
75	20	Continued discussion of interest priorities, decision reached.
95	15	Planning or suggesting possible procedure (discussion, tape recording, role playing, etc.) for studying the problems identified as first priority. Responsibilities fixed where necessary.
110	10	Filling out post-meeting reaction sheets (by all members) to aid in further planning.
120		End.

Comment: Many workshops begin in this way, and this may be a good design to use where members have not had experience with more vigorous, experience-centered methods. The approach demands less skill from the trainer than do other designs described below, and it does involve members actively in planning. The design can be easily used with students (ex: a first meeting of a leadership clinic for committee chairmen).

The primary weakness of this design is its heavy reliance on talk, rather than on experience. Only a brief amount of time is devoted to analysis of "how we're doing"—the training group is scarcely used as a laboratory at all. Also, the design is perhaps too "rational"—it assumes that group members will be able to locate and decide on meaningful needs in a neat stepwise order. Actually, the more potent the goals involved, the more difficult it will be to reach a good decision, especially in a new group where the situation is unclear and uncertain. Comments like "We've spent nearly two hours just organizing. When are we going to get at it?" are likely to be heard. If the trainer can capitalize on such comments, and help the members analyze what is happening, they may well learn a lot about problems in new group situations, how to set group goals, effective decision making, and so on. Plan II, below, makes more explicit provision for such process analysis and learning.

FIRST SESSION: PLAN II

Time: 2 hours.
Setting: As in Plan I.

Minutes		
Total	**Each**	*Activity*
0	10	Orientation as in Plan I, plus comment by trainer on the use of the group as a laboratory (see Chapter V, pp. 102–03).
10	10	Introductions.
20	15	Analysis and evaluation of how the introduction process went ("Why did we tend to stereotype each other as 'typical kindergarten teachers,' 'typical principals'?" "Why did we seem hesitant and cautious in expressing ourselves?" "Did we really get acquainted? Why not?" etc.).
35	5	Summary of needs and interests, as in Plan I.
40	15	Discussion of needs, clarification, priority-setting, as in Plan I.
55	15	Analysis and evaluation of problems of agreeing on group goals ("Why did we get into such conflict?" "Does everyone feel his needs will be met?" "Were good decisions reached? Why or why not?" etc.).
70	10	Coffee break.
80	10	Plan-making (by total group) for next time.
90	20	Analysis and evaluation of planning and of entire meeting.
110	10	Post-meeting reaction sheets, as in Plan I.
120		End.

Comment: This design emphasizes attention to the here-and-now, that is, the actual behavior occurring in the group, as it happens. Such an approach is considerably more interesting than that taken in Plan I, although it may also bring forth comments like "What is this, anyway?" The trainer needs skill to know when and how to intervene as he encourages analysis of what's happening. (For suggestions, see Chapter IV, p. 80; Chapter V, pp. 102–03; and Chapter VII, pp. 210–14.) Thoughtful questioning and interpretation are also needed to help members learn from what's going on in the group.

One weakness of this design is that it may prove frustrating for members with strong needs to "get things done." Almost certainly, the meeting will end with incomplete decisions on plans and next steps, and some members will not have seen the analysis periods as "getting things done." Encouraging the group members to discuss what they feel has and has not been accomplished is usually helpful. Group members may come to realize that they differ considerably in their pictures of what this group— or any group—should accomplish.

First session: Plan III

Time: 1½ to 2 hours.
Setting: A series of afternoon-evening meetings held once every two weeks on "Understanding Group Behavior," size 10–200. Can also be used for first session of a workshop.

Minutes		
Total	Each	Activity [8]
0	10	Orientation as in Plan I.
10	10	Summary of needs and interests from pre-meeting questionnaire.
20	5	Orientation to demonstration. Role-playing situation is explained to audience, and they are asked to watch the demonstration and jot down "things that help" and "things that hinder" the group as it works.
25	10	Demonstration: a typical group of 5–7 members puts on a skit (role-playing scene) showing part of a meeting, which runs into substantial difficulty. (Film scene, such as Scene I of *Meeting in session*,[9] may be used instead.) Meanwhile people watching are jotting down helps and hindrances they see in the scene. [8, 9 Footnotes on page 77]

35	5	After scene ends, watchers keep writing any additional helps or hindrances.
40	10	Watchers talk with one another in groups of 4–5 people about the helps and hindrances they saw.
50	20	General discussion reporting helps and hindrances. Written on chalkboard, these form a functional agenda for the future (how to supply helps, make hindrances less frequent, and cope with hindrances when they do appear).

CUT TIME AFTER THIS POINT IF DESIRED

70	15	Trainer or consultant talks on the general nature of group behavior, drawing from the helps and hindrances on the chalkboard.[10]
85	20	General discussion.
105	15	Plans for the next meeting (via discussion, post-meeting reaction sheets, or reference back to helps and hindrances).
120		End.

Comment: Variations on this basic design have been used by the author in a wide range of settings. It is concrete, highly interesting, and lets participants get right down to work. Members, trainer, and consultant (if used) can get a good idea of where other people are in their thinking about groups. The design can be used for evaluative research: if a tape recording is made of the scene and played back at the end of the workshop, members can usually see many more helps and hindrances than they could at first—they have become more sensitive. The design is easily used in the classroom; students, like adults, enjoy portraying and watching a snarled-up committee meeting.

If a role-playing scene is used, the role players need to be carefully warmed up ahead of time and the scene must be a plausible, rich one,

[8] This plan does not include the time for registration, giving out name badges, etc., that may be required for a workshop or a series of meetings involving more than twenty people or so.

[9] *Meeting in session: human relations in a group process,* sound, black and white, 16mm., 20 minutes (Teachers College Bureau of Publications, 1953). The film shows two meetings of a nursing staff which vary in effectiveness. Discussion guide included.

[10] Content might come from general review, such as M. Horwitz, "The conceptual status of group dynamics," *Review of Educational Research,* 33:309–28, 1953; or M. B. Miles, "Human relations in cooperative research," in *Research for curriculum improvement,* 1957 Yearbook, Association for Supervision and Curriculum Development (The Association, 1957), esp. pp. 210–16; or G. Lippitt, "How to get results from a group," *Office Executive, January* 1955, pp. 13–15.

with plenty of conflict and difficulty built in. See Chapters V and VI for suggestions on role playing.

<h3 style="text-align:center">FIRST SESSION: PLAN IV</h3>

Time: 1¾ to 2½ hours.
Setting: A continuing study group, size 10–15; or subgroups of a larger workshop.

Minutes Total	Each	Activity
0	10	Orientation as in Plan I.
10	15	Subgroups of three persons each are formed. In each subgroup, the members listen successively as each one describes the problems that he personally faces in groups.
25	15	Subgroups break up, are scrambled, and new subgroups are formed with different members. The process of describing one's own problems is repeated. A third set of subgroups may be gone through if desired.

ADD TIME BEFORE OR AFTER THIS POINT IF DESIRED

40	25	General discussion: (1) How did members feel in the two or three group situations (any warmer in the second or third one? clearer? easier to express real problems? why? (2) What were some of the problems and concerns which members expressed? (Listed on chalkboard.)

ADD TIME AFTER THIS POINT IF DESIRED

65	15	Group members decide on areas of highest priority for work at next meeting.
80	15	Evaluation and analysis of session.
95	10	Post-meeting reaction sheets.
105		End.

Comment: This is a good design for creating a warm atmosphere and developing feelings of mutual support. Being able to admit one's problems —and to see that others share them—tends to create psychological safety. Members may leave the session with the desire to get help from others and change one's own way of doing things. Participants are, in effect, introducing themselves as whole persons, not as "Joan Hunter, second grade, Lincoln School."

Some attention is paid in this design to the group as a laboratory, but there can be a tendency to become over-interested in the problems listed, while ignoring the processes going on in the session itself. This is not serious, however; the trainer can draw attention to the fact, for example, that "many of us are listing problems of *others'* behavior rather than our own," and help the group examine this.

First session: Plan V

Time: 3½ to 2½ hours.

Setting: Session to train leadership teams (chairmen, recorders, resource people, observers, etc.) or individual chairmen for a forthcoming conference or workshop (ex: an in-service day on language arts). Size 10–50.

Minutes		
Total	*Each*	*Activity*
0	25	Orientation as in Plan I, plus description of the general task which leadership personnel face in the forthcoming conference or workshop. Also information on meeting rooms, special procedures, etc.
25	10	Set up dry-run meeting. If possible, this should have approximately as many members as the actual groups which members will be working with later on. One member acts as "chairman." If teams are being trained, an actual leadership team who will be working with a group in the forthcoming conference takes over.
35	50	Dry-run meeting and recurrent analysis.

The "chairman" begins the meeting as he might with a real group. From time to time, the trainer, serving as a clarifier, interrupts the dry run and helps the group analyze how well it's going. ("In the introductions, the first person just gave his name and the rest followed around. How did we feel about that? What could a chairman do that would help make introductions most useful?")

Then the group returns to the dry run, continues, is "cut" again by the trainer, analyzes, does more dry run, and so on. Different "chairmen" and "recorders" may try their hands at working with the group.

85	5	Brief summary of learnings so far.

[First session: Plan V cont'd]

| 90 | 15 | Coffee break. |

CUT TIME AFTER THIS POINT IF DESIRED

| 105 | 15 | Listing of additional problems that members feel they will be facing as they work with groups in the actual conference or workshop. |
| 120 | 40 | Shorter dry runs set up to cope with particular problems, such as "handling the excessive talker," "what to do when the group is apathetic," and the like. |

CUT TIME AFTER THIS POINT IF DESIRED

160	20	Each team meets to plan how they will begin their sessions at the real conference. If individual chairmen are being trained, small groups of 3–4 discuss their plans.
180	20	Reporting plans, getting reactions from other members. Clearing up items like "Does my group's room have a chalkboard?"
200	10	Evaluation sheet and/or plans for a clinic session during the conference to share how well meetings are going, get help, etc.
210		End.

Comment: This is a helpful and direct way to train people for a specific job of working with specific groups. If the session is held shortly before the conference itself, motivation is generally high, because the leadership personnel are concerned about doing a good job. The design is most helpful for people with little previous experience in working with conference or workshop groups. It can be easily adapted to help student committee chairmen when a class is new to working in small groups.

The design assumes that "getting started" is a big problem for most special leadership personnel. Where this is not a central need, less time should be spent before the break and problem listing.

The design can also be varied by starting with the problem listing, which may give more security to group members, but may also let them "run away" from the need to practice and try out things actively.

Knowing when to interrupt as a clarifier is difficult, but can be learned by practice. Some good points at which to intervene are: when the "chairman" has just started doing something new; when there is uncertainty, discomfort, or dissatisfaction in the group; when the chairman has just done something that made the group feel good. See also Chapter V, pp. 125–28, for comments on use of a clarifier.

First session: Plan VI

Time: 2 to 2½ hours.
Setting: One-day institute on "Understanding Group Behavior" for teachers or other school system staff, size 20–400.

Total	Each	
Minutes		*Activity* [11]
0	10	Orientation as in Plan I.
10	5	Summary of needs/interests from pre-questionnaire.
15	5	Audience is divided into four sectors to watch for different things in the film to be shown (below): Sector 1: What does the leader do to help? Sector 2: What do the members do to help? Sector 3: What does the leader do to hinder? Sector 4: What do the members do to hinder?
20	15	Scene I of *Meeting in session* [12] is shown; audience watches.
35	5	Members in same sector talk with one another in groups of 3–4 to pool what they saw.
40	20	Reports from the four different sectors; information put on chalkboard.

ADD TIME AFTER THIS POINT IF DESIRED

60	5	Clarifying and summarizing comments by trainer.
65	15	Scene II of *Meeting in session* is shown, with sectors watching again.
80	5	Sector members discuss what they saw in groups of 3–4.
85	15	General reporting and listing on board.

ADD TIME AFTER THIS POINT IF DESIRED

100	10	Comparison of the two scenes, and summary.
110	10	Coffee break, then move to next activity (usually small training groups).
120		End.

Comment: This is a good design to help people dig beneath the surface of what goes on in groups. When members are looking actively for helps and hindrances of leaders and members, they are less likely to stereotype

[11] Registration time not included.
[12] See p. 77, Note 9.

("The first scene was awful, but the second scene was very good," or "It was all the leader's fault").

The main skills required from the trainer are: keeping the reporting moving vigorously; guiding the discussion; and identifying common threads as they emerge. If the total group size is much over 50, the timing above is too tight (add more time for reporting and discussion).

The film shows nurses, and so training group members' attention usually tends to stay focused on the human problems in the film instead of on school "shop talk." One risk is that the film may be rejected as being too far from school people's concerns, but experience suggests that this rarely happens.

Summary: first-session planning

The sample session designs above share one characteristic—careful planning. Formality of planning will naturally vary. More thorough preparation is usually required for large groups, groups of relative strangers, and groups meeting intensively for a block of time. Some general guidelines to planning are:

1. Clarify the purposes, both general and specific, for the session.

2. Design specific procedures to meet the purposes, not vice versa. Get the session plan on paper.

3. Make sure that responsibilities for all parts of the session are clearly placed: "master of ceremonies," trainer, registration personnel, warmer-up of role players, etc. A good procedure is to go through the plan step by step to be sure "who does what."

4. Check the room setup to be sure it is adequate for what you want to do. Re-check arrangements just before the session.

5. Brief any special personnel involved in the session. This briefing may include, if desired, a dry run of difficult or unclear portions of the session.

6. Relax and enjoy the session. Most opening sessions meet or surpass expectations, since they have been much more carefully planned than the typical large meeting.

So far this chapter has dealt with the planning that takes place before the program gets under way. Below are discussed the planning problems encountered as training proceeds, and as the program is terminated. The material is put here for convenience under the general topic of "planning," but the reader may wish to go directly at this point to the next chapter, which gives illustrative training activities and methods.

Continuing and Maintaining the Training Program

It is almost impossible to supply detailed directions for coping with the planning problems that appear while a training program is going on. The answer to nearly any question about the operation of any given training setup is likely to be, "It depends." This section is aimed at suggesting what it depends on. Here, then, are some general guides for making administrative and training decisions as the program proceeds.

Organizing for planning

By the time the first session plan is complete, it should be clear who is to have continuing responsibility for planning. The suggestions made above on page 60 about the composition of the preliminary planning group are still applicable, although the same group may or may not continue. In general, the planning group should represent all major categories of members, including people who have strong reservations about the way things are going. As with the pre-planning group, it should be crystal clear who the planning committee are, and what kinds of decisions they have responsibility for.

As training proceeds, it is probably even more important than before to involve many members in the planning process. Sometimes training sessions can be used to make planning decisions about important general matters, such as extra or fewer meetings, or the content of a forthcoming session. All members can also be involved through the medium of reaction sheets and evaluation questionnaires (see pp. 111–13 and 242–44). The results from such questionnaires can be used to guide further planning of content and procedures.

Representation in the making of specific training decisions is important too. If more than one training group is involved in the program, each group may send representatives to a Steering Committee. Each successive planning session may involve some continuing members, and others new to the committee, so that many different people get a chance to take part.

As a training program gathers momentum, many planning procedures get easier and more routine. Often, however, the over-all organization may get more complex. Thus the role of the planning committee chairman or coordinator becomes quite important. Someone needs to be sure that the committee faces all the issues in front of it. These issues are of many kinds: "We have some visitors who would like to come to one of the general sessions next week"; "Nearly everyone in Group III seems to be disgusted with the workshop"; "Mrs. Walker says she can't get us coffee on Friday because the kitchen people are leaving early for the holiday."

The coordinator must also see to it that someone thoughtfully and accurately interprets the progress of the training program to other interested parts of the school system—especially the parts that are paying for it.

Steering from data

Which way the program goes should depend on carefully-gathered information. As things proceed, the ups and downs in the participants' reactions need to be charted as accurately as possible. As new interests develop, and new needs for learning appear, the planning committee must know about them as it decides what to do next in the program. Data for planning may be obtained in many ways:

Informal chats with members about how the program is going.

Bull sessions scheduled as part of the program, where members can relax and express their gripes and satisfactions.

Evaluation sessions where all group members discuss progress to date, and plan what might come next.

Post-meeting reaction questionnaires, responded to immediately or in the interval before the next meeting. Sometimes such questionnaires can be designed by using questions suggested by the total group.

Planned interviews with members designed to get particular information (ex: "In what ways is the training helping or hindering you on the job?).

Discussions with representatives from each of several training groups (as in the discussion of the Steering Committee, above).

The more fact and the less haphazard opinion about what people are thinking, the better. It should be pointed out that feelings are facts. If Tom flushed and retorted angrily to a question on whether the training group was being helpful to him, then his responses are facts. They need to be looked at and taken into account during planning—not ignored or explained away.

Centering the program's direction in facts can free planners to work in an experimental way—trying out something new, getting feedback of results, revamping the program. That is, while the planning committee works together, it can *learn,* much as the individual participant in the program learns (Chapter III). At first, it is difficult to face up to a group meeting that failed or a session that left participants frustrated. But accepting an experimental approach to training can help a planning committee to feel relaxed, less concerned about achieving perfection, and more effective all the way around.

Designing training experiences

Given reasonably accurate information on needs and interests, and on people's reactions to previous training activities on the program, a planning committee should be able to assemble, continuously, a curriculum of learning experiences.

In Chapter V following, many different training activities are outlined. Any given activity needs to be chosen on the basis of certain criteria. These may include, for example, the activity's appropriateness to the needs expressed, its "potency" or degree of emotional impact, how adequately it can be handled by the person or persons who are serving as trainer(s), and how it fits into the sequence of activities before and after it. These and other criteria for choosing training activities are discussed at the beginning of Chapter V.

Here, it may be important to comment on some problems of sequence and over-all design, remembering that specific training design problems are discussed at length in Chapter VI. In general, training activities need to follow each other in a psychological, learner-centered sequence, rather than in a purely logical progression. That statement is easy to make, but often puzzling to implement. Some examples of general session topics for a three-day workshop may help.

Logical order
1. The history of group dynamics as a field.
2. General characteristics of groups.
3. The nature of leadership.
4. Membership responsibilities in groups.
5. Personality and group work.

Psychological order
1. The new member in a group (with illustrations from the present workshop).
2. Hidden feelings in group situations.
3. How groups set goals.
4. Leadership and problems of authority.
5. Group morale and cohesion.

The latter set of topics, presumably, reflects more clearly the psychological readiness of members as they proceed through training. For example, at a first session, participants are much more concerned with how they are going to relate to the new situation than they are with logically-correct outlines of the history of research in group dynamics. This points up again the need to know "where people are" at any given point during the program. (See the discussion below of trends during training.)

Another general design principle is that training activities should follow each other in an alternating sequence. General sessions should be interspersed with small groups; sessions demanding active theoretical thinking should be followed by opportunities to apply ideas to job problems; sessions where conflict and tension build up should be followed by open-end, loose situations like coffee breaks or meals, so the tension can be worked out informally to aid in learning.

Whatever design is decided on, it is quite important that everyone be clear about how firm it is, how much change in it is legitimate once things have gotten under way. If people are uncertain about how flexible the training design is, they feel anxious. Sometimes group members who feel unclear about design flexibility accuse planners of being excessively rigid, or, on the other hand, of being "wishy-washy." The author vividly remembers an opening session full of conflict on this very issue.[13] It took some time before the trainers and group members were all able to examine the conflict of expectations about flexibility versus pre-planning, and to learn from it.

The trainer's approach to design flexibility depends on how his role is set up, and of course on his personal style or unique way of working with groups. However, experience suggests that it is good to have enough firmness in plans so they can keep their shape under non-realistic

---

[13] M. B. Miles and S. M. Corey, "The first cooperative curriculum research institute," in *Research for curriculum improvement*, 1957 Yearbook, Association for Supervision and Curriculum Development, esp. pp. 309, 335–38.

or anxious attacks by members, but can change when change seems realistically desirable. For example, some training groups are designed to start without any fixed agenda or leader, to help the group understand the problems of achieving independent, responsible cooperative planning. In such a group, if several members complained bitterly that "we aren't getting anywhere," it would be undesirable for the trainer to shift the plan and suggest action goals for the group. He should help the group analyze *why* no movement was taking place, and support their own efforts to plan together.

On the other hand, in this same kind of group, suppose that members discussed and clearly understood the reasons for the unstructured procedure, and went on to decide they could benefit by analyzing a tape recording of their own meeting. Then the trainer might profitably help the group plan such an activity. If shifts in training design are made experimentally, capricious or meaningless changes are less likely to occur.

Finally, in designing training programs, some thought needs to be given to the planning of "bridging activities." Such activities are aimed at helping to link the things group members are learning to the everyday demands of their jobs. The usual danger is to get involved in bridging activities too early. Some members can talk interminably about the sins of other people, and the terrible burdens of chairing this or that committee— mainly as an escape from really looking at *me* and *my* contribution to it all. Ordinarily, bridging activities should not come until people have had a chance to re-examine their own behavior, and until new frames of reference have begun to take hold. Then the question is less likely to be, "Isn't this idea rather unrealistic?" and more likely to be, "Now, how could I use this with my committee?"

As suggested earlier, a serial program with several spaced meetings is useful because it offers group members the chance to engage in bridging activities repeatedly, and as a result to try out more things on the job.

Many different bridging activities are described in the section on "Relating Training and Job Experiences" in Chapter V (pp. 156–75).

Developmental trends in training

Any training group (and, by extension, any training program involving several groups, such as a workshop) seems to change and develop over time. If planning committee members anticipate such changes, they can work more constructively than if they believe the changes are caused only by their skill (or unskill) in planning. The trainer, too, may get emotionally involved—he may be quite discouraged during a negative phase. As with child-rearing, it helps to know that "it's a stage," and better times lie ahead if we can help the growth process.

The changes over time suggested below are far from inevitable, but seem more likely to happen than not, especially when the training design leaves the group members free to plan whatever activities they wish to.[14] Most groups or workshops seem to progress from initial disorganization and resistance to more effective organization and better learning. If some of the changes outlined below do not appear in a program—at least in analogous form—the author's guess is that learning is incomplete. The changes, then, can be thought of as a series of markers. They may give an indication of how a training program is progressing.

1. *The new situation.* Before expectancies and the general nature of the situation are clarified, there is likely to be much caution, and defensiveness. In some cases exaggerated behaviors of attack and withdrawal appear. New, unstructured situations do cause much stress in people, in or out of training. As is suggested above, some training designs are made deliberately vague and ambiguous at first so that people's usual patterns of defending themselves and controlling others will appear and can be analyzed for learning. But a minimum working structure has to be clear to everyone before much can get done.

2. *Conflict over goals and expectancies.* Once the situation has become less new, and members are generally acquainted with one another, conflict often begins to develop—usually on a polite or covered-up level at first. Anyone coming to a training program has some personal goals and needs he hopes to work on. The big, unvoiced uncertainty is: "Will I be able to learn what I want to, or are others' needs going to assume prior-

---

[14] For some diverse accounts of developmental changes in small training groups, see W. G. Bennis and H. A. Shepard, "A theory of group development," *Human Relations,* 9:415–37, 1956; M. B. Miles, "Human relations training: how a group grows," *Teachers College Record,* 55:90–96, November 1953; and H. A. Thelen and W. Dickerman, "Stereotypes and the growth of groups," *Educational Leadership,* 6:309–16, February 1949. There are at least a dozen different accounts of developmental changes in training groups; the common denominator seems to be that clear changes do take place, and that groups operate much more effectively and satisfyingly after they have moved through a series of growth crises. One of the trainer's jobs is to help group members analyze and cope with these developmental changes, since many of them also occur—in less dramatic and visible form—in work groups on the job.

ity?" People seem motivated to "prove themselves," establish their identity as persons who have good ideas about what the group should be doing. At this point, for example, there may be much difficulty in setting up an agenda for work. Or if topics have been pre-set for the first meeting, there may be concern as to "whether we should really work on *that*."

So far, no really durable "culture" or set of working agreements has developed, and therefore differences among group members stand out. Besides differences in the kinds of problems which participants wish to work on, there may be differences in basic motivation, sophistication about groups, willingness to experiment, and rate of learning. It is very important that these differences be expressed as fully and completely as possible, and not be covered over by politeness, otherwise the training group will lose valuable resources. However, resolution of these conflicts usually cannot be hurried.

3. *Resistance.* Any human relations training program, by definition, requires participants to become personally involved, and to change their ways of behaving in some respect. People naturally find this prospect partly painful, and usually resist the program in various ways. Resistance may be quite direct—for example, attacks on the group or the trainer, or open assertions that the training program is useless. Or it may be relatively veiled—long intellectual dissertations, complaints that "this doesn't apply to us," cries of "Isn't this *fun!*", withdrawal to the sidelines, or superior assertions that "this is old stuff."

Resistance is a sign that a training program is taking hold, is making a difference.[15] The job of the trainer(s) and planning committee is to assess expressions of resistance as carefully as possible. To explain away *every* negative comment as resistance is just as undesirable as to feel that each negative comment is realistic and dictates an immediate and drastic overhaul of the program.

During this stage, and as other apparently negative behaviors show up, planners may very well decide *not* to invite important visitors to the workshop sessions, unless quite careful interpretation can be made to them of what the griping is all about.

4. *Factional crisis.* As training continues, conflict and resistance often mount, and are further expressed through subgrouping and the develop-

---

[15] For two practical discussions of resistance, see H. A. Thelen, "Resistance to change of teaching methods," *Progressive Education,* 26:208–14, May 1949; and J. R. Gibb and L. M. Gibb, "Obstacles to training," in *Applied group dynamics,* Chap. II, pp. 10–16.

ment of factions. The training group, or sometimes the program as a whole, may become split over crucial issues. These may be: hearing the experts vs. working on our own; having an appointed leader vs. no leader at all; working on specific pre-planned tasks vs. "planning by ear"; analyzing group process here and now in the training group vs. talking about group experiences on the job; deciding things by vote vs. working from only a full consensus; focusing on feelings vs. focusing on the task to be done.

In most cases these factions have spokesmen or leaders, who in effect are more or less openly vying for control of the group. This comment applies most clearly when the training group is taking a laboratory approach and is doing its own planning, instead of moving through pre-planned activities. However, experience suggests that subgroup conflict and leadership striving may also exist under the surface in pre-planned programs.

To planners or trainers, the situation may seem chaotic and upsetting. Actually, factional conflict is usually a good sign. It is a symptom that the group or workshop is making progress in getting organized and building good working agreements.

At any rate, much of the conflict seems to center around problems of authority and control. Things often get easier following a symbolic demonstration of the group's power to act and work. Here are some examples from the author's experience:

A planning committee gave in to group demands that more time be devoted to on-the-job problems in the program.

The group asked the trainer to observe and report his impressions, then failed to call on him.

The group decided to permit each of three factional leaders a ten-minute try at leadership, to see how they would handle the group.

Hostile joking or horseplay was directed at the trainer, who accepted it.

The workshop staff admitted in a general session that they were puzzled about where to move next, and asked for member suggestions (which came thick and fast).

During factional crisis, the main idea for planners or trainers is to—in effect—trust the developmental process, and try to make it possible for participants to work out, through action, the limits of "what we can decide."

Rational discussion of authority problems sometimes seems only to prolong them.

5. *The golden glow.* Following the resolution of subgroup conflict, feelings in the group may change strikingly. The group may find it can work much more effectively with the trainer or other authority figures (less rebellion, less dependence, more realistic use of expert knowledge). Group members appear unusually satisfied, and there may be a great deal of harmony. Old conflicts are buried, and members may feel that the program is immensely valuable and that the other people in it are especially wonderful.

As with the other changes described, much of this may represent a realistic view ("We have suffered and accomplished together"). Many workshops end right here. But the golden glow may also be a needed resting period, or even resistance to continued hard work and learning. Here the problem of the trainer(s) and planners is not to feel complacent too.

6. *Getting involved more deeply.* But as the group continues, the golden glow may give way to something that seems like a cold gray cloud. Members say, "We are not a good group," "We are not accomplishing what we should," and so on. In many cases, this seems to be a realization that members of the group must be willing to get involved at a deeper level, give up something more of themselves in order to learn more. In some groups, as the end of the training program approaches, the discussion may turn to the topic of mutual evaluation ("telling each other how we've worked as individuals in this group"). Whatever the topic, there may arise in the group once more a kind of crisis, sometimes with factions. New crucial issues may appear: "giving all of ourselves" vs. staying aloof; being frank with each other vs. being polite; evaluating group progress vs. evaluating the roles of individuals.

7. *Productive work.* The conflicts mentioned above may, again, be resolved by some symbolic or crucial action. A member may spontaneously ask the group to evaluate his role, or the group may experiment with an evaluation procedure and see that it works. Group members come to see that individuals, through admission of their real willingness to be helped, can in fact fulfill themselves as persons more completely. Persons feel freer than ever to drop their usual defenses (arguing, withdrawing, trying to dominate others, over-harmonizing). Now, they can really work with each other on problems of mutual concern.

At this point it might be said that the group is in full flower. Really accurate and meaningful communication is going on. "Feelings" and "the job" are not separate entities, but parts of one whole—getting work done productively and satisfyingly. Clear and efficient work procedures can be set up quickly. Decisions can be made rapidly and effectively, and the atmosphere is full of excitement and learning. Sometimes groups do, at this point, discuss each member's role thoughtfully and thoroughly, providing him with good feedback on how he has been behaving. Sometimes groups review their history as a means to understanding group growth. Sometimes a group plans and carries out projects to test its own skills of working together. In any event, groups that reach this stage of development are highly exciting and creative. It is sad but true that few groups on the job seem to reach this level of ability to work in a shared, productive fashion. Showing just how good a group can be is by no means the least valuable contribution of training.

8. *Deceleration.* Assuming that the training program is finite, its chronological end must approach at some point. The group must find ways of closing, wrapping up loose ends, clarifying puzzling learnings, applying balm to wounds, and in general putting its emotional affairs in order. All this may involve a gradual slowing-down of the earlier excitement and involvement. If the group is not to meet again, there are sobering thoughts of losing the warmth and support that have grown up. The day-to-day demands of the job begin to re-intrude themselves. Planning for termination, closure, and bridging to the job situation is discussed in more detail in the final section below, and appropriate activities are described in Chapter V, pp. 156–75.

A final comment

What is needed if a planning committee is to do a good job of continuing and maintaining the program? The planning group must be composed of the right people. They must work steadily during the program, using the best data they can get, to plan each next step. An experimental approach can turn failure into learning, and helps considerably to reduce planner tension. Matters of over-all design need to be considered, as well as the setup of any particular training activity. All planning activities need to be related to the developmental changes over time that seem to take place in small training groups, and in a program as a whole. Above all, good planning takes time and thought.

Planning for Program Closure and Follow-through

Ending the program

As the termination point for a program approaches, a number of planning problems are likely to come up. People usually will have been working very hard. Especially in an intensive block-of-time program, they will be nearly saturated with new insights and questionings about group life. Under these conditions, a planning committee may find that there is some pressure to go at full tilt right up to the closing time, then flop into blessed relaxation. This may feel good, but experience suggests that it is less than desirable for good learning. The end of a program should seem more like a comma than an exclamation point or a period.

In effect, the latter part of a program ought to consist of activities which help the learner get gradually unhooked from the strong feelings of the training experience. And, as suggested above, he needs to build better and better bridges for himself between the training program and his job. Bridging activities like these are usually helpful: planning what to say about the program to others on the job; evaluating the training program for its relevance to job problems; planning new things to try on the job; and practicing difficult and needed skills.

The entire question of how training and job are related is an interesting one. Some people may see them as in separate, watertight compartments. Others may feel that the job is "real" and training not real. Still others reverse this view and assert that all job problems would disappear if only "everyone would act the way we have in this training group." A good training program must help members express and examine their views of the difference their personal learnings can make on the job. Specific planning of next steps on the job is desirable. Other members of the training group can help plan, and back on the job, may also provide ideas, advice, and support.

Any training program that is set up to help participants learn new behavior inevitably influences and is influenced by the surrounding organizational setup. For example, suppose that a principal, after training, begins to experiment with talking less in faculty meetings and encourages teachers to participate more. If this practice is sharply at variance with what the teachers have come to expect from him, stresses and strains are set up in the system. Until an equilibrium is reached, people will be unhappy. Perhaps the principal will revert to his old talkativeness, thus meeting the teachers' expectations for his behavior. (Some training studies suggest this does happen.) Or perhaps his new approach meets a real need, and will come to be standard operating procedure in faculty meetings.

Training is more likely to be successful if the learner has had a chance, with the aid of other interested learners, to diagnose his job situation carefully and make specific action plans. The plans should include not only immediate action steps, but ideas on what to do when stress and strain appear as the result of whatever the first step is. Ideally, a training program should include bridging activities at a number of points during the latter part of the program, and not just during the last session. Spreading application over several sessions permits tryouts on the job, analysis, and re-planning with the support of others in the training program.

Not all the problems of closure in a training program are "official" ones —people ordinarily have many informal, personal needs to work out. A planning committee may find that requests for a picnic, dinner, or party begin to mount at this point. It is wise to try to fit in such activities along with more formal work sessions. Informal activities at this point let members unwind, blow off residual steam, deepen and strengthen the new friendships they have made during the program, and in general act like people instead of organization men.

Continued self-training

Perhaps the crucial test of a training program is whether or not it is able to encourage participants to keep taking an inquiring approach to their job problems. No training program can ever supply all the answers to a person's group-relevant job problems. But it can supply him with better methods for finding his own answers. As suggested in Chapter III, the person who gets the most from training is probably the person who has *learned how to learn*. When he is faced with a difficulty he backs off, makes a diagnosis, and tries things out experimentally. From this point of view, good training never really ceases. The focus has shifted from a public, official program of training to continued individual questings for improvement. An experimental attitude toward problems in group behavior has been built into the person. If the training program has been good, he sees it not as an isolated incident but as a helpful experience in the larger context of his own continuing development.

Planning for future programs

Self-training is essential. Even so, people may again feel the need for intensive work on group problems in an off-the-job setting. Experience suggests that planning for future training is more likely to result if decisions about its desirability are made during the training program. A decision like "Let's get together again the next in-service day," even when made during the excitement of a training program, often has considerable durability. This holds true for the decision to invite others ("Let's see if we can get some of the sophomores in on this.").

It is usually helpful to have a steering committee or interim planning group that can keep sensitively in touch with program "alumni" and their needs for further work together. Such a group may also assess the needs for training being expressed by persons who were not involved in the original program. In effect, the training function should be built into the surrounding system—classroom, building, or school district—just as it should be built into the individual as he copes with his job problems. The steering committee may well be asked to collect systematic data on members' reactions to and learnings from the program, and to assess new needs.

Periodic training sessions, from this point of view, can be thought of as a good habit for a school system to get into. Then particular sessions are less likely to be seen as isolated phenomena of majestic but unclear significance, and more likely to be viewed as valuable episodes in a long, shared sequence of continued professional development.

Summary Comment

To review the material on ending a program successfully: Members need to examine the demands of their jobs tough-mindedly, in the new light shed by the training experiences. Since they need also to clarify their feelings, to put their relationships with others in order, and to gain support for job innovations they are considering, informal activities should be planned along with work sessions. Better job performance will result to the degree each person has picked up "self-training" skills during the program. Finally, organizational provision should be made for the planning of future programs.

CHAPTER V

TRAINING ACTIVITIES

What actually goes on in a training program? This chapter is devoted to illustrative examples of training activities.* These examples are, deliberately, not recipes in which each substep is outlined. To present such recipes would be misleading and unhelpful to trainers and members alike. Instead, the attempt has been made to describe training activities clearly enough so that a trainer without extensive previous experience can adapt them to his own situation and skills. How this adaptation can be done is described in Chapter VI. The reader may wish to turn to that chapter before getting too deeply enmeshed in the detail of this one, which involves 25 broad types of training activity and 115 specific examples.

The chapter does include in passing many specific comments and suggestions about the planning and operation of particular training activities. It is organized as follows. After introductory comments, there is a discussion of criteria for choosing training activities. Then specific activities are described, with considerable detail, in three broad categories: (1) studying ongoing group behavior; (2) learning through specially planned situations; (3) relating training and job experience. There are two indexes, broken down by *training problem* (the initially-presented difficulty in group work which is to be tackled via the activity), and by *type of activity* (the procedure employed).

As members of a training group or workshop identify their needs and problems, the question of "How do we proceed?" assumes much importance. A major task of the trainer is to supply technical help on pro-

* Several members of the Horace Mann–Lincoln Institute staff, especially A. Harry Passow, helped supply original materials for this chapter.

cedures for learning. The chapter is designed as a source book for planning, to which trainer and planning committee can turn for ideas.

The assumption is that at those points during training when new procedures are needed, trainers and group members may wish to look through the chapter and choose specific activities for adaptation with the help of the criteria suggested below. Through revision, group members can come up with experimental training activities that make sense for *them,* given their needs, in their job settings.[1] It is, quite literally, impossible for a trainer or a group to lift out bodily any activity in the chapter, turn a crank, and produce group members who are "trained." The chapter is best seen as a reservoir of ideas for planning. Each activity described includes several variations, and these do not exhaust the possibilities.

Almost all the activities listed in this chapter have been experimented with vigorously and revised as the author and others tried them out in groups they were working with. It is expected that the reader will need to do the same. It is not always easy for a trainer to take this sort of an experimental approach, especially if he is working as a trainer for the first time. Of this, more in Chapter VII; here it is suggested that it is easier to be experimental if the trainer has a confidant (friend, relative, or other trainer) with whom to talk over his trials and successes. If he can admit his own fallibility to the group and ask for help, so much the better.

As an aid to his experimentation, the reader who owns the book is encouraged to comment in margins, and to use the space provided at the end of each activity description for notes.

Nearly all of the training activities outlined below are appropriate for a training group of eight to 20 members. The opening session plans of Chapter IV included some designs for larger groups, since the beginning of a workshop or institute often involves all participants in a general session. But the activities in this chapter are focused on small groups, on the assumption (discussed in Chapter III) that a small, cohesive group is the major medium for personal growth in group behavior. A large workshop would ordinarily be broken into several subgroups, each with

---

[1] For an anecdotal account of how a human relations training group moved through a series of learning procedures, aided by a skilled trainer, see H. A. Thelen, *Dynamics of groups at work* (University of Chicago Press, 1954), Chap. 5, especially pp. 140–67, "The laboratory method in operation: a case study." The approach is not suggested as a model for the reader to follow—considerable background in human relations training is implied—but the sequence and flow of activities may help supply the flavor of what an experimental approach to training is like.

a trainer to help. Some training programs, of course, involve just one training group which meets periodically over a length of time.[2]

Many of the activities can be easily and directly used with students (in and out of the classroom) and these are indicated. Most of the other activities in the first two sections can be adapted for use with students.

The index on page 100 indicates that the array of training activities available is quite formidable. How to choose?

Guides to Selecting Training Activities

This section suggests a series of criteria to use in deciding whether a particular training activity can and should be adapted for a particular group. To see how the criteria work, the reader may wish to apply them to the training activity described in Chapter III, pages 28–31.

Appropriateness to member needs. The proposed activity should be aimed at meeting member needs for improved group behavior that are real and compelling. When on-the-job problems are too compelling, it is sometimes useful to construct a hypothetical situation, but even here the activity must tie in to member dissatisfactions and desires for change.

Helpfulness in relating the training and job situations. The proposed activity should help members test their job demands against the events of the training situation, and vice versa. Training, after all, exists to improve job performance. The links between "what we just did here" and "the meetings with the supervisors I have next week" must be made explicit. Even further, the proposed activity should encourage and support on-the-job experimentation, the active trying out of new learnings. Pre-planning, dry runs, and the like are helpful here.

Location within the trainer's range of competence. This is a crude but realistic criterion; trainers should not try things they feel they cannot handle. However, some insecurity is natural, and much skill can be learned.

[2] It is worth saying, however, that many of the activities described here can be altered for use in large-meeting situations (anything over, say, 20 people). Many devices can be used to increase participation and involvement in large meetings (ex: buzz groups, listening teams, audience representation panels, and the like). See, for ideas, National Training Laboratories, "Leadership and participation in large group meetings," Bulletin No. 4 (1951); "Improving large group meetings," *Adult Leadership,* December 1952, entire issue; M. B. Miles, "Your professional meetings," *Nursing Outlook,* 2:469–71, 1954; W. W. Reeder, "Some methods and tools to increase interest, participation and teaching effectiveness," Cornell Extension Bulletin 907 (1954).

Optimal emotional impact. The training procedures themselves—aside from the importance of the job problems being dealt with—should encourage active interest. The individual needs to become emotionally involved in the learning process. On the other hand, the procedures should not arouse excessive anxiety or concern.

Multiple learning. The proposed activity should take account of the fact that "whole persons" are involved. It should provide for intellectual, emotional, and action types of learning. An activity which is likely to invite attempts at quick-answer solutions to complex human relations problems is undesirable. A given training activity usually should focus rather narrowly, but its place in a sequence of training activities should round out a larger picture, show the whole situation, assist the member in many different aspects of his own struggle to learn.

Self-correction. A good training activity should contain provision for its own evaluation and self-correction. Members need to be able to criticize the activity as a learning experience, or its improvement is unlikely. This holds especially true where the trainer is new to training, or if the group is thought of as a means of training trainers for subsequent programs.

Presence of support for learning. The proposed training activity should provide for guided practice of specific skills—learners should get feedback on the consequences of their acts. The situation must be psychologically safe enough for participants to unfreeze, and try out new ideas and actions. (For example, a role-playing scene that is too uncomfortably close to the way a real principal in the group behaves in real staff meetings ought to be revised or discarded.) The procedure should protect and enhance the personal integrity of the learner—never threaten it.

These seven criteria, then, suggest how activities may be selected, and how they may be revised to fit the needs of a particular group at a particular point in a training program.[3] Now, on to the training activities.

The index below organizes the training activities according to the training problem the activity is designed to help with. The problems are here only named, taken out of context. For indications of how training problems appear when groups are at work in schools, refer back to

---

[3] Although these criteria are most appropriate to the special problems of training for better group behavior, they are also clearly applicable to any procedure designed to bring about changes in people. In the classroom, for example, students are protected in a psychologically safe atmosphere (school is different from adult life). The use of planned situations (for example, a mock election) can extend the value of the "not for keeps" idea. Or, to take another example, some criticisms of traditional education can be restated as: The learning activity is inappropriate to member needs, and does not have optimal emotional impact.

the incidents described in Chapter II (pp. 11–15) and to the comments on ineffective group work in Chapter IV (pp. 51–52, 56–57). A second index, organized by type of training activity, appears at the end of the chapter.

I. Studying Ongoing Group Behavior

How does one go about studying group behavior? One approach consists of studying what happens naturally in the training group, as contrasted with using a pre-planned situation. That is, a training group, like any group, faces certain common problem areas—identifying goals, creating a comfortable climate, developing clear procedures, making decisions, and the like. As a training group copes with these problems from its first meeting onward, it is profitable for members to discuss the processes taking place, just as they are happening. The analysis of group events as they occur right here and right now gives concreteness to concepts of social psychology. Such analysis is also quite compelling, because each member is learning *observant participation*. He is the guinea pig and scientist, all in one. He is the watcher of events which concern him deeply, because he is *in* the events as well as watching them. Some of the other reasons for the power of the small group situation as a place to learn have already been discussed in Chapter III (pp. 45–47).

The study of ongoing group behavior usually does not happen by itself—or all of us would be much more sophisticated about groups than we are. Methods for analysis have to be built in, so that group members see it as legitimate to take time out from *what* is being discussed and can easily turn to analysis of *how* it is being discussed. Below are outlined a series of methods—training activities—for the study of a group's processes by its members. (For comments on why or when to use a particular activity, see Chapter VI, pp. 180–83.)

After each activity is explained briefly, an example is given. The example includes an informally-stated training need or problem, the actual procedure, general comment about the use of the procedure, suggested variations, and space for notes. The discussion assumes that the training group (size 8 to 20) will have a number of meetings totaling at least eight hours. Many of the activities could probably be used in a single, isolated training session, but they are likely to be more productive when used in a supportive group that has some degree of continuity and stability. Such a group may be meeting on its own, or in the context of a workshop or other training program. One or two persons are assumed to be taking the role of the trainer, with specially-assigned responsibility for helping the group learn.

Trainer comments

Initially, at least, the study of ongoing group behavior gets its greatest impetus from what the trainer does. When he comments directly on what is going on in the group, there are a number of consequences. By indicating his awareness of what is happening in the group, and his interest in using this as discussion content, the trainer illustrates how the sessions themselves can provide raw materials for analyzing and gaining greater insight into group phenomena. As a model, the trainer demonstrates that noticing, commenting on and discussing group behavior are not only possible but desirable. Trainer comments (*a*) illuminate the immediate problems facing the group and (*b*) help build in the process-analysis function as a central feature of the group's work structure.

EXAMPLE OF TRAINER COMMENTS

Training problem: Why do new groups often have decision-making difficulty?

Procedure: The trainer intervenes at a point when the group has bogged down, and can't reach agreement. He asks the group to examine what's happening. (If the group is blocked over how the members should introduce themselves, the trainer may say, "I wonder why we seem unable to make this apparently simple decision about introductions," or "It's been repeatedly urged that we give personal details about ourselves, and no one objected, yet we don't do it. What's blocking us here?") The group members, with the trainer's aid, begin analysis of the situation ("Since the situation is so new, we are afraid to stick our necks out. Maybe someone would jump on us"; or "We don't know yet whether we really can make decisions as a group.")

Comment: Trainer skill here lies in selecting a salient point for comment, and commenting in a way that will lead the group toward self-analysis. The trainer does not try to bring members to admire his insightfulness, or hunt for the answers he wants, or simply feel guilty because "we are a bad group." He does try to help members begin to examine the immediate situation and learn from it.

At first, trainer comments may seem to be ignored, or followed by silence. This seems to happen because members are not yet sure how to respond, or do not believe that talking about what is happening is a safe and legitimate thing to do. As the group develops, trainer comments are more and more likely to start the group into analysis of ongoing processes. The group may feel more comfortable, too, in criticizing the effectiveness of comments made by the trainer.

Focusing on negative events and difficulties does increase motivation to learn at first, but it is also important for the trainer to comment on successful incidents if members are to learn more than "what *not* to do."

Trainer comments should usually deal with the behavior of the group as a whole rather than with what particular members have done. (For more on this, and on other aspects of the trainer's role, see Chapter VII, pp. 204–15.)

This method of studying ongoing group behavior can be easily used in classroom situations. Most teachers normally make comments on classroom group behavior in the course of their teaching, so the method is not new.

Variation: The trainer, on his own or at group request, may restrict his comments to specific times, such as the end of meetings or phases of a meeting, or every fifteen minutes.

Notes:

Intermittent process analysis

Given some experience with trainer comments, a group may develop a basic ground rule: All members have the right and responsibility to comment frankly on what is happening here and now in the training group. Once this agreement has been developed and individuals feel free to comment on what is happening in the group, practically any phase of the group's ongoing activity becomes grist for learning. At any point, group members can discuss what is happening, make generalizations from their learnings, and move on, if desired, to setting up related training activities. Thus intermittent process analysis, instead of being seen as an "interruption," comes to be the most important part of the group's work. In effect, group members are asking continuously, "What is happening? What is making these things happen? How can we change our behavior for the better?"

EXAMPLE OF INTERMITTENT PROCESS ANALYSIS

Training problem: How does a group go about building an agenda, agreeing on specific objectives?

Procedure: As the training group begins to plan its agenda, members feel free from time to time to comment and raise questions about what's happening. For example:

"I didn't feel free to say what I felt about Jim's proposal. Did anyone else have that feeling?"

"We are trying to assign priority to these items, but not everyone has agreed that we should work on them all in the first place."

"Why are we taking so darn long on this?"

"I think there's a conflict here between the people who want agenda item 4 and those who think item 5 is the most important."

"Aren't we all really worried that our own pet idea won't get discussed?"

After such comments, the group may, depending on the interests and skills of members:

Move into extensive analysis of agenda-making problems.

Look at specific members' behaviors that blocked or impeded agenda-making progress.

Ignore the original comments and simply continue with agenda-making.

Make analogies with other agenda-making situations in groups on the job.

Alter the agenda-making procedure being used to see if a new method (ex: "Let's not discuss the items until they're all up on the board") will work better.

Comment: Not all member interventions are accepted by the group—some comments are ignored, some are resented. At first, member comments may be either superficial or too threatening. Some statements by members may be made to control the group rather than to aid learning. Sometimes a group gets divided into a "process" faction, who wish to analyze everything, and a "task" faction, who want to get on with the agenda. But all this can be studied too. Good intermittent process analysis that simultaneously results in member learning and group progress doesn't come naturally but must be learned. It can be.

Notes:

Diagnostic periods

Sometimes the members of a training group, when carrying on a critique of their methods of learning, feel that intermittent process analysis is too sporadic, too much a hand-to-mouth existence. They may set aside specific periods during a meeting, or at the end, for extended discussion of what has taken place. In these periods, complete attention can be paid to examination of process.

EXAMPLE OF DIAGNOSTIC PERIOD

Training problem: What causes confusion in a group?

Procedure: The discussion in the training group seems to be unusually confused. The group members agree to stop working on the immediate group task (ex: discussing Mike's back-home committee as a case study). They agree to spend fifteen minutes in trying to understand more about the causes of group confusion. The events of the past few minutes in the group are analyzed to shed light on this:

"I don't know what you were talking about. I haven't been able to follow for the past five minutes."

"Why didn't people who were confused speak up?"

"Doesn't a chairman have some responsibility here? Bill, don't you think you should have flagged us when you saw what was happening?"

"We jumped into Mike's topic so fast that many of us weren't clear about what we were discussing."

"Most of us were quite confused, but assumed that everyone else in the group was crystal clear. Yet we didn't ask. Why?"

"I was angry about the way we jumped into the topic, and so I just wasn't listening. Then when I came in to disagree with Jane, it really gummed up the works."

Comment: Setting a clear starting and stopping time for the diagnostic period is a good idea. The group may not use all the time (though wanting more time is more typical). Usually, at first, groups underestimate how long a thoughtful analysis really takes.

It should be made clear at the start of the diagnostic period what the phenomena to be diagnosed are (ex: this meeting, the history of the group, one specific incident). Otherwise the diagnosis may well be diffuse, off-target, or otherwise unproductive.

In the classroom, using diagnostic periods halfway through a class dis-

[Diagnostic period cont'd]

cussion can be very helpful. ("Let's take the next ten minutes to evaluate how our discussion is going.")

Variations: (1) The group breaks into several small subgroups. They diagnose what's happening, and then report their ideas back to the total group. This approach is helpful when group members are finding it difficult to participate in the large group, for whatever reason. The subgroups may well be asked to discuss "What factors are making it hard for us to participate in the large group?"

(2) Either in subgroups or as a whole, "critical incidents" are listed— things which happened that seemed especially salient or crucial for the group. For example:

"George's interruption of the chairman."
"The place where we got bogged down on agenda item 3."
"Our decision to experiment with using an observer."
"Our semantic conflict about 'leadership'."
"When Lois admitted she didn't know the answers."
"When we first criticized John [trainer] for remaining silent."

Listed on the chalkboard, these can form a useful backdrop for further analysis of the development of the group so far, or the sequence of events in a single meeting.

(3) Diagnosis is done by "brainstorming." A topic, such as "What is blocking this group from reaching decisions?" is chosen. Ideas are listed on the chalkboard as rapidly as possible, with the ground rule that no idea may be criticized. Under these circumstances, many bright ideas can appear quickly.

A sorting out and refining period follows; here some wild ideas are discarded and others prove to be highly creative answers to the problems facing the group.

One training group, completely immobilized because it had no clear decision-making method, used brainstorming and came up with thirty-seven ways of reaching decisions (ex: majority vote, consensus, leader ruling). This took ten minutes. The sifting-out process that followed led to the use of a modified consensus-testing procedure, and the group was able to move on productively.

Notes:

Use of group observer

The training group may decide to ask one or more members to stop participating in the discussion, watch what is going on in the group, keep some record, and report back what was seen. The assumption is that dispassionate observing, in addition to the sort of participant observation all group members are doing, can help members learn more about why groups behave as they do.

EXAMPLE OF USE OF GROUP OBSERVER

Training problem: What functions are needed for effective group problem-solving?

Procedure: Group asks one member to watch the discussion and check off the functions (such as summarizer, clarifier) played by group members as the discussion continues.[4] After fifteen minutes, the member reports back the sequence of functions performed. He leads a discussion of how group members feel the sequence of functions can be improved. ("We should stop proposing solutions to the problem until we can do a better job of clarifying what the real problem is.") Then the group returns to its discussion for a second fifteen minutes, with the same member observing again.

Comment: The observer should be sure the group has told him what to look for.[5] If he stays within the limits of what the group wants, his report is more likely to be helpful and less likely to be threatening.

The skill of reporting (that is, supplying feedback to the group) is not a simple one.[6] The observer role can, however, be learned—by students or adults—through practice (see pp. 109–11). When an observer admits fallibility and asks for suggestions on how to be a better observer, the group is much more likely to make optimal use of his comments.

In general, the observer should report ascertainable facts. If he is giving his own impressions and feelings, he should so label them. He should avoid making evaluative judgments, and unless explicitly asked to report on individual behavior, he should comment only about the group as a whole. The observer's failure to observe these rules of thumb will usually lead the group

---

[4] See Chapter II, pp. 17–21, and footnotes.

[5] There is a great deal going on in any group. J. R. Gibb and L. M. Gibb, in *Applied group dynamics* (National Training Laboratories, 1955, pp. 52–54, list 27 different things an observer can look for, such as: who talks to whom, roles missing in the group, pressures for and against decisions, attempts by members to control the group, leader behavior, group standards, subgrouping or coalitions, quality of work going on.

[6] For a useful discussion, see D. H. Jenkins, "Feedback and group self-evaluation," *Journal of Social Issues*, 4:50–60, Spring 1948.

to reject the feedback, scold the observer, or become self-conscious in an unproductive way.

The observer must also resist the temptation to play social scientist or epigrammatist. The test of feedback is not: Is it brilliant? but: Does it help the group understand what it wanted to understand in the first place? A good observer report does not stop discussion; it starts it. Reports in the form of a few questions (*not* a barrage) are often very helpful. ("Did some of us really object to the decisions we made without saying so?" "Do we have any guesses why the discussion has been so slow during the last half hour?")

Variations: (1) Two or more observers working at once also aid in objectivity, and can also help the group see how the richness of subjectivity can deepen the observer's role:

Chuck (observer 1): As you know by now, I'm the kind of guy who is quite rebellious toward leaders in general. So what I reported to you may have been rather biased.

Grace: No, Chuck. I thought you pointed up some things that were very important in what Dave was doing as chairman. They didn't stand out for me until you put your finger on them.

Walter (observer 2): Now, maybe this is defending myself, but I thought that Chuck missed several things about what was going on at the blackboard, just because he was watching Dave so much.

Grace: Yes, but that was OK because you filled us in. I don't think we can all be sensitive to every little thing that happens. Everybody is different.

Chuck: Thanks, Grace. (laughter)

(2) Observer feedback, like trainer comments, may be given only at specified times, or cover limited segments of a meeting. An observer report at the midpoint of a meeting is often very helpful. It encourages the group members to *act* on the diagnosis resulting from the feedback, whereas end-of-meeting reports mainly encourage adjournment.

(3) A group member in the recorder role (keeping notes on the content —what is said) may be useful to the group in the same way an observer is. He may, for example, report that "the group has discussed the following six topics in the last fourteen minutes, apparently without reaching any clear decision on any: reasons for lateness to meetings, the room temperature, the agenda, a newspaper article, Topic 7 of the agenda, negative feelings about the workshop. . . ." From this, the group members may be able to

[Use of group observer cont'd]

draw conclusions about their productivity as a group and why it is not greater:

"No one was exerting leadership."

"Many topics in the old agenda are no longer important to us."

"We were upset by Joe's comment way back at the beginning but didn't want to admit it."

"Maybe we are feeling frustrated about the workshop but don't want to come out with it in the open."

Using the recorder role this way can help the members clarify the relationship between content and process in group situations.

Notes:

Practicing service roles

Most groups have one or more formal service roles, such as chairman, recorder, observer, and resource person.[7] A training group offers members an opportunity to practice these service roles, and understand more clearly what effective chairing, or recording, or observing is like. Such learning can be applied directly and easily to the job situation.

If members take turns in carrying out the different service roles, they feel less tense ("I'm not the only one who worries about chairing meetings") and also can see new needs for training. When the "practice" aspect of service roles is emphasized, needs for perfection are cut down. Individuals tend to view mistakes not as crises but rather as opportunities for learning more skillful behavior. Also, the trainer and other group members can give support to a practicing chairman, recorder, or observer if the group gets into difficulty.

Practicing service roles also helps the group understand the trainer's role, and makes clear that he is *not* the chairman, recorder, observer, etc.,

[7] See "The service roles which groups require," in K. D. Benne and B. Muntyan, *Human relations in curriculum change* (Dryden, 1951), pp. 154–59; also A. Miel, "How to use experts and consultants," in the same book, pp. 208–10.

but stands in a general, helping, facilitating relationship to the group. Basic decisions about "where we move next" are thus seen to be the group's responsibility, not the trainer's.

EXAMPLE OF PRACTICING SERVICE ROLES

Training problem: What should a chairman do when conflict arises?

Procedure: During a time when disagreement in the group is reasonably vigorous, one member agrees to serve as chairman. After a half hour of discussion chaired by him, the group suspends discussion on the previous topic. The members turn to an analysis of the chairman's behavior. Many different questions can be explored:

(from chairman)

> "What did you think of it when I tried to smooth over things?"
> "I gave my own opinions; how did you feel about that?"
> "Do you think we were getting anywhere?"
> "What mistakes do you think I made?"
> "I was puzzled when the group suddenly went off on a tangent there. Was that something I caused?"

(from group members)

> "How did you feel?"
> "What incidents bothered you the most?"
> "Why did you cut off Joe like that?"
> "Did you notice that we were getting divided into two factions?"
> "How would you handle that?"
> "It was excellent when you summarized."
> "Who do you think you could count on for help?"
> "Can you say what you've learned about how to handle conflict?"

The original discussion can be resumed with the same or a new chairman, and the analysis repeated.

Comment: Exposing oneself to direct or indirect criticism in this way can be threatening. Threat is reduced when the member knows that other members will be practicing the role after he does, and when he sees his practice as real, but not necessarily "for keeps." Sometimes, for example, members prefer to "try out a way of chairing that I thought of" rather than present their chairing performances as really *theirs*. In any event, difficulties and mistakes must be seen by the group as an inevitable, developmental part of learning. Sometimes the trainer needs to support an individual who is being belabored for his attempts as a chairman by reminding the group why they decided to practice the chairman role in the first place.

Role practice also helps people to understand the demands of a specific service role more clearly. After six persons have worked as observer, all members are much clearer on the difference between fact and inference, and the difference between process and content.

This may seem obvious, but provision for feedback and analysis should be built in before the service roles are undertaken. Sometimes a member will work as group recorder for two hours, only to discover that there is no time left for the group to discuss the adequacy of his note-taking skill.

As with any training activity, time should be taken to criticize the effectiveness of practicing service roles as a learning experience. This activity is, incidentally, a straightforward and effective way to improve committee work in the classroom.

Variations: (1) A special observer is used to watch the behavior of chairman, recorder, or regular observer (One group member said, "Let's have a watchbird to watch the watchbird"). He reports back his notes, and they are compared with the perceptions of other group members.

(2) The group specifies service-role behavior ahead of time ("The chairman is only to summarize, restate opinions, and encourage people to speak"), both to support a member taking the role and to experiment with different patterns of service-role behavior.

(3) The group makes up a roster for its next few meetings, specifying who will play the different service roles. The chairman, recorder, observer, etc., form a Planning Committee for each meeting.

Notes:

Use of reaction forms

Pencil-and-paper questionnaires, filled out by all group members, can be extremely useful in understanding group behavior. Each member has a chance to respond personally, in writing, to questions about a group meeting or part of one. When these responses are summarized and reported back, the full, diverse range of member attitudes and reactions is made clear. Too, group members may find, unexpectedly, that they share some perceptions with others ("I thought I was the only one who . . .").

EXAMPLE OF USE OF REACTION FORMS

Training problem: What factors affect overt participation in groups?

Procedure: At the end of the meeting, members take ten minutes to respond to a prepared form with ratings and open-end questions on it. For example:

Post Meeting Reaction

1. How did you feel about this meeting? (check)

Very dissatis- fied	Somewhat dissatis- fied	Neither satisfied nor dis- satisfied	Quite satis- fied	Very satis- fied

2. Please comment on why you felt this way.

3. Were there any times when you wished to speak but did not?

Never	A few times	Fairly often	Very often	Almost all the time

4. What things *helped* you to take part in the meeting?

5. What things *hindered* you from taking part in the meeting?

6. How could our next meeting be improved?

Members need not sign their names. The reaction forms are summarized by a committee and reported back to the next meeting as the basis for diagnosis and planning (ex: "Most of the people who were dissatisfied also said they could not get into the discussion." "The most helpful thing was when we were in subgroups").

Comment: As in the example above, reaction sheets can be used not only to improve immediate group functioning, but to help members understand the needs and reactions of others. They may, indeed, alter a member's picture of his own needs ("This discussion has helped me realize that I like to go off in the corner and pout when no one asks for my ideas").

The experience of selecting and building a reaction sheet and using it can itself result in learnings: how to word questions; how to analyze open-end data; how to interpret findings; how to report back information accurately and helpfully.

Sometimes individuals or groups resist using reaction sheets. Attitudes toward them usually depend on: whether the group members actively decided to use them; who will see the results; the kind of questions asked;

how they will be reported back; and the practical results of the report.

To be helpful, any form must be planned to meet the needs for which it is proposed. If group members help to plan and use the form, they are less likely to (1) resist the sheets; (2) get carried away with a mechanical, superficial approach.

In general, reaction sheets are easy to use with students or adults, and, since they are a very useful planning tool, can be very profitably used in job groups where the emphasis on training is minor.

Variations: [8] (1) The group builds the questions for the sheet at the end of the meeting instead of using a prepared sheet.

(2) A reaction sheet is used halfway through a meeting, summarized during a break, then reported back. This method lets the group take immediate advantage of the results.

(3) Members take a sheet home and react after several days.

(4) The same rating question (ex: on satisfaction with the meeting) is used over several meetings. A graph of average scores shows the course of feelings about the group. Different meetings can be compared, and trends over time detected.

Notes:

Use of tape recording

Often a training group finds it useful to record part or all of its meetings. The tape provides an impersonal record of audible behavior,[9] and can be played back and stopped at will for analysis and comment. (See Chapter VI, pp. 198–202, for a discussion of tape recording as a training method.)

---

[8] *Adult Leadership,* April 1953, devoted to "Evaluating program and performance," contains a number of suggestions on end-of-meeting evaluation sheets.

[9] Video tape recording is now used to reproduce TV programs. If this method becomes available at low cost, playback during training could be even more effective. The individual would get a visual as well as an aural report and would have a much fuller idea of how he strikes others as he works in a group.

EXAMPLE OF TAPE RECORDING

Training problem: To understand the dynamics of conflict in a group.

Procedure: Group agrees to tape-record all training group meetings. One meeting especially marked by conflict is picked out, and the tape for that meeting is played back. Each time a member wishes to analyze, or make a comment illuminating what is happening on the tape, he raises his hand, and the tape is stopped. ("Now, right there, I felt sort of irritated about the way Joan pushed us right on into the next topic. I don't think we really had a group decision at that point.")

After discussion, the tape playback is resumed. Sections where interpretations differ can be repeated.

Comment: This is a very concrete and productive way to learn about group behavior (and incidentally one's own contribution to groups). Group members usually have a successful, supportive experience in analyzing the behavior of others, and being analyzed. The tape provides an objective record against which different perceptions can be checked.

Discussing tapes is time-consuming. For a rule of thumb, multiply the time taken by the taped meeting by at least four. One training group took twenty-five minutes to analyze what happened in the first minute and a half of a tape-recorded meeting. Also, much material on the tape may be boring or not helpful—selecting critical episodes is often desirable. Getting a technically good tape (audible, little extraneous noise) is important.

People are rarely bothered by tape recording when they know that the tape will be heard only by other members of the training group. Sometimes members are self-conscious for the first few minutes of recording, but this generally disappears quickly and the machine is ignored. It is usually a mistake to make an issue out of whether or not to tape record. The idea should be presented matter-of-factly as a way to get at desired learnings.

Variations: (1) At each meeting of the group, the first half of the meeting is tape-recorded. After a break, portions of the tape selected by the group are played back and analyzed for the second half of the meeting.

(2) The group may play back a section of tape and use role checklists or other process-recording devices to analyze what happened.

(3) Specific "critical incidents" which proved especially important for group learning or progress can be isolated and played back. The same procedure can be used for incidents about which markedly differing opinions are held. (For this method, the tape recorder must be equipped with a revolution or footage counter, or other device for rapid location of episodes on tape.)

(4) The behavior of a chairman (or recorder, observer, etc.) can be analyzed via tape playback.

(5) A tape being played back can be stopped after each member contribution on the tape. In the listening group, each member jots down +, −, or o, according to whether he felt the comment was helpful, hindering, or neutral. These ratings are reported to the group, and analysis is done of why members gave the ratings they did. Then the tape is turned on for another comment.

(It's very easy to lose continuity this way. One solution is to reverse the tape for a minute to get the context immediately preceding. Another is not to stop the tape so frequently, but to rate only "critical" behaviors, or to rate a behavior only when some member raises his hand as the tape is playing.)

Notes:

Alter ego comments

Tape recording, and analysis of the recording, can deepen group members' understanding by providing much useful data about what *has* been going on in the group. But how to get at members' feelings just as they take place, here and now?

In most meetings on the job, the persons involved do not say all they are thinking.[10] In training groups, however, it is possible and useful to examine the unvoiced thoughts and feelings that are present around the table—just when they occur. In the alter ego method, the group agrees that any member may make a public guess about real, unvoiced feelings of any other member (see example below). Each guessed feeling is then checked with the person to whom it is attributed. General group discussion may illuminate reasons why persons do not express real feelings, and clarify the factors behind accurate or inaccurate sensing of others' feelings.

---

[10] Thank goodness.

EXAMPLE OF ALTER EGO COMMENTS

Training problems: To be able to sense others' real feelings more clearly; to understand the role of covert feeling in groups.

Procedure: As a normal group discussion proceeds, any member signals that he is making an alter ego comment, and does so. Then checking of the comment, and discussion, follow:

> Bill: I'm very much disappointed in this group. Why can't we get down to business instead of fooling around?
>
> Hilda: Bill, I don't think you understand what this group is for.
>
> Walt: Yes, I agree. What we're doing is fine as far as I'm concerned.
>
> Lois [*raises hand*]: Alter ego for Bill: "I feel squelched." (This is checked with Bill, who agrees.)
>
> Hilda [*raises hand*]: Alter ego for Walt: "I really feel impatient with people who want us to get down to business."
>
> (This is checked with Walt, who says he does *not* feel impatient. Some group members suggest that maybe Hilda is assuming he is, because *she's* impatient.)

During discussion, besides checking and correcting member perceptions the group can analyze how the process of making covert feelings explicit has influenced group movement and feelings of people about each other.[11]

Comment: Making alter ego comments may look like risky business. There are risks in any procedure which supplies extra information about feelings which people have about others. Members could be misunderstood, or seriously misunderstand others, or feel psychologically naked.

There are several reasons why these anticipated risks are unlikely to materialize. Ordinarily, if a procedure like alter ego comments is proposed in a training group, it is not accepted unless members feel a considerable degree of trust in and security with others. Where a group has met for some time and has developed increasingly durable working relationships, the members are quite sensitive to the possibility of hurting each other, and will discuss the pros and cons of the procedure extensively before starting to use it. Early alter ego comments are often made experimentally, and the group will decide either to abandon the procedure if it is evoking too much tension, or to continue it if it proves to be helpful. If all members of the group really want to use the procedure, and the first few trials are successful, considerable learning can take place.

[11] A sequence of alter ego comments, combined with "soliloquizing" (see variation 4 below), is presented in M. K. Barron and G. Krulee, "Case study of a basic skill training group," *Journal of Social Issues*, 4, 2, Spring 1948, pp. 25–28.

The reader is also referred to the discussion in Chapter III (pp. 36–37) on the differences between training and therapy. The implication here is that alter ego comments are restricted to *group*-relevant matters (the alter ego for George says: "I feel angry about Bill [chairman] saying my topic wasn't relevant," *not* "Bill reminds me of my father and all of the problems I have with authority figures"). The trainer can be helpful by demonstrating what kinds of comments are appropriate. He should not urge the group members to use this—or any other—procedure if they do not understand and accept it.

A frequent consequence of successful use of alter ego comments is that the whole level of feeling in the group changes. People become warmer and more spontaneous as they understand, with the aid of the alter ego procedure, how others really feel.

Variations: (1) Each member steadily acts as alter ego for the person on his right, or the person across from him, etc.

(2) Half the group sits in a circle, with the other half grouped around. Each member's alter ego sits in back of him.

(3) Using variation (1) or (2), checking is suspended until five or ten minutes have gone by, so people can get an over-all picture of how they are seen by others. Then these pictures are examined.

(4) Each person acts as his own alter ego—soliloquizes at points where he would not ordinarily express his feelings. Usually more and more informal soliloquizing happens naturally anyway, as the training group progresses.

Notes:

Relationship charting

In any group, differential relationships exist between members. These relationships may involve liking, prestige, and influence, among others. Often people form informal subgroups on the basis of these relationships. Such subgroups influence the effectiveness of the total group.[12]

---

[12] For evidence of this, see M. Horwitz, "The conceptual status of group dynamics," *Review of Educational Research*, 33:309–28, 1953, and D. Stock and H. A. Thelen, *Emotional dynamics and group culture* (National Training Laboratories, 1958).

In a training group, relationships can be profitably studied by asking in a systematic way for members' reactions to other members, and charting them on a chalkboard or large sheets of paper.

EXAMPLE OF RELATIONSHIP CHARTING

Training problem: Understanding how subgroups develop during a struggle for leadership.

Procedure: Each member writes down the name of the one other member "whose ideas I feel most sympathetic to so far during this meeting." The slips of paper are read off and plotted on a chalkboard,[13] with arrows from chooser to chosen:

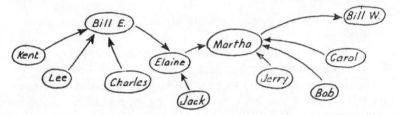

(Read as: Kent named Bill E. as the person whose ideas he felt most sympathetic to; Bill E. named Elaine, etc.)

When the charting is complete, the group discusses its implications, and interviews individuals about the reasons behind their naming the persons they did. Analysis is made of the subgroup patterns in relation to leadership phenomena.

For example, the chart above came from a training group of college student leaders. They proposed and carried out the idea of relationship charting. In the analysis, it developed that the persons called "Bill E." and "Martha" were seen as spokesmen for two different factional points of view about what the training group should do next. "Elaine," it will be noticed, is a "bridge" person between the two factions. It turned out that she was chosen to be leader for the next session of the group, which proved unusually productive.

Comment: Here again risks are present. On seeing a relationship chart, some members may feel that their worth as persons is being challenged, that they are not accepted by others, or that they are being accorded special

---

[13] A relationship chart is a form of sociogram. For help in plotting choices this way, see Horace Mann–Lincoln Institute Staff, *How to construct a sociogram* (Teachers College Bureau of Publications, 1957 printing).

acclaim, even when the charting has been done on the basis of impressions "in this meeting so far." The word "sociogram" usually is applied by someone, and this may make members feel the chart is primarily a matter of personal acceptance or rejection.

As with alter ego comments, however, hurts to individuals are least likely to occur when careful cooperative planning has been done ahead of the charting. Hurried or pushed decisions, where everyone does not foresee the consequences of a procedure, are extremely undesirable. The trainer's skill here lies mainly in supporting the group as it clarifies alternatives and makes clear plans about which everyone feels good.

In charting, it is best to use items like "Whose ideas have I felt most sympathetic to during this meeting?" Such items are concrete and specific in time, and do not imply long-term judgments of persons. Items like "Who is the most likable person?" or "Who is the best leader?" should be avoided. Negative items are also hard to handle, in general (but see Variation 3 below). The focus should be on *group*-relevant behaviors, not personality factors.

Variations: (1) Repeating the charting procedure several times during the life of a training group can help show developmental changes very graphically.

(2) Making two simultaneous charts (ex: "person whose ideas are most like mine" and "person who I think clarifies others' ideas most frequently") is useful. The two charts invariably differ a good deal, and can show how different persons have different kinds of skills needed by the group for problem solving.

(3) To study communication blocks, group members use an item such as "person I think understands me least well." After charting and analysis, members who do not understand each other well break into pairs to discuss and clarify reasons for misunderstanding. They report back to the group, and factors making for communication difficulty are identified.

(4) To study communication patterns, group members use an item such as "the two people I agree with most in the group." Linkages between each pair of chosen members are plotted, with the chooser's name left out.

Notes:

Role analysis

As a series of training sessions proceeds, members may feel they would like to get the reactions of other members of the group to the way they have been behaving during the sessions. Such feedback has, of course, been provided frequently during training, but on an intermittent, sketchy basis. When the need for systematic feedback is shared by all members of the group, they may plan and carry out a careful discussion of the way each member's behavior has been seen by others during the life of the group. This discussion can provide substantial insight for members, as they learn from trusted, objective, accepted others "how I affect a group" and get a deeper understanding of "how a group affects me."

EXAMPLE OF ROLE ANALYSIS

Training problem: Understanding how individual behaviors affect group processes.

Procedure: The group carefully plans a procedure as follows: any member invites comments on his role as the group has seen it, listens, asks for clarification, raises questions about his own behavior as it has come across to others. Reference is made to significant events in the group's history, how they affected the individual's participation, and vice versa. Discussion on the individual's role ends when he requests it, and another member asks the group to focus on his behavior.

Comment: After a training group has worked together for several sessions, the members can usually supply the sensitivity and skill needed to do a good job with this procedure. It is not easy and may be painful at times, but ordinarily it is greatly rewarding to members.

A frequent tendency is to put off role analysis until near the end of the training program ("We only have one more meeting, and I would like the chance before we break up to hear the impressions you have of the way I've participated"). This is less than desirable, because members then have very little time to react to the feedback they get from others, and to experiment with new behavior. On the other hand, role analysis should not be attempted too early in the life of the group—members simply do not have very clear impressions of each other as yet.

As with the two previous training activities, thoughtful, non-pressuring group planning is needed. One group of teenagers spent over an hour carefully specifying what was to be in and out of bounds in discussing each others' behavior as they had seen it during the sessions of the training group. (For example, requests like, "OK, now tell me what's wrong with me" were to be clearly out of bounds.) Whatever the final procedure is, it should respect all reservations held by members about such a thorough-going discussion of individual behavior.

Another group, using brainstorming, listed over thirty different methods of doing role analysis, including writing poems about each other, doing role-playing skits, making alter ego comments, interviewing, and filling out rating scales. Then they gradually winnowed these down and came out with a procedure much like that described under *Procedure*.

Often a group experimentally tries out a role-analysis procedure with several members who have requested reactions to their behavior, and then decides to continue, revamp, or abandon the procedure.

In doing role analysis, there are some useful rules of thumb:

1. The focus should always be on *perceived behavior*—the way a member's actions in the group have been seen by others.
2. Questions of intent and inner motivation should be referred to the member whose role is being discussed.
3. No judgments!
4. Each person should speak for himself.

Illustrations of these principles are shown on page 122.

No training group is likely to follow these rules of thumb exactly during role analysis. The important thing is that the group be clear on *some* ground rules, and be alert to how well the procedure is going as it is tried out.

Variations: (1) Members write comments about each other member's role on cards, which are then sorted out. Each member reads those about his role, and asks for clarification and discussion.

(2) Each member interviews the group, asking questions about the way others have seen him.

(3) The members make up a series of rating scales ("How skillful is this member in helping the group accomplish its tasks?"). Each member rates each other member, and the results are discussed. (This procedure is difficult because of the judgmental aspect implied. A more effective variant is to use a role checklist,[14] which deals with concrete behaviors.) Results from the ratings or checklist can be summarized, so the individual sees how he stands in relation to others.

---

[14] For example, see *Adult Leadership,* January 1953, pp. 17–23, for a "Tool Kit" with which member functions can be observed and recorded.

EXAMPLES OF ROLE ANALYSIS COMMENTS

NOT "You were insecure." (personality imputation)

BUT "It seemed to me you often did not speak when the group was tense or upset." (report of perceived behavior)

NOT "You were trying to take over the group." (attack, imputed motives)

BUT "I don't know how you saw it, but the impression that came across to me was that you were trying to control me. How did you feel about it?" (Here is my reaction to your behavior; what is your view of it?)

NOT "You are a pleasant, well-adjusted person." (personality generalization, stereotyping)

BUT "Whenever you spoke, I felt warm and accepted. You never did anything that threatened me." (report of the way you affected *me*)

NOT "The group thinks you are very capable intellectually." (imputation of opinion to group)

BUT "You struck me as making a real contribution to our thinking, for example, during our analysis of decision-making. Do other group members share this feeling?" (Here is my view, what is that of others?)

(4) Alter ego comments, checked with the member, may be used.

(5) Group members may recall and list on the chalkboard a series of critical incidents from the group's history so far (see p. 106). This method is usually extremely helpful; the incidents serve as an objective, stimulating background for role-analysis comments. Individual behavior is seen in the context of the group situation where it took place.

Notes:

A final comment

The activities described above can be adapted for use in any training group. All of them are designed to help the group study its own ongoing processes as they take place. Although the reader will have seen that the activities are arranged in rough order of increasing emotional involvement, much variation is possible. Most of the activities can be planned for use on a relatively matter-of-fact, intellectual level; any of them can be deepened to include strong personal feelings relevant to group participation. As suggested at the beginning of this chapter, activities planned to evoke moderate emotional intensity are most effective in bringing about real self-examination and learning. In general, activities planned to evoke high interest and involvement require more skill from the trainer in helping the group set up and move through the activity. As we have noted, high involvement also brings risks, and the trainer must be clear on what he wishes to help the group undertake. An old rule of thumb can be applied here: "Don't start something you can't finish."

To repeat once more, if there is careful cooperative planning, a training group will tend to seek a stable level of work where members are participating in a challenging but not personally threatening fashion. The important thing is that the trainer not hurry or trick the group into activities for which they are unprepared.

Finally, time spent in a critique of the procedure a group has been using, with an eye to judging its value as a way to learn, deepens the skills of both trainer and group. Without such evaluation it is difficult to improve the program as it proceeds.

Perhaps these comments may be read to imply that studying ongoing group processes is first of all a matter of being rational, of controlling emotions via the intellect. The position taken here is rather that feelings and emotions are the heart of the training process, and that confusion, disruptions, puzzles, and frustrations are a normal part of any training group's development. (See again the discussion of developmental trends in training, Chapter IV, pp. 87–92). The question is: How can we learn to function *intelligently* in group situations, synthesize the rational and emotional aspects of social man?

The next section deals with planned situations as another general type of training activity.

II. Learning through Planned Situations

In a training program it is often useful to construct situations which are tailored to the requirements of solving a particular problem. For example, a training group may do a role-playing scene between a "supervisor" and a "teacher" to learn some of the skills of helping people change. Or, the group may analyze a film of a group meeting in order to understand how the vested interests of members can operate to block progress.

In short, the training group members take time to deliberately *alter* their usual rules of procedure, and set up a special, marked-off situation in order to work on a particular problem. Planned situations are usually less open-ended and more pre-structured than some of the activities described in the preceding section. Usually too, they focus less directly on the here-and-now processes spontaneously developing in the training group.

It should be pointed out that most of the training procedures discussed above in Section I, "Studying Ongoing Group Behavior," can also be used in deliberately planned situations. For example, if a role-playing scene of a difficult meeting has been set up, the alter ego procedure can be used to study the feelings role players express during the meeting. Or, if a film is being shown, observation forms can be used as members watch. The basic thing about planned situations, however, is that the raw material being looked at is specially set up, marked off from the normal ongoing processes of the group, selected with forethought. In short, a certain group situation has been *caused* to happen, instead of appearing naturally.

Below are described eight different types of planned training situations. For each type, one or more examples are given. The format of this section differs somewhat from that used above. First a training need or problem is named. This is followed by the procedure for setting up the situation, the action phase, and subsequent analysis of the action. As in the section above, general comment, suggested variations, and space for notes follow.

Planned situations naturally have advantages and disadvantages. They can increase group focus on a problem, and add to interest and involvement. They can enable systematic, point-by-point **learning**, rather than the sometimes haphazard learning which occurs when members study ongoing group processes as they take place. And, since the situation is by definition "not for keeps," group members can safely and repeatedly analyze the problem, try out solutions and evaluate them. In short, planned situations are more controllable.

On the other hand, when planned situations are used, the problem chosen may be looked at in isolation from its real context, and partial, inadequate solutions may be accepted. The training group may come to accept a superficial approach to learning and problem solving. The best safeguard against these dangers is careful assessment of group members' problems and needs. Then a situation can be built around real concerns, instead of being jumped into because it's fun, easy to do, or a convenient way to escape from other problems and stresses in the life of the training group.

The basic characteristics of the planned situation, then, are: (1) careful planning to meet a focused, specific group need; (2) deliberate, temporary alteration of usual training-group procedures; (3) creation of a psychologically safe atmosphere, often by the use of role playing. In practice, there is no *sharp* division between planned situations and methods for studying ongoing group processes—the latter obviously require planning too—but there are differences in emphasis, as will become clear from the examples below.

Use of a clarifier

Group members often need—especially at the beginning of a training program—to understand features of ongoing group behavior which cannot be simply or easily explained. It is very difficult for a group of people, hearing verbal explanations alone, to get insight into how problem solving proceeds, the nature of a "non-directive" approach to interviewing, or ways of getting started at the first meeting of a committee. A common, concrete situation is needed as a background for verbal explanations.

Setting up a skit or demonstration scene, and using a "clarifier" to stand outside the scene and comment on what is happening, can be very helpful. Those who are watching the scene and listening to the comments of the clarifier get a fuller understanding of what is going on in the scene than would otherwise be possible.

EXAMPLE OF USE OF CLARIFIER

Training problem: How does the process of defining a problem take place in a group?

Setting up the situation: The group sets up a hypothetical situation in which people must, as a first step, define their problem (for example, a committee which has been asked to study the way in which reports are made to parents). Volunteer role players [15] for this group leave the room to decide who will play what roles and get "warmed up" to the scene.

Meanwhile, the rest of the members of the training group discuss problem definition, and attempt to decide what things they will look for in the demonstration. One person (usually a trainer) is named to act as a "clarifier." Once the role-playing scene has started, he will stand to one side and comment on what is happening. He is to be "invisible" to the demonstration group, but can be "seen" by the audience.[16] That is, the demonstration group is to pay no attention to him, except to keep silent while he is talking.

Action: The role players return, and the clarifier procedure is explained to them. The role-playing scene starts, and the clarifier occasionally intervenes with comments:

Cooper (chairman): I'm glad to see you all here today. Uh, the superintendent has asked us to meet and discuss the problem of reporting to parents.

McCoy: Well, Bill, I do think it's a problem. The report cards I'm using with my second-graders haven't been reprinted since 1942.

Miller: Yes. I wonder about really doing a job on those. We could really make a contribution if we revamped them.

CLARIFIER: [*To audience*] You notice that the problem has already gotten defined as a matter of report card revision only. Other aspects of reporting to parents are being left out.

McCoy: For example, on this 1942 card, rating kids on "Obedience" and "Deportment" is not exactly consistent with what we're trying to do with children in our elementary program, I think.

COOPER: Well, I think so too, but let's think of the whole system a minute. The superintendent, when he talked to me yesterday, said he

---

[15] Role playing, or spontaneous acting-out of problem situations, is discussed in Chapter VI, pp. 191–94. The reader who is unfamiliar with role playing may wish to refer ahead, since many examples of its use are given in the present section.

[16] The term "audience" will be used throughout this section to mean those watching a demonstration, even if only a handful of people is involved.

felt that high school reporting practices might be looked at as well as what we're doing in the elementary schools.

CLARIFIER: The chairman is supplying information on the product expected of the group, but it still is not clear what the focus of attention is to be today.

McCoy: Did he specifically say he felt the report cards should be improved?

The scene continues until the clarifier has been able to point up as many principles or features of the process of defining a problem as he thinks are useful, or until the problem is thoroughly defined by the demonstration group.

Analysis: The demonstration group can be interviewed on their reactions. The audience can compare their observations of what happened with the comments made by the clarifier. Generalizations or principles of problem definition can be listed on the chalkboard.

Comment: This is a good design for increasing members' sensitivity to what is going on in a group. A skillful clarifier can catch events immediately, as they happen. Terms like "defining the problem" are illustrated concretely, specifically, and realistically in the context of an ongoing situation.

Clarifier comments usually do not seriously affect the course of events in the role-playing scene. Some of the methods described in Section I above, such as process observation, sometimes alter the situation drastically. (For example, an observer's mention of the amount of participation by members usually causes people to talk more or less, depending on the judgment of appropriateness they feel is implied.)

Naturally, clarifier comments do alter things somewhat (for example, Cooper's second comment in the scene above may have been made because of the preceding clarifier comment), but this is not serious; in fact it illustrates what happens when explicit attention is paid to process factors in a group's work.

The job of clarifier can be learned by practice with "live" groups, or by listening to a tape recording with others, and stopping it from time to time to make comments. It requires good sensitivity to what's happening, some conceptual background in the study of group behavior, and a ready flow of words.

The danger of the clarifier method is that it keeps members from doing their *own* thinking about what's happening in the demonstration group.

[Use of clarifier cont'd]

It may encourage dependent reactions to the clarifier ("You're so capable and understanding. I'm sure *I* could never put things into words the way you do.") After all, the sensitivity and diagnostic ability of the clarifier are skills *all* members of the training group should be acquiring (see Chapter II, pp. 23-25). The clarifier method should be used to aid member learning, not to generate puzzlement or dependence. Taking time to evaluate the procedure after using it is a good idea.

Variations: (1) Tape record the scene without a clarifier; then replay and have clarifier make comments, stopping the tape to do so. This approach has the advantage of not interrupting the scene as it is played originally.

(2) Using tape, stop it at certain focal or crucial points. Have all members write down a clarifying comment; then read these aloud and compare. This approach gets all group members actively thinking about what is happening in the scene. Allow four or five times as long as the original taped meeting took.

(3) Use two clarifiers, each focusing on different aspects of what is happening in the demonstration group. They must be careful not to comment too frequently, or the demonstration group may be thrown off stride.

Notes:

Study exercises

When a training group wishes to study a specific aspect of group behavior, exercises can often be set up to help. The focus is not so much on practicing a skill, or demonstrating a social-psychological phenomenon (as in some of the types of situations described below), as on presenting the training group with an opportunity to explore a problem area systematically. Study exercises are usually most helpful when a training group is just beginning to move into a new area of work, and the members' training problems are not highly focused.

Example of study exercise, No. 1

Training problem: How do organizational relationships affect small group behavior?

Setting up the situation: Before the meeting, the trainer, with the help of a subgroup, constructs a scene where organizational relationships, rather than personality factors as such, are likely to influence what happens.

For example: A junior high school lunchroom committee has four teachers from different grade levels and subject fields, and a guidance worker. Some are respected old-timers, some are newcomers; some are friendly with the principal, and some not. One of the teachers is chairman.

The meeting was called by the principal. He is very upset because some 8th-graders were acting up in the cafeteria, and spilled milk on the dress of a new School Board member who was visiting. He implies that the committee has failed, and demands that they *do* something.

The role players are briefed before the training group session.

At the session, before going on to the role-playing scene the trainer gives a short lecture on aspects of organization, such as authority relationships in a hierarchy, communication problems, influence, prestige, and the like.[17] The audience members do not know what briefings have been given to the role players, but are asked to watch for things that happen in the scene because of apparent organizational loyalties and pressures. The setting (lunchroom committee, etc.) is briefly explained by the trainer.

Action: Scene starts and proceeds for ten or fifteen minutes, until cut by the trainer.

Analysis: Audience members list on chalkboard the organizational influences, both helping and hindering, that they felt were present, for example:

"The principal, in calling the meeting, by-passed the authority of the committee chairman."

These influences are checked with the role players for accuracy.

Chairman: "Yes, that's right, and I was furious with him. I kept thinking, 'Brother, if you don't want to let me run this committee, why did you make me chairman in the first place?' "

Generalizations are made about organizational effects on group work:

"When authority relationships are by-passed or are unclear, this creates frustration and anger as well as added insecurity in group members. These feelings can prevent the group from working on the problem at hand."

[17] See, for example, M. R. Goodson, G. Jensen, and J. Jackson, "Workshop on the larger organization," *Adult Leadership,* 3:13–29, September 1954.

[Study exercise, no. 1 cont'd]

Comment: This sort of procedure is straightforward and simple to carry out. It is usually most effective as an exploratory, opening-up device when a training group is just beginning an area of study.

Incidentally, this particular scene, if roles are carefully built, usually brings out a rich variety of feelings about group work in the school organization. About an hour and a half should be allowed.

Variation: The group lists unanswered questions and problems at the end of the session to build an agenda for further work in the problem area.

Notes:

Sometimes study exercises can be built around a social-psychological concept rather than a situational problem.

EXAMPLE OF STUDY EXERCISE, No. 2

Training problem: How do members of a group perform the different leadership functions needed as a group proceeds?

Setting up the situation: The training group (if larger than eight persons) breaks into subgroups of size 6 to 8. Each group locates two observers, who leave the room for briefing by the trainer. He gives them observation sheets, one for "task" functions, such as summarizing, clarifying, asking for opinions, and one for "maintenance" functions, such as encouraging, supporting, testing for consensus.[18]

Action: The observers return, and each subgroup is given a simple task, such as "You are a special committee of teachers. Decide on a list of criteria for determining how a $500 Lions Club college scholarship should be awarded in your school system."

Analysis: After each subgroup has worked for about 10–15 minutes, the task observer leads a discussion, in his subgroup, of what he has seen. (It helps if there are enough extra copies of the observer sheets for each member to have one to follow.)

---

[18] For help in making up such sheets, see Gibb and Gibb, *op. cit.,* pp. 82, 91; or the discussion in *Adult Leadership,* 1:8:2–23, January 1953. The reader is also referred back to the earlier review of leadership functions (Chapter II, pp. 17–21).

After ten minutes or so, the maintenance function observer also reports. Each subgroup is thus discussing who supplied what functions, whether all functions on the sheet were filled, the relative flexibility of members (some filled only one function, some many), the approximate sequence of functions filled, and the like.

Subgroups can report their findings to the total group, and generalizations can be made ("All groups reported they had more task than maintenance functions—maybe because the goal was clear and few conflicting feelings were present").

Comment: This study exercise was developed by the National Training Laboratories, and has been extensively used in short training workshops. It is simple, brief (time about one hour), and extremely useful in helping group members see quite concretely what has to go on in a group if it is to get a satisfying job done. The idea of a *function* is illuminated clearly, and members may come to see that better group behavior is not a mysterious mumbo-jumbo but can be learned.

The observer task is not difficult if function categories are kept to five or six per sheet. If subgroup members are numbered, record-keeping goes rapidly.

The exercise is very easy to use with students. As with adults, one has to watch out for the use of function names as stereotypes—"You're a harmonizer," "You're an opinion-seeker."

Variation: Instead of a made-up task, use a real one currently facing the training group, such as "Develop a list of criteria for deciding who should attend workshops like this one." Tasks that are likely to get a response from all group members quickly and easily are best for this exercise.

Notes:

Perception check

For most people, it is difficult to perceive quickly and accurately the feelings being expressed by others in a group, without making good-bad judgments about these feelings. Yet such sensitivity is essential for good group work (see Chapter II, pp. 23–25). Ordinarily, people get very little chance to practice and improve their ability to understand what another person is thinking, feeling, and trying to express. Immediate feedback on the accuracy of one's perception is rare—except for indirect indications, such as impatience, repetition of points, frowns, smiles of understanding, and the like. The perception-check procedure attempts to short-cut this indirect process. Each member guesses the reaction of each other member to a specific statement; these data are then tabulated and analyzed by the whole group.

Example of perception check

Training problem: How to increase our sensitivity—our accuracy in perceiving what others are saying and feeling.

Setting up the situation, and action: Members agree on a verbal statement about which they feel some difference of opinion has recently been expressed in the group. ("Teachers should be expected to attend in-service training meetings on their own time.") This statement is written on the chalkboard. Each group member first reacts privately to this statement (on a sheet of paper), using a plus or minus sign to indicate his own agreement or disagreement. Then he writes the names of all other group members, putting a plus or minus sign by each name to indicate how he thinks that member feels about the statement.

Analysis: Each member's real feeling ($+$ or $-$) is set down on the chalkboard. Then the group is polled ("How many people guessed Bill right? 7"; "Walter? 3"), and the results are put on the board.

In addition, each person's perception-skill score can be tabulated. ("Bill was able to perceive the feelings of 6 out of the total group"; "Walter guessed right on 8 . . . .")

People interview members whose feelings they misjudged, to discover the reasons for their misunderstanding. ("Walter, when you disagreed with Bill that time, I was *sure* you felt negative. But then I guess I stopped listening to what you said next, because I was angry.") Members whose feelings most people misjudged may explain their position more fully.

Ways are suggested for people to improve their accuracy ("Watch for nods and frowns of other listeners, while you are listening to what a speaker is saying"). Factors that keep people from perceiving accurately are discussed.

For best results, the exercise should then be repeated several times with new statements, to give people a chance to apply their learnings about accurate perceiving.

Comment: This exercise is easy to run if done slowly and clearly, a step at a time, with plenty of time for people to exclaim in delight or dismay at what shows up in the data. The first run usually takes about twenty or thirty minutes, if group size is over a dozen, but subsequent runs go more quickly. Practice and thoughtful generalizing are needed, or people may get wrapped up in their specific successes and failures at guessing the feelings of other members.[19]

Variations: (1) Instead of a general statement, the group can use an actual statement just made by a member of the training group.

(2) The group picks out a statement from a tape recording of the meeting.

(3) Members respond to a rating scale ("How satisfied I am with the meeting right at this minute"), and try to guess the ratings made by other members on the same scale.

(4) After a statement is agreed on, the group engages in discussion of it for 15–20 minutes; then the perception check is made. This usually boosts accuracy scores, and shows the effects of trying to be sensitively aware of other members' feelings, either about discussion content or about group processes.

Notes:

Role reversal

Misperceptions of the feelings of others often occur because people are unable to empathize (take the role of another). They rely instead on stereotypes, assumptions that the other is "just like me," or pure guesswork. In role reversal, the parties in a two-person situation change places and try to continue their discussion. Analysis of what happens can illuminate the difficulties of really "standing in someone else's shoes" and making a valid estimate of how things look from that position.

[19] How this procedure worked out with one training group is described in A. H. Passow, M. B. Miles, S. M. Corey, and D. C. Draper, *Training curriculum leaders for cooperative research* (Teachers College Bureau of Publications, 1955), pp. 36–38.

EXAMPLE OF ROLE REVERSAL

Training problem: What factors influence empathy—how well one can feel what another person is feeling?

Setting up the situation: The group members identify a situation where perceiving feelings accurately is likely to be difficult (ex: a principal interviewing a teacher who is not keeping up with her routine record-keeping tasks).

Two volunteers are located. One leaves the room while the other is briefed by the group ("You feel guilty about the records, but you as a teacher just do not have time for all the paperwork that is required by the office. You would rather spend your time on more constructive things").

Then this role player steps outside and the other one returns for briefing ("You as a principal are very concerned about accurate record-keeping, since State aid depends on it. You cannot see why anyone with a little sense cannot do the amount required by making an effort to be more efficient"). Then the first role player is brought back into the room, and the scene is set up (ex: it is taking place after school in the principal's office).

Action: The scene starts and runs for a few minutes, or until evidences of conflict and non-understanding begin to appear. The trainer cuts the scene, and asks the participants to reverse roles ("principal" is to take "teacher" role and vice versa). They change seats (and roles) and continue their discussion.

Analysis: Each role player is interviewed to find out what happened after he had to take the role of the other person. He discusses difficulties he experienced in doing this, and what helped him. Group members may also analyze whether the problem (routine record-keeping, in this case) got anywhere near solution.

The group members may also identify principles of empathizing ("Try to restate what a person says and check this with him, instead of jumping ahead and assuming you know what he means").

A new scene with different content can be set up. Here the emphasis is on trying out the ideas or principles for increasing empathy.

Comment: If the role players are emotionally involved in the scene, they usually find changing places fairly difficult, even if they have been expecting to be asked to do so. This difficulty in itself can provide a useful insight for the group.

If the role players have *not* been expecting to be asked to reverse roles, they usually find it very difficult indeed, and there may be considerable learning ("I never realized before how completely I ignore how the other person must be feeling"). However, the danger in the trainer's asking the players to change places without forewarning is that the trainer-group relationship may suffer. Feelings of manipulation or dependence may develop. In the long run an active co-planning relationship is best for learning. If everyone shares in making training decisions, unexpected consequences in training experiences do not lead to mistrust, but to better learning.

Variation: Instead of one scene with others watching, the group divides into two subgroups (one "principals," one "teachers") for separate briefings. Then people assemble in principal-teacher pairs for the scene in the principal's office. All pairs work simultaneously. After 5 minutes, the trainer cuts and asks for role reversal. General discussion follows. This variation has the advantage of involving everyone in a basic insight experience.

Notes:

Case analysis

Case analysis as defined here[20] means the construction (or adaptation from a description on paper) of an over-all human relations situation. Specific interpersonal or group incidents taking place in the situation are role-played. The incidents are analyzed, and new incidents are planned, role-played, and discussed.

EXAMPLE OF CASE ANALYSIS [21]

Training problems: Defining an effective role for the consultant who is working with a new group; how to help a group identify and work toward solution of real problems.

Setting up the situation: The training group specifies general characteristics of a case situation (ex: a new supervisor in a small city school system

[20] The case method of teaching human relations involves thorough and complete discussion of a case described on paper, and will not be discussed in this book. For good material describing the case method as an approach to learning, see K. R. Andrews, *The case method of teaching; human relations and administration* (Harvard University Press, 1953).

[21] For more detail on this example, see M. B. Miles and S. M. Corey, "The first cooperative curriculum research institute," *Research for curriculum improvement,* 1957 Yearbook, Association for Supervision and Curriculum Development, Appendix B, esp. pp. 323–24.

[Case analysis cont'd]

with relatively formal operating procedures, a principal with rigid tendencies, etc.). A subgroup agrees to write up details of the case before the next meeting.

At the next meeting, all group members read the case, and identify specific problem incidents they would like to work on (ex: faculty meeting where principal announces impending arrival of the new supervisor and asks group how they would like to work with her; supervisor meets with faculty; several teachers discuss her later in the teachers' room). One or several such incidents are set up for role playing.

Action: The incidents are role-played and tape-recorded.

Analysis: The tape is played back, and interrupted for comment and analysis. ("The supervisor is in a tough spot because the principal fears she is competing with him for leadership of his staff.") The original role players are interviewed to check the interpretations made.

As new problems appear, possible solutions to them can be tested by additional role-playing scenes (ex: the supervisor meets with the principal, hoping to gain his cooperation and reduce his fears that she will "take over"). The training group may also break into subgroups to share learnings and map out desirable next steps for the central character in the case.

Comment: In effect, the training group constructs a shared, hypothetical, compelling situation, and uses it as a vehicle for analysis and skill practice. The case can be altered so that any desired problem or situation is produced, but still provides a realistic context for any particular role-playing scene.

Needlessly complex cases should be avoided, and focus should be on specific incidents. Everyone should have the same common information, so that role players do not escape from a predicament by suddenly making up a new piece of information that everyone else is presumed to know (ex: "Why doesn't your committee have its report ready?" "Surely you remember the snowstorm last week that kept us all out of school?").

The case should be open-ended. That is, a resolution of the state of affairs in the case is not presented, and should not be easily attainable or readily apparent. The case is not set up for members to solve like a detective story. Rather, it offers practice in analyzing situations and choosing crucial "leverage points" for taking action. (The group referred to in footnote 21 decided that such a point involved the new supervisor's talking with the principal to discover who the influential teachers in the school were.) Good case analysis is a useful way to reduce the tendency to oversimplify.

Plenty of time should be available for case development, analysis, and

[Case analysis cont'd]

thinking-through. The same group spent a half hour developing the case outline, three hours reading the case and doing the first scenes, and about five hours analyzing, role playing new scenes, working in subgroups, and pulling together final learnings. During a critique of their work, they felt this time was rather short for what they had hoped to do (which included intermittent analysis of ongoing processes in the training group itself).

Variation: The group uses an existing case,[22] and develops incidents from it; in this way less time is needed for case construction. The risk is that the case may be less likely to represent all the kinds of problems which group members want to work on. The same is true if a case is drawn from the experience of one member.

Notes:

Experimental demonstrations

Sometimes it is useful for training group members to improve their understanding of social science concepts by experiencing them directly. If the trainer is familiar with research studies of small groups, he may be able to identify concepts or generalizations relevant to problems being discussed in the training group. (Ex: how group influence is exerted on the deviant members of a group; how interpersonal liking and formal status are related in a group; how clear and unclear goals affect member behavior and group progress.) The trainer may set up, either alone or with the group, miniature laboratory experiments which clarify these concepts or generalizations.

[22] For casebooks, see H. Cabot and J. A. Kahl, *Human relations: concepts and cases in concrete social science* (Harvard University Press, 1953); M. Hamburg, *Case studies in elementary school administration* (Teachers College Bureau of Publications, 1957); E. Lloyd-Jones, R. Barry *et al.*, *Case studies in human relationships in secondary school* (Teachers College Bureau of Publications, 1956); D. E. Griffiths, *Human relations in school administration* (Appleton-Century-Crofts, 1956), pp. 345-450.

EXAMPLE OF EXPERIMENTAL DEMONSTRATION, No. 1

Training problem: How does a group exert pressures on its members to conform to group decisions?

Setting up the situation: In this design, all group members, except for two observers, participate in role playing. The training group identifies a situation, and a topic about which a decision must be made (for example, a workshop planning committee deciding whether or not to invite principals to a workshop like this one next year).

Two observers are recruited. Two other members agree to take the part of latecomers to the meeting. These four persons step outside.

The role players remaining in the room are briefed to agree very strongly on a decision (for example, that principals should *not* be included). They discuss reasons for this decision while the trainer briefs observers and the two latecomer role players outside.

The latecomer role players are briefed to take a deviant position ("principals *should* be included"), but are *not* told that it is deviant. Independently, one role player is told he likes the group very much and wants to belong to it; the other is told he does not respect or like the members and thinks their meetings are usually a waste of time.

The two observers are briefed by the trainer to tally the number of comments directed to the two latecomers by other group members and if possible to jot down the nature of the comments as they are made. When they are fully briefed, they return to the group, and sit where they can observe easily.

Action: The meeting starts and runs for a few minutes; then the "latecomers" are brought in, observers watch, and the role-played meeting continues until a decision (or the impossibility of reaching a decision) is clear.

Analysis: Using the chalkboard, various data are listed (how the other role players felt toward each latecomer; feelings of each latecomer; observer data on number and type of comments directed toward each latecomer).

The group members generalize from the data. ("When deviance arises in a group, nearly all the comments are directed toward deviant members, until they give in or psychologically leave the group"; "A deviant member who is highly attracted to the group can be more influenced than one who does not care about belonging.")

Implications are drawn ("Does this mean everyone must always go along, or be rejected?").

Comment: This demonstration can produce very dramatic and meaningful data, corresponding fairly well with studies of deviation and rejection.[23]

About an hour and a half should be allowed.

A planned situation of this type is usually more complex than those presented earlier in this section. The trainer needs to be comfortably familiar with social-psychological concepts. He also must be able to plan and stage-manage so that the "experiment" will be likely to come off. Usually, the trainer will need to have a detailed working plan on paper before the session starts.

If, as sometimes happens, the desired phenomena do not appear (for example, the deviant members do *not* have most of the communication directed at them), then the trainer needs to be able to help the group analyze why ("Maybe we didn't want to hurt their feelings and so politely ignored them").

For a good learning experience, members in the scene must be carefully and thoroughly briefed. When people are asked to leave the room during part of the preparations, they may naturally feel apprehensive or threatened. These feelings are much less likely to arise if the planning to this point has been shared as much as possible by the total group, and if the people out in the hall are themselves actively engaged in "warming up" for the scene, planning their approaches, etc. If a role-playing scene involves the use of special information unknown to some members (in this scene, for example, the fact that one of the latecomers does not feel attracted to the group), this information should be made clear to all soon after the scene itself is over.

Variations: (1) Use a written case study as the vehicle for decision making.[24]

(2) If the training group has over 12–14 members, several simultaneous groups can be run. (Miniature experiments of this sort have been used with audiences up to several hundred, working in many small sub-

---

[23] Compare S. Shachter, "Deviation, rejection and communication," in D. Cartwright and A. Zander, *Group dynamics* (Row, Peterson, 1953), chap. 17, pp. 223–48. A trainer can get many ideas for experimental demonstrations by looking through research studies of group behavior.

See also P. Hare, E. F. Borgatta, and R. F. Bales, *Small groups* (Knopf, 1955), which contains, like the Cartwright and Zander book, a large number of studies. An annotated bibliography of 584 items, plus a subject index, is included.

[24] See National Training Laboratories, *Report of the Tenth Summer Laboratory Session* (1956) for an experimental demonstration like that above, using the case of "Johnny Rocco." The role players are asked to be a citizens' group which a new school superintendent has appointed to react to a case of a delinquent boy. The same reference, and the reports of prior and subsequent NTL summer sessions, give examples of other experimental demonstrations, as well as study exercises and skill practice sessions (see pp. 147–55 of the present book). They are worked out in step-by-step form.

groups.) Reports from the subgroups at the end are useful in outlining the general principles involved, since circumstances particular to any particular group tend to even out.

(3) This design can be used to study problems of status and group acceptance and rejection of members. The two latecomers are given no special briefing. The rest of the group is briefed to treat the latecomer who happens to sit in one particular empty chair as if he were the superintendent of schools, but not to use his title. They are briefed to treat the latecomer who sits in the other empty chair as if he were an inexperienced second grade teacher. After the scene, analysis can show how the ideas of high-status people are often accepted without regard to merit, and how feelings of being rejected cause withdrawal, anger, and refusal to present one's good ideas to the group.

Using the empty chairs is important, to indicate that who falls into the accepted or rejected role is a random matter. The trainer and the group need to supply support during the analysis, since the accepted high-status person suddenly learns he was not being accepted for the worth of his ideas, and the rejected low-status person may feel relieved but tricked.

Since this variation may thus develop more tension in members than does the original example, it is a good idea to use a role-playing scene as a vehicle, rather than a real problem facing the members.

Notes:

EXAMPLE OF EXPERIMENTAL DEMONSTRATION, No. 2[25]

Training problem: How do the characteristics of group goals affect group behavior?

Setting up the situation: The trainer discusses the general nature of group goals ("a place the group members want to get in order to reduce some tension or difficulty they all feel") and how these goals are made explicit through a coordination of individual motives and needs.

The training group is divided into subgroups of six or seven persons.

[25] This demonstration was devised by I. Knickerbocker, and developed further at the National Training Laboratory in Group Development. It is described fully in the NTLGD Delegate Take-home Packet, Summer Session 1954 (National Training Laboratories, 1954).

Each group nominates an observer. The observers are briefed (by the trainer, outside) to watch (1) for the number of times members attempt to clarify the goal, (2) for disruptive, ineffective behavior by members, (3) for general productivity.

Action: Observers return, and the trainer gives the groups a short time (7–8 minutes) to accomplish a vague, abstract, complex task ("Reach agreement on this statement: What are the most appropriate goals to govern the best development of group experiences in order to maximize social development in a democratic society?").

After the time is up, the trainer then gives the groups a concrete, clear, simple task ("In 7–8 minutes, list all the names you can of clubs or organizations appearing in a typical community").

Analysis: Observers report back to the total group what they have noticed (ex: "The first scene had long silences, considerable angry feeling, much asking for clarification, long vague intellectual comments. The second scene produced an initial burst of laughter, very rapid discussion, and nearly everyone took part, which was very different from the first scene").

The group members generalize about characteristics of effective and ineffective types of goals (ex: "attainable, clear, challenging"), and examine the reasons for the negative, disruptive behaviors appearing in the first scene.

Comment: This is a clear, simple experimental demonstration to run. With a new training group, it often shows powerfully how group characteristics (in this case, clear and unclear goals) can make a decided difference in the way members behave—that "personality" is not all-determining. The demonstration takes about one hour.

This exercise can be easily used in the classroom to point up the importance of clearly defining the goals of a committee. One social studies teacher said, "It made me uncomfortable when I realized that the kids were doggedly plugging away at the first task, really taking it seriously. I thought, 'Are the assignments I usually give them *that* bad?'"

Variation: Repeat the exercise after the analysis period, with new group tasks, to give members a chance to practice goal-clarifying skills.

Notes:

Experimental tryouts

Frequently, a training group discovers that members are making assertions about desirable action-taking methods ("The way to cope with the guy who won't shut up is to step in as tactfully as you can and . . ."). If training is to be more than sharing of dubious wisdom about what to do, members need to try out actions and examine the consequences. Experimental tryouts permit the training group to focus on particular kinds of action problems, and to understand "what leads to what," and *why*.

EXAMPLE OF EXPERIMENTAL TRYOUT, NO. I

Training problem: What are the results of different methods of making group decisions?

Setting up the situation: The training group agrees to use, temporarily, a decision-making procedure different from the one they have been employing (ex: after several meetings' experience with consensus, trying out parliamentary procedure).

Any required service roles (ex: chairman, recorder) are filled, and the role responsibilities are outlined ("The chairman is to act according to Robert's Rules"). Observers are recruited, and observer tasks are specified ("Keep a record of who talks to whom, and of the number of decisions reached"). Time limits for use of the new procedure are specified.

Action: Discussion proceeds, the new decision-making method being used for the agreed-on amount of time. The topic(s) can be ones left over from an earlier agenda, or they can be decided on here and now by means of the new decision-making method.

Analysis: When the discussion period is over, all members individually record on paper their reactions to the method (ex: ratings of satisfaction with the decisions made, amount of personal tension, opportunity to speak when desired). These are tabulated on the chalkboard, along with observer data.

Generalizations are made ("It looks as though we made more decisions than usual, but the commitment to them is low. Also, many people felt tense, and said they couldn't get into the discussion. Perhaps this is because everything had to go through the chairman").

Implications are drawn ("Strict parliamentary procedure is probably inappropriate for a small, informal group like this, but it may be useful when the group is large or the problem is complicated").

Comment: This is a good example of a planned situation which does *not* involve role playing, but the creation of a special marked-off situation within the context of the training group's actual situation. The procedure is a good one to use with students or adults who have never tried any other decision-making method than majority vote in working groups.

Usually 30–45 minutes, at least, should be allowed for trying out the new procedure. Ideally, it is best to compare *two* methods systematically (first consensus, then voting, for example) rather than to rely on hazy memories for data on a method used in the past. Getting data from observers as well as from members helps to insure a careful record of results. Tape recording the sessions also provides useful evidence.

Variations: (1) The group uses a simpler (and funnier) procedure, such as 20 minutes of majority vote by hand-raising on *every* issue facing the group, no matter how minor.

(2) The group may experiment with other aspects of procedure such as: agenda written on the chalkboard vs. chairman announcing each successive item; steady summarizing vs. no summaries; brainstorming vs. critical discussion in trying to find solutions for a problem.

Notes:

Sometimes, rather than experimenting with a general aspect of group work (as above), members may want to experiment with different approaches to handling difficult situations in groups. Successive tryouts by individual members can be analyzed with profit.

EXAMPLE OF EXPERIMENTAL TRYOUT, No. 2

Training problem: How to encourage the expression of genuine feelings when you are the chairman.

Setting up the situation: The training group identifies a setting and a topic (for example, a school staff, chaired by their principal, is discussing the fact that end-of-semester grades are late in getting to the office).

Two or three "principals" are identified and leave the room to plan their individual approaches to getting out real feelings about the lateness of grades. The remainder of the group discuss some of the forces that keep people from expressing true feelings. (The "principal" is seen as the "superintendent's fair-haired boy," some members are new teachers and do not want to be seen in a bad light, etc.) Some underlying feelings about the topic are also discussed (teachers' resentment of petty record-keeping tasks, professional pride about doing careful marking, guilt about lateness, etc.).

As in planning for any role-playing scene, underlying feelings and motives are put into briefings, but no *behavior* is specified ahead of time. Each role player is left free to behave as a person with his background and feelings would be likely to behave. This way, the approach taken by the "principal" can have a definite effect on the role players. If, on the other hand, behavior is briefed ("Keep talking a great deal"), then no matter what the principal does, it will be ineffective.

Action: One "principal" returns and tries his hand at starting the meeting in a manner he hopes will encourage the expression of genuine feelings. The scene is cut after five minutes. Members and the "principal" write down their reactions to the approach tried, but do not discuss them. The group "thinks itself back" to where it was before the first "principal" appeared, and the second "principal" is brought in. He tries his approach, and it too is commented on in writing, after a few minutes. The third "principal" follows.

Analysis: The different approaches can be compared. Both the "principals'" and group members' viewpoints can be brought in. ("George's tendency to keep the group focused on the problem kept feelings hidden, while Jane's willingness to let the group wander brought out frank feelings. However, Jane herself felt that progress on the problem of lateness of grades was slow, and she felt dissatisfied.") General characteristics of effective and ineffective approaches to bringing out true feelings in groups can be tentatively identified.

Comment: The persons (principals, chairmen, or others) who are trying approaches should be encouraged to try "a different approach" rather than their usual or typical one. This helps to reduce feelings of threat during the analysis period. Using three persons, or discussing more than one aspect of behavior helps to reduce stereotyping ("Mike's approach is good and Paul's is bad"). Time: up to two hours.

Variations: (1) An immediate re-trial, using the same or new chairmen, can be made to test some of the generalizations appearing from the analysis. ("Let's try the approach of making direct comments like 'What's the trouble here?' and see what happens.")

(2) The approaches can be tape-recorded and played back for analysis.

[Experimental tryout, no. 2 cont'd]

(3) Before the approaches are tried out, all members write down what they believe a good approach would be. After tryouts and analysis, members write down their beliefs once more. These can be compared and discussed to see what apparent changes the training experience has induced in the persons participating.[26]

(4) All the chairmen remain in the room. Chairman I is observed by Chairmen II and III. After he finishes, they jot down reactions and revise their approaches if desired. Then Chairman II works with the group, followed by Chairman III. In this way, the approaches can draw from each other, and become cumulatively more effective. Sharp differences between approaches are less likely, however.

Notes:

A third type of experimental tryout requires the use of an existing audio-visual stimulus (tape or film), followed by role playing.

EXAMPLE OF EXPERIMENTAL TRYOUT, No. 3

Training problem: What are the best ways to resolve conflict in a situation?

Setting up the situation: A subcommittee, before the training session, locates a film excerpt which includes a conflict situation.[27] Exact stopping and starting times are located on the excerpt, and a list of the characters is made.

In the actual training session, one role-playing volunteer is located for each character in the film excerpt. Each role player is to identify himself as closely as possible with the character in the film while it is being shown. One member is briefed to attempt to reduce the conflict as soon as role-playing begins. The audience is briefed to watch for behaviors which reduce conflict or built it up.

---

[26] For an account of how this variation worked out, see Passow *et al., op. cit.,* pp. 31–36.
[27] See, for example: *Meeting in session* (Teachers College Bureau of Publications); *All I need is a conference* (Strauss-General Electric); *Working together* (Encyclopedia Britannica Films); *Fury* (Teaching Film Custodians).

[Experimental tryout, no. 3 cont'd]

Action: The film excerpt is shown. When it is cut, role players are asked to continue the scene. Action continues until the conflict is resolved or shows clear signs of persisting indefinitely.

Analysis: The observers report, and role players are interviewed for their perceptions of how effective the conflict-reducing attempts were.

Comment: This is often an effective and rapid way for a group to move into active experimental tryouts. Role players should empathize as much as possible with the film characters (extra briefings and showing of portions of the film prior to the conflict incident are sometimes helpful).

Role players should also know that they will be asked to continue the scene.

One large class comprising about twenty subgroups followed this design (using as stimulus a role-played demonstration rather than a film). Members in each group were asked to empathize with characters in the demonstration. After a few minutes they were unexpectedly requested to continue the scene. Over three-quarters of the groups did so, but with some disruption and initial readjustment of their expectations. (Even so, the three-quarters figure suggests the relative ease with which continuations of this sort can be done.)

Variations: (1) As above, a role-playing demonstration can be used. This has the advantage of flexibility; it can be tailored to the immediate problem the training group is concerned about.

(2) Pre-recorded tape, either of role playing or of an actual meeting, can be used. If the scene is kept simple, and the group is not large, continuation is fairly easy.

Use of the training tape discussed in Chapter III (Corey, Halverson, and Lowe, *op. cit.*) has indicated that a group using it can warm up to role playing very rapidly. Usually the group listens to the first taped episode, and discusses it generally, suggesting what a chairman "ought" to do. After one or two taped episodes, group members often begin spontaneously to say things like this, "Now, if I were that chairman, I'd say, 'Bob, it seems to me you are a little off the track.'" Someone leaps into the role of Bob, and the scene continues. One group spent an entire day doing nothing but listening to episodes on this tape and role playing different approaches to the problems presented.

(3) If the training group is large, several subgroups can continue the film or tape scene simultaneously, analyze what happens, and report back what they found. This has the real advantage of demonstrating that (*a*) many different approaches to resolving conflict may be equally effective;

(*b*) the "same" approach may be more or less effective, depending on how it is carried out; (*c*) there are, however, some general principles underlying conflict resolution.

Notes:

Skill practice sessions

One outcome of an experimental tryout session may be that some approach is clearly seen to be desirable and helpful, but members feel unable to carry it out. For example, in one training group studying "resistance to the chairman," members agreed that when resistance mounted, the chairman should stop trying to work on the group task, and make a process comment on the interpersonal problems besetting the group. However, members felt very pessimistic about their actual ability to *do* this effectively ("People would resent it"). Such feelings may well lead the members of a training group to construct some skill practice sessions.

Skill practice sessions enable people to improve through *practice* some rather specific and defined behavior. The situation must not only permit, but definitely contain specific provision for a practice process like this:

1. Isolating and defining a desired behavior (*intention*).
2. Trying out the behavior (*action*).
3. Collecting evidence on how the try worked out (*feedback of results*).
4. Noting discrepancies from the original intention (desired behavior) as a basis for further *refinement and correction* of the behavior.

This process is like that involved in learning the behaviors of riding a bicycle, driving a car, or using a dictionary. The focus is on *how* an agreed-on goal can be reached most effectively. In the area of group work, we might think of such desired skills as: being able to sense the real feelings of others; building an agenda cooperatively with a group; summarizing at appropriate points.

The term "skill practice session" is loosely used by many trainers to mean any planned situation, such as a study exercise or an experimental demonstration. It is here used in a more precise sense to signify an actual practice process like that outlined above.

EXAMPLE OF SKILL PRACTICE SESSION, No. 1

Training problem: How to sense accurately when another person is feeling threatened.

Setting up the situation: The group members begin with a discussion of why people may feel threatened in a situation (ex: the person is mobilizing his defenses against potential or actual attack). Then a two-person situation is set up in which it is likely that one or both members will be threatened (ex: a principal's calling in a secretary to talk about her work, which seems to him to be inadequate).

Two volunteers are found to play these roles. Each person is briefed separately on the way he or she sees the situation. ("You feel quite angry about her spelling errors, and think her telephone-answering creates a bad impression for callers. Also she is often late. But you feel guilty about not having mentioned these things six months ago. You have never been very good at criticizing people"; and, for the secretary, "You like your boss very much. You worry some about what he thinks of your work—he never really tells you. You are *very* anxious to keep working in this school. You feel guilty about coming to work late.")

The rest of the training group is divided into two subgroups. The members of one subgroup are to watch one of the role players, and record each point in the conversation when they think he feels threatened. The members of the other subgroup do the same with the second role player.

The scene is to be tape recorded.

Action: The tape recorder is turned on, and the scene between the principal and the secretary starts and continues for ten minutes or so.

Analysis: The tape recording is played back. Each time a member notices in his notes that he recorded a "threat," he raises his hand and the machine is stopped. The role player concerned reports how he was feeling at the time (threatened or not threatened, with explanation). In this way, the training group member gets immediate feedback on how accurate his perception was. With discussion, he can see mistakes and generalize ("Don't assume that something is threatening just because the person doesn't reply to a question immediately").

Then the tape playback is resumed, and members get additional feedback on their sensitivity to "threats." (For good skill practice, members should not be restricted by their notes. They may see threats not noticed before, or may realize that something seen as a threat before is not actually a threat.)

Comment: This is ordinarily a very interesting exercise, and is quite easy to set up and carry out. It "takes apart" an interpersonal situation for analysis, and aids learning through repeated practice. As with any tape playback and analysis, plenty of time must be allowed (see pp. 114 and 136–37 in this chapter).

Variations: (1) Use another interpersonal behavior, such as "reduction of threat," "hurt," or "support." [28]

(2) Have an asymmetrical situation, where one role player (for example, a teacher) is more likely to threaten the other (a student) than vice versa. Under these circumstances, it is profitable for one subgroup to empathize with the teacher to see when he thinks he is threatening the student, and for the other group to empathize with the student to see when he *feels* threatened. It is very illuminating to examine the times when the teacher turns out to be threatening the student without realizing that he is doing so.

(3) In setting up the situation, one person can be a chairman and the others his group members. Watchers or empathizers can focus on the chairman, on separate members, or on their picture of the group as a whole.

Notes:

Another group-relevant skill is being able to predict accurately what is likely to happen next in a situation, as suggested in Chapter II (pp. 24–25). Usually a given member's private decision to speak up or remain silent in a meeting depends very closely on his prediction of the immediate future. It's as if he asks:

> "Will things get worse if I remain silent?"
> "Will things get better if I make a certain kind of comment?"
> "What will people think of me if I say something?"
> "What does the group *need* from me right now?"

[28] A session using "hurts" is reported in S. M. Corey, *Action research to improve school practices* (Teachers College Bureau of Publications, 1953), pp. 113–18.

Good predictions, plus action skill, mean effective group work. Poor predictions tend to lead to inappropriate actions (no matter how skillfully one can summarize, if a summary is not needed at that moment group movement is not aided).

EXAMPLE OF SKILL PRACTICE SESSION, No. 2

Training problem: How to predict what will happen next in a group.

Setting up the situation: Before the session, a subcommittee or the trainer locates an audio-visual record of a group meeting (tape of another group, or excerpts from films like those suggested under "Experimental tryouts"). Critical points are located where prediction of next steps would be important in actual operation.

Action and analysis: The film or tape is played to the training group. Playback is stopped at the first critical point, and members are asked to predict, in writing, what is likely to happen next in the group. Then the next minute or two is played, and stopped for discussion. Members can check the accuracy of immediate predictions, and as the playback proceeds, how their longer-term predictions turn out.

Discussion should include analysis of correct cues—the specific behaviors on the tape or film which members use to guide their judgments. ("When several members shift in their chairs at once, something has been said that stirs them. Watch for a burst of talk on a topic related to what has just been said.") It's also important to learn which cues are irrelevant and misleading.

Comment: To be effective, a substantial chunk of material should be available (at least 20 or 30 minutes), otherwise there will be little opportunity to *practice* prediction-making as the tape or film proceeds. The stimulus material should also be as plausible and real as possible. Few films fit this requirement in the sense of including genuinely-evolving group dynamics, and so a tape of a live meeting may be better. However, other things being equal, tapes may have longer periods of "doldrums" than films. Excerpting to by-pass dull periods is not desirable because it destroys genuine continuity.

Variations: (1) Rather than use pre-selected critical points, the group agrees before playback starts that any member can ask to have the tape stopped at a point where he is sure (or not sure) about what will happen next. This procedure emphasizes the fact that people vary widely in how puzzled they are about what's happening in a group, and also insures that points of maximum interest on the tape are discussed.

(2) A fascinating variation involves using a film excerpt (10–15 minutes) and dividing the training group in half. One subgroup leaves the room. The other members watch the film with *sound off* and make predictions at two or three pre-selected points in the film. After the film excerpt is finished, they leave the room to discuss what they have seen, and compare their predictions.

Meanwhile the members of the first subgroup return, and listen to the *sound track only* (by facing away from the screen). They too make predictions at the same two or three points.

The "sight only" group then returns. The members of the "sound only" group report their predictions for the first critical point, the "sight only" group members add, argue, correct, and expand. The film is then played, with sight and sound, up to the first cut point. Analysis of the relative importance of visual and aural cues can be made, and the total group moves on to analyzing the next segment of the film, this time with the "sight only" group reporting first.

One consequence of this exercise is that individuals may extend considerably the range of cues they attend to in groups. (A person who looks at his notes most of the time in a meeting is much more likely, after this exercise, to look for frowns, gestures, squirms, nods, and other non-verbal behavior.)

Specific behaviors can often be practiced quite simply without role playing if the nature of the behavior is clearly defined.

EXAMPLE OF SKILL PRACTICE SESSION, No. 3

Training problem: How do you state a problem so that (a) no one feels guilty, (b) no predetermined solution is implied? [29]

Setting up the situation: The training group identifies a context (such as a school staff meeting) and a problem (several teachers have complained to the principal that the cafeteria is too noisy during lunch).

Action and analysis: Each member takes a minute to write down what he would say, as a principal, to state the problem for consideration without implying a solution. Members read their statements one by one. Each

---

[29] N. R. F. Maier has discussed this matter in *Principles of human relations* (Wiley, 1952), pp. 215–19. He points out that an apparent statement of problem like "The office secretaries use the phone too much for personal calls" really contains an implied solution ("fewer personal calls"). A better statement might be, "What can be done to make the office more available to the public by phone?" This statement contains no pat solution (added phone lines, a new switchboard, prompter answering, fewer personal calls, using students for phone answering, etc., may all be solutions.) Also notice that it is situationally oriented, and is less likely to make anyone feel criticized and guilty.

statement of the problem is reacted to and discussed: Does it make anyone feel guilty? Is a "hip-pocket" solution implied or not? As the analysis of statements proceeds, general principles of problem-stating may become clear, and members may try their hands at new statements which can be analyzed.

Comment: This is a somewhat cognitive, but extremely interesting exercise. Avoiding predetermined solutions is surprisingly difficult. A training group may react to this procedure as an enjoyable hunt for ingenious solutions to a puzzling situation. The procedure is often a good change of pace from more emotionally-involving procedures.

Variation: The training group members need not attempt to build a common situation, but can simply practice problem-stating skills like those above by writing down, reading aloud, and reacting to many different problem statements. One training group produced a series like this, with thoughtful analysis and discussion between each statement:

"The business manager says that no more money is in the fund for classroom art materials. This is March 1, and I believe many of us have plans for classroom art work."

"The problem is that the bus behavior of the junior high kids is simply intolerable. We have to *do* something."

"I noticed that the telephone rang for some time this morning before anybody in the outer office answered it. Does this happen often?"

"Today is the day for electing class officers. Before we begin, I would like to say that it is very important to elect officers whom you feel really represent you. In the past, this has not always happened."

"Our salary schedule is below 56% of the school systems in the state."

"Mr. Johnson of the AFL-CIO Council visited with me yesterday. Our problem is whether or not our association should affiliate with them."

The group members seemed to have no difficulty in adjusting rapidly to the context implied by each statement, and showed keen interest in refining their problem-stating skills.

Notes:

Another form of skill practice session involves *coaching* for members who are attempting to cope with a group situation effectively. Coaching has some important features. It is prompt, not delayed. The coach and learner can rapidly develop an informal, supportive relationship. And the learner gets very individualized, specific feedback on his efforts.

EXAMPLE OF SKILL PRACTICE SESSION, No. 4

Training problem: How to make effective decisions in a group.

Setting up the situation: The training group sets up a scene where some explicit decisions must be reached (for example, reassigning classrooms in an elementary school building). Public facts about the situation (who is chairman, experience and tenure of teachers, type of classrooms, etc.) are agreed on.

Half of the group members become role players and decide individually what their private feelings are in relation to the problem. The role players sit in a circle. Each role player has a "coach" from the other half of the training group sitting behind him.

Action and analysis: The role-played meeting begins. After five or ten minutes, it is cut. Each role player turns to his coach, who suggests ways in which his behavior could be improved to help the decision making along. They plan together what the role player should do next. The scene resumes, and goes for another few minutes, is cut, and the coaching is repeated. When a final decision is reached, the entire training group analyzes the effective and ineffective decision-making behaviors that have taken place, and their influence on the final decision.

Comment: This design evoked very high interest when used recently in a training group. People seem to appreciate the unusual opportunity to turn to a confidant in the middle of a meeting and ask, "How'm I doing?" and then return to the fray.

Notice that role players are getting skill practice in how to aid group decision-making, while the coaches are getting practice in (1) how to diagnose a group meeting; (2) how to help another person with his behavior.

It is important that role players have a clear sense of their role, so that they do not find themselves doing silly or capricious things that are highly inconsistent with the basic picture of the role they started with. For this reason, it is sometimes easier to take a real problem rather than to use role playing. The topic "What kind of report, if any, should be made of this workshop to the Board of Education?" was used very successfully by the training group mentioned above.

DECISION-MAKING OBSERVATION GUIDE

Directions: Each time you hear someone make a comment or do something that fits one of the steps, put a tally mark beside the step. Jot down examples of what is said at the **right**.

STEPS	TALLIES	EXAMPLES
Stating the problem		
Clarifying and elaborating		
Developing alternative solutions		
Keeping discussion relevant		
Summarizing		
Testing the consequences of proposed solutions		
Testing responsibility and commitment to the emerging decision		
Decision making		

[Skill practice session, no. 4 cont'd]

Variations: (1) The action phase can be preceded by a trainer lecture or general discussion of steps in decision making. The coaches can use observation sheets like that printed on page 154. Both these additions can help members clarify their conceptions of decision making, and relate them to concrete, specific events in the action phase.

(2) This design can be used to study subgroup conflict and its resolution. Here two factions might be set up (for example, "Salary advancement" vs. "Professional dignity" in a teacher's association). When the scene is cut, all the role players in one subgroup meet with their coaches, and the members of the other faction meet with *their* coaches. This may have the effect at first of increasing tension and conflict—especially if the coaches slip over into giving advice on the *problem* rather than on problem-solving behaviors. Trainer commentary here can often be quite helpful.

As a second step, after the conflict has continued, some coaches may be asked to cross over and advise the other faction. This usually aids in conflict reduction, and demonstrates the importance of the liaison person, who has membership in each of the two conflicting groups.

Notes:

Clearly, the designs above do not exhaust all possible types of skill practice situations.[30] The essentials are that the person have a supported opportunity to try a desired behavior, learn the results, think, and try again.

This concludes the material on planned situations as a method of learning improved group behavior.

---

[30] See, for example, National Training Laboratory in Group Development, *Explorations in human relations training* (National Training Laboratories, 1954). Two skill practice sessions are quite thoroughly described (pp. 34-44). They deal with decision making in groups, and with perceiving and reacting to group members who like or dislike you. Each session involves an opening-up portion ("study exercise," in the terms of the present book), followed by actual skill practice. Each member rotates through several different roles, and gets a chance to try out the learnings he gets via feedback from other members.

III. Relating Training and Job Experiences

Two previous sections have discussed methods of studying ongoing processes in the training group itself, and procedures involving deliberately planned situations. Neither of these types of training activities *necessarily* deals with actual job problems faced by training group members. This section presents activities specifically designed to help members *bridge* between the training situation and the demands of their jobs. As such, the section is not logically parallel to sections I and II.

The training activities described in this book assume improved functioning in job groups as the general outcome desired. Whether ongoing group processes are studied or situations are especially planned, the compelling reason for trying to learn and improve one's group behavior lies in the problems and pulls of the job situation.

Explicit attention must thus be given to the relationship between training and job. How can the training experience be interpreted to others on the job? Can the skills learned in the training group be brought to bear on a *particular* back-home problem? Do members of the training group share certain kinds of problems on the job, and can a concerted attack on them help? In what ways can members of the training group support each other as they try out new things in their job environment? All these questions are urgent, and their urgency mounts as the end of the training program approaches.

The basic assumption here is that thorough interaction between training and the job situation must be maintained. Training experiences are unlikely to be effective if they teach something which is to be grafted, somehow, onto the job. Rather, the real and pressing demands of the job situation and the new skills and understandings of training must be brought together, so that analysis, planning, and evaluation can take place. Only thus can the individual learn to operate more effectively on the job, long after the training group has dissolved.

Some experience suggests that this sort of interaction takes place best during the latter part of a training program. Then new viewpoints have begun to crystallize ("refreeze," in the terms of Chapter III), and new skills have been picked up. Premature focus on job problems sometimes encourages shop talk and griping rather than realistic attempts to solve problems.

Below are described seven types of training activities designed to aid the job-training relationship, and to help training be effective, rather than remain an exciting but isolated experience. For each type, the framework used earlier to describe activities for studying ongoing group processes will be used (training problem, procedure, comments, variations, notes). Most of the activities can be used either with intact groups, whose members work together closely in the same school organization (for example, a building faculty), or with *ad hoc* groups, where a workshop or training program contains members from many different working groups in a school system (or from several different school systems).

The classroom teacher who is experimenting with training activities may wonder where the "job" comes in, as far as students are concerned. When training goes on in the classroom, students must be helped to make bridges to many other settings: other classes, co-curricular groups (clubs, student organizations), community groups, the family. All these other settings are, in effect, the student's "job." The classroom teacher is simply urged here to make translation to these settings whenever the word "job" appears in the material below.

Sessions on the theory of application

Although some training programs have sessions spaced over time, with job experience interspersed, many involve an intensive block of time (for example, Friday and Saturday away from the job). As a program of this intensive sort moves past its midpoint in time, the demands of the job, which have been in the background, usually begin to reassert themselves. It is often helpful, then, to have a session which deals explicitly with the general nature of the relation between training and job. The title above is not a misprint for "application of theory." What is meant here is a genuine attempt to help members think through the problems inherent in application as such, before moving on to tackle job problems more specifically.

EXAMPLE OF SESSION ON THE THEORY OF APPLICATION

Training problem: What are the general problems of moving back to the job after an intensive training program?

Procedure: Before the session, a subcommittee of the training group plans several short role-playing scenes (vignettes) showing a member of the

[Session on the theory of application cont'd]

group in his job situation. (ex: He meets a friend in the corridor, and responds to a joking query about the "vacation you had at the workshop"; he is asked by his principal to present a report at the next faculty meeting; he is soliloquizing alone at his desk about his feelings.)

During the training session itself, the trainer outlines some general ideas about moving from training back to the job.[31] He asks the group to empathize with the member in the vignettes.

After the vignettes, the other group members discuss the problems faced by the member, and test the general ideas about application which were presented earlier. Some action generalizations may develop (ex: "Don't use special language that sounds mysterious"; "Be concrete about what the workshop was like"; "Find out first what happened while you were away, and if anything needs to be done.")

Comment: If the training program has been intensive, the vignettes can often help to point up very poignantly the uncertainties and pressures group members feel as they contemplate returning to the job. The vignettes should be kept short (two minutes apiece).

If the session is held, say, two-thirds of the way through the training program, it can help to identify further needs for learning. For example, if the discussion suggests that members are relatively inarticulate about the training experience, and tend to have the "expatriate" reaction ("Oh, if only our faculty meetings were like this training group, what a difference there would be!"), then a session on the principles of training and the difference between training groups and action groups may be in order.

Variation: Particular stress situations on the job can be identified by the group, and vignettes produced spontaneously. This approach may be less focused but will probably reflect members' concerns most clearly.

Notes:

[31] See J. Watson and R. L. Lippitt, *Learning across cultures* (Institute of Social Research, 1956). The discussion is of a U. S. training program for visiting German nationals, but the general approach is highly applicable. That is, in the case of an intensive workshop held in a setting away from the job, members are going to a "cultural island" (in a foreign country, in effect) and must return to their homeland. They may return as gratefully homebound "tourists," as complaining "expatriates," etc. For further discussion, see National Training Laboratories, *Report of the Twelfth Summer Laboratory Session,* "Transferring laboratory learnings" (National Education Association, 1958), and "Training foreign nationals in the United States," by S. O. Lesser and H. W. Peter, in UNESCO, *Some applications of behavioural research,* R. Likert and S. P. Hayes, eds. (Paris, UNESCO, 1957), pp. 160–206.

Situational diagnosis and planning

Given some understanding of the problems of application in general, members usually need to examine their job situations and plan new actions. Training sessions focused on the job situation can accomplish two things: (1) improved planning for the immediate problems ahead; (2) a general increase in the member's disposition to diagnose and plan systematically. It is unlikely that either of these outcomes will appear on the job itself, unless thorough diagnosis and planning take place during training.

Such sessions may take several forms, including analysis of the general job situation facing a member, diagnosis of a particular job group's problems, or exploration of specific skills a member needs to function effectively in his job. An example of each is given below.

EXAMPLE OF SITUATIONAL DIAGNOSIS AND PLANNING, No. 1

Training problem: In a formal organization how do forces, such as status, prestige, informal communication, affect individual behavior?

Procedure: One member of the training group works at the chalkboard. His task is to draw a picture of his job organization, with his own role included. This may possibly begin with the usual line-of-authority chart, and go on from there to include informal relationships of all sorts, as in the chart below.

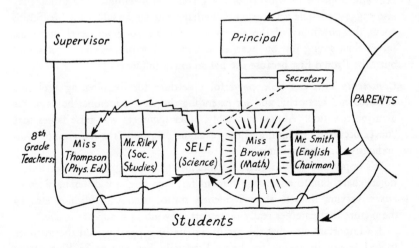

[Situational diagnosis and planning, no. 1 cont'd]

Other members of the training group then begin asking questions about the organizational relationships shown in the diagram.

"Who do you feel has more influence over you—your principal or the supervisor?"

"What is there about your work relationship with Miss Thompson that leads you to get into arguments with her?"

"You said parents were concerned about science teaching. Do they mostly come to you, to Mr. Smith, or to the principal, or what?"

They also ask questions which raise issues not covered by the member:

"What about your relationship with the other teachers? You haven't mentioned art, industrial arts, or homemaking. And doesn't the guidance counselor come to grade level meetings?"

"You say Miss Brown as an older teacher has the most influence in grade level meetings. Who are the teachers who agree with her viewpoint most?"

"Whom does the supervisor feel responsible to? You have him hanging in space. Same for the principal."

"What do you and the office secretary talk about when you have coffee? Does that bear any relationship to Mr. Smith's feeling that you're 'bypassing' him?"

The group can gradually move on to identify the major work difficulties being faced by the member as he attempts to apply workshop learnings and improve the quality of the grade-level meetings. The group may also suggest possible action steps ("Perhaps you might talk with Mr. Smith about the possibility of the supervisor's coming to grade level meetings, rather than seeing just one teacher at a time. But maybe you better sound out Miss Brown first because she has so much influence").

Comment: This can be a powerful procedure for illuminating problems of status and hierarchy, and for extending the view a member holds of his own job situation. Almost inevitably, other members will raise issues that "never occurred" to him, and the resultant diagnosis is usually quite comprehensive and penetrating.

It's important not to restrict the member to drawing the usual organizational chart, but to encourage him to feel free to draw different sizes of boxes, varying lines to show influence, status, friendship, dislike, etc., so the picture that emerges really represents "my job as it appears to *me*."

It's important also that the group climate be supportive, aid the member to feel secure in asking for help. Especially for persons in high status

[Situational diagnosis and planning, no. 1 cont'd]

positions, admitting problems may seem like expressing weakness or inadequacy. In using this organizational charting procedure, members should remember that they are beginning to move back from the special, "not-for-keeps" atmosphere of training to the real rewards and penalties of day-to-day life in school. A leisurely pace, and sensitivity to the member's readiness to tackle particular aspects of his job, are helpful.

The procedure is best fitted, for these reasons, to a group who do not ordinarily work closely together. However, it can be adapted to an intact job group if they have had some time to work together during the training program. Using an intact job group means, in a way, that the general method of "studying ongoing group processes" is translated into "studying our ongoing work situation."

Members of an intact job group can often share previously-private concerns about their work. This helps to reduce worry and aid planning. ("I thought I was the only one who thought the department meetings were so dull, but since we all feel they need improvement now maybe Jim and Carol and I could get together and plan some better procedures and report back next week.")

As charting proceeds, it is a good idea for members to feel they can make general statements of broad learnings applicable to the work situations of all other group members. ("This business of being overconcerned with everything an authority figure says, just because of his status, is true of me too. Does anyone else feel that way?") Such generalization-testing can keep the session from being an altruistic procedure designed to help one member alone, and moves it toward being a learning vehicle for all. In this way, many members can get insight about their own situations. They begin to think about "how *my* chart would look."

Finally, the charting procedure and discussion following it can expose the need for additional training activities. It can help members define and focus the kinds of help they need in order to function effectively on the job. ("I didn't really realize how little I pay attention to what people say. Could we set up a session to practice listening?")

Variations: (1) Trainer may precede the charting with some general comments about formal organization.[32]

(2) Instead of using an organizational chart, the member may take a "life space" approach [33] showing how the job-relevant parts of his life look to him. The following diagram is an example.

[32] See M. R. Goodson, G. Jensen, and J. Jackson, *op. cit.,* or G. Jensen, "The school as a social system," *Educational Research Bulletin,* 33:38–46, February 10, 1954.
[33] See K. Lewin, *Resolving social conflicts* (Harper, 1948), pp. 94–102, for illustration of this approach in a husband-wife situation.

The person drawing the diagram explains and comments on it:

"The dotted lines show where one thing affects another. For example, the complaints from parents and also, right now, my little boy being sick really bother me and I can't concentrate on teaching the way I should. Mrs. Lane [supervisor] helps though, so the line is dotted there too. The solid lines show where one thing doesn't affect the other."

Other group members comment:

"It looks as though you think you don't have much energy left for teaching at all."

"Doesn't the guidance you do affect your teaching and vice versa? You have them separate."

The member who drew the diagram begins to think aloud and make plans:

"If I could have drawn that line around the Curriculum Committee any blacker, I would have. They are really isolated off in a corner. Maybe I should suggest at the meeting to focus more on real classroom problems instead of being so vague.

I suppose if I brought some parents in to be resource people on the next unit we're doing, then the pressures might be less there. At least they wouldn't seem so strong to me."

Notes:

Often, it is profitable for the training group to diagnose and plan for action in a specific future meeting that a member is facing.

EXAMPLE OF SITUATIONAL DIAGNOSIS AND PLANNING, No. 2

Training problem: How can new ideas and procedures be introduced in a meeting on the job so that those attending will be more likely to use them in their work?

Procedure: One member of the training group who is facing an actual job situation describes it briefly to the training group. (For example, a newly-prepared resource unit is not being used by teachers, and the training group member, who is a supervisor, is planning to call a meeting of teachers to explore the reasons.)

The training group helps the member diagnose existing barriers and aids to the new procedure (in this case, use of the unit by teachers). These are listed on the board graphically, perhaps with force field analysis (see Chapter IV, p. 57, note 1). The group proceeds through careful analysis of how to reduce the barriers and encourage the positive forces during the proposed meeting.

Experiences from comparable situations are cited to help in developing a general strategy for the meeting, and in planning specific things the member might do. ("Maybe the meeting ought to start with a bull-session approach to let people express their feelings fully about the resource unit. That means your job as chairman will be mainly to state the purpose of the session clearly so no one feels blamed or threatened, then lay off and let people talk.")

When it seems appropriate, situations may be planned to help the member involved (and others) practice the skills needed in the future meeting, or test the appropriateness of a general strategy.[34]

Optimally, at a later session of the training group, the member should report back what was done in the actual meeting, and how it worked out.

Comment: As with the previous example, one risk is that individuals may pontificate, freely counsel, or reminisce from their past in ways which hardly aid the individual whose situation is central at the time. Voluminous suggestions may not get at the important problems; they may even reveal faulty understanding of the situation. This danger is reduced substantially if trainees are motivated to concentrate on the *situation,* rather than on their own status or competitive relations with others. It may be a good idea to take time out for a diagnostic period, and examine whether status problems in the training group are jamming up attempts to diagnose someone's job situation and help with planning (see pp. 173-74).

---

[34] For an account of how this worked out with one training group, see Passow, Miles, Corey, and Draper, *op. cit.,* pp. 51-53.

The training group must also guard against suggesting action on the basis of inadequate or inaccurate analysis of the situation. First answers may shoot wide of the mark. For example, help-seekers may present over-all problems so vaguely that diagnosis is superficial and incomplete. ("The teachers aren't interested"; "The trouble is that this committee just won't cooperate.") Help in such circumstances may well begin with thorough, supportive, open discussion as to the nature of the problem situation—before over-all diagnosis is attempted. If "snap diagnoses" are spotted and commented on when they occur, the entire group becomes more aware of the problem-solving processes it is employing, and is less likely to "jump to confusions," as one group member called it.

A similar difficulty arises when trainees state problems with built-in solutions, closing their eyes to the possibility of alternate solutions. ("The trouble is that Mrs. Green dominates the meetings and criticizes the new resource unit.") This implies fixed solutions: if Mrs. Green can be removed from the group, or if she can be persuaded to be less vocal, the group will move ahead smoothly. Actually, Mrs. Green's domination may be a symptom rather than the cause of the group's behavior. An open-minded diagnosis of the existing situation may suggest other underlying factors (for example, the fact that group members feel passive and have low involvement in meetings because they do not help to plan agenda), and appropriate corrective actions can be planned.

Another member may insist, "They won't use the resource unit because it's too long." Here the implied solution is: shorten the unit. Actually, there may be a half dozen more pertinent reasons—perhaps not related to the unit at all—why the teachers do not use it. If the full resources of the training group are brought to bear on the complexity of an action situation, then better diagnosis and action planning are likely to result.

Variation: The training group breaks up into pairs, who diagnose and plan in relation to specific situations each one is facing on the job. This tends to cut down on the richness and completeness of the diagnosis, but brings forth high participation and involvement. One member said, "This is the first time in months that anyone has listened to me for half an hour without arguing or trying to sell me their ideas."

Notes:

A third form of situational diagnosis and planning involves examination of specific member behaviors needed to cope with a particular situation.

Example of Situational Diagnosis and Planning, No. 3

Training problem: Improving chairmanship skills in a decision-making group.

Procedure: One member of the training group is dissatisfied with the way things are going in a group he's chairing on the job. He wants to find out what contribution his own behavior may be making to the difficulty.

The member describes the setting of his group and some typical roles. Volunteers are located to be "group members." Other training group members serve as observers to watch the behavior of "chairman" and group.

The "chairman" starts off the group as he usually does. Observers watch for behaviors that help or hinder the group. The scene is cut after a few minutes to see if the "chairman" feels his behavior and the group's are typical enough to make good diagnosis possible. If not, the scene is restructured, and continues. The scene is cut when a number of relevant chairman behaviors come out (usually not over 10–12 minutes).

The "chairman" describes his feelings as he worked; the "group members" give their perceptions. Observers report their observations of helping and hindering behaviors; these are listed on the board. General discussion is focused around the problems, "What's the difficulty?" and "What should the chairman do next?"

If a general consensus is reached on the trouble points, the scene may be replayed to test the diagnosis, and to have the "chairman" practice ways of improving the situation. Replaying may indicate that the first diagnosis was incomplete or faulty, and more analysis like that above may follow.

Comment: Trainer and group need to be sensitive to threat to the group member most centrally involved in this procedure, since analysis and discussion are of his real-life role rather than an assumed one.

A common mistake during a briefing period is trying to reproduce the actual on-the-job situation precisely. This is, of course, impossible. The group can, however, observe and diagnose the chairman's efforts in working with a group roughly resembling his actual job group. The focus is thus on the member's here-and-now behavior. From this point of view, an imprecise portrayal of the actual job situation is good, since it permits the member a safety valve—"I'm not this way usually." Here-and-now analysis

[Situational diagnosis and planning, no. 3 cont'd]

also provides more involvement for all group members, instead of the half-involved feeling that "We're solving Jim's problem for him." Common learnings are more likely.

This procedure is a good one to use with students who are chairmen. For example, in a student leadership clinic, the chairman of the Student Council can demonstrate the problems he is facing in getting seniors and seventh-graders to participate and solve problems together.

Variation: Successive "chairmen" may try their hand at coping with the "job group." The approaches can be tape-recorded, then played back for analysis, as suggested in the example of an experimental tryout (No. 2) on page 144, variation 2.

Notes:

Problem-centered groups

Another way of relating training and job involves group members' meeting to work on a common, persistent job problem. Procedures may vary widely.

EXAMPLE OF PROBLEM-CENTERED GROUP

Training problem: What methods can be used to improve school faculty meetings?

Procedure: Through discussion, the members list typical problems faced in faculty meetings (low involvement, differential participation, etc.). Then they list specific devices and procedures that can be used to aid improvement (ex: building agenda by the use of questionnaires, using subgroups during the meeting, using observers, using post-meeting reaction sheets, having teachers chair meetings). This general list is winnowed down for feasibility. Items that look most promising are explored in more detail. Role playing is used when particular skills (for example, how to propose to the faculty the idea of using a process observer) are needed.

Comment: This sort of session often proves fruitful, since all members by definition are actively interested in the problem, which may not be the case when a heterogeneous training group decides to work on something. Topics for problem-centered groups may range widely, from specific skill items like "How to criticize a teacher effectively," through general topics like "How to evaluate the success of group meetings," and "Implications of this workshop for improving home-school relations."

Problem-centered groups should usually be set up on an *ad hoc* basis as they are needed, and terminated promptly when the problem is coped with to the members' satisfaction. The temptation to have them persist through many meetings, discuss at length, and make extensive reports to other problem groups (who, after all, were not interested in this particular problem in the first place) should be vigorously resisted.

Variation: Members of the problem-centered group split up to read materials bearing on the group's problem, and report back.

Notes:

Role-centered groups

From time to time during a training program, it may be helpful for persons who occupy the same occupational role to get together to discuss common problems raised or intensified by the training experience.

EXAMPLE OF ROLE-CENTERED GROUP

Training problem: What are the special problems in group behavior faced by elementary principals?

Procedure: All elementary principals in the training group meet together to identify problems they face because of the unique demands of their roles. ("I am expected to do a great deal of cooperative planning with the staff, but teachers complain that the staff meetings deal with trivia, and I wonder if I shouldn't be making more of the decisions myself.") Similarities and differences in the way principals cope with these problems can be explored ("You mean you have teachers chairing the staff meeting? How does that work out?"), and action plans can be made.

Comment: This procedure helps occupants of a role to see more clearly what the demands of the role are, as contrasted with the special problems which they as a person bring to the role. Considerable support and blowing off of steam is possible too. The most needed trainer skill is aiding thoughtful analysis and planning, since, if members feel at all threatened, much self-justifying shop talk is likely to take place. The trainer should remember, however, that a certain amount of expression of negative feeling at the beginning of the session helps later work.

Variation: (1) Two roles may be studied at once. For example, several principals meet to discuss problems they face in relating to supervisors. Simultaneously, several supervisors meet to talk over what principals do that makes life difficult. Then principals and supervisors have a joint meeting to confront each other with their different role expectations and perceptions:

Principal 1: We discussed the fact that many supervisors do not notify the principal when they enter a building. This bothered us.

Supervisor 1: This is a problem for us too. We often do not know whether to check with the principal or not, especially if he is busy.

Trainer: It sounds like an authority conflict here. That is, who is authorized to speak with the teacher? Must all visitors check through the principal, or does the supervisor have special entree?

Principal 2: Well, I do know it irritates me at times and then I can't work well with the supervisor at the next meeting we're in.

Supervisor 1: Well, what is the best thing to do here? Our big job is to help the teacher who needs help, and how can that best be done through our relationship with the principal?

Such a session is not easy to run, because it may bring out long-standing feelings which role occupants have about other roles—and their occupants. Playing out "critical incidents," as in the material on case analysis (pp. 135-37), can help because it increases psychological safety.

(2) Another helpful (and quite dramatic) procedure is for each role group to meet separately as above and then name a couple of representatives. The representatives' job is to communicate clearly what was said in their role group—*not* to argue. (All other members of the role groups sit back and listen to the four representatives, without taking part.) This can be followed up by new role group meetings to discuss the implications of "what they said about us," and then by a final joint meeting.

Notes:

Intervisitation on the job

Often, members of the training group can profit from watching other members as they work in their own job situations. (This method requires that the working situations of training group members be geographically near each other. Also, it is best used when there are a number of spaced training sessions, between which visiting can be done.)

Such visits can help in clarifying the nature of a job problem, in extending a diagnosis of a job group's difficulties, and in illustrating the job use of an approach previously tried out during training. If a feedback period is built in, this helps make the job situation into an extension of the training group.

EXAMPLE OF INTERVISITATION ON THE JOB

Training problem: How to reach decisions effectively in large meetings.

Procedure: The training group helps one member who is to conduct a large decision-making meeting (ex: a monthly meeting of a teachers' association) by making a general procedural plan for the session. Steps in systematic decision making are discussed, and the member practices behaviors he feels unsure about (ex: stating the problem clearly and completely).

The member invites interested members to attend the actual meeting. They plan a checklist method of recording the steps in decision making used in the meeting.

They attend the session and keep records, using their forms. After the meeting, they meet with the member who acted as chairman to discuss their observations, raise new questions, and aid in planning for the next session. ("One big hindering factor was that the group never really seemed clear on whether they had the power to decide this question, or whether they were just to make recommendations to the Executive Board. Maybe that should be clarified early in the next session by the Board members. Also, your attempt to use consensus in the meeting was confusing to people, because they have been used to parliamentary procedure. Better clarify this procedure or drop it.")

Comment: Planning for intervisitation needs to take into account the probable effects of visitors or observers on the meeting. In small groups this can be disruptive, unless a participant-observer role is taken.[35]

[35] For a discussion of the participant-observer role in general terms, see "Participant observation," pp. 134–44, in M. Jahoda, M. Deutsch, and S. W. Cook, *Research methods in social relations,* vol. 1 (Dryden, 1951); also in vol. 2, see "Observational field work methods," pp. 494–513.

Intervisitation is most helpful when clear feelings of need for help are expressed by the person being visited, when the purposes and procedures of the visit are clarified by all concerned, and when follow-up discussion of the experience is a normal part of the procedure.

Careful planning reduces the threat involved in having one's job behavior examined. Usually intervisitation should not be used as a training method until a reasonably supportive climate has developed in the training group, and members have acquired some common meanings for terms relevant to the visitation (ex: "group maintenance function," "leadership skill," "goal clarity").

Good intervisitation usually leads to new problems, and to new activities at the next session of the training group.

Variations: (1) Intervisitation can be rather effectively carried out on a two-person basis. The pair, working together, plan meetings at which one of them will be active, the other observing. Then after the meeting they meet to evaluate and make new plans. This approach can be quite helpful in planning classroom activities, if two teachers' schedules can be dovetailed for purposes of mutual planning, observing, and evaluating.

One training group of central office personnel, all of whom worked this way between training sessions, found it in general quite helpful. The major problem was finding time to meet when the pairs had job commitments of drastically different sorts.

(2) Intervisitation may not necessarily imply attendance at meetings. For example, a principal may spend part of a day sitting with another principal in his office, looking at the kinds of decisions and choices that his friend has to make steadily without recourse to "meetings" as such.

To take another example, two supervisors in the central office group mentioned above wanted to do a better job of talking with principals and teachers over the telephone. The two people worked in the same large room, and so decided to evaluate the way they handled their phone conversations immediately after concluding them.

(3) Rather than focusing solely on the improvement of the skills of the person being visited, visits may also serve as a demonstration. A member who is trying out a new practice (for example, co-operative agenda planning in faculty meetings), more or less successfully, may find that several other members of the training group would like to see for themselves how the new practice works out. The demonstration idea is the usual reason suggested for intervisitation in education, as when teachers visit lab schools, or school board members visit other systems. Demonstration

has validity as a way of introducing new practices in group behavior. Presumably it has most effect when the new practice is perceived as desirable but impractical or difficult. Ideally, intervisitation should be followed up with skill practice sessions.

Notes:

Interim team activity

If the training program has sessions spaced over time, it may be quite helpful for teams of members to tackle common problems between sessions. "Team" here refers to persons in the training program whose work brings them together on the job. They may be able to try out new things relevant to both training and job—together. Feelings of support may be increased, and individuals may be more inclined to experiment than if they were working alone.

EXAMPLE OF INTERIM TEAM ACTIVITY

Training problem: How to deal with apathy.

Procedure: Persons whose jobs demand that they work together (for example, an elementary principal, two committee chairmen, and a supervisor) form a team to work between training group sessions. They analyze the situation they are facing ("The reaction sheets from the past three in-service days indicate that people feel somewhat apathetic about them"), and plan experimental actions ("Let's have a two-hour clinic session for the chairmen next week to talk over what they think is causing the apathy, and plan ways of coping with it").

These actions are carried out, and evaluation is made of the results. ("Five of the seven chairmen said they would like more clinics like this one. But the real payoff is what the reaction sheets from their groups look like on the next in-service day.") The team reports back to the training group at its next session for further reactions and suggestions.

Comment: Team activity offers an excellent method of interweaving job and training experiences. The job situation offers a testing-ground for ideas and methods experienced during training; the training group provides

[Interim team activity cont'd]

encouragement, technical help, and balm for wounds received during the testing process. Any member of a training group is in the difficult and interesting position of trying to resolve the demands of two different cultures—the familiar, compelling, earn-my-bread-and-butter job situation, and the novel, intense, learning-centered training group situation. Making explicit provision for interaction between these two cultures is essential. Near the end of the training, especially, the training group must more and more stand at the elbow of the member as he works in his job situation. If an actual team can stand at his elbow, so much the better.

During team planning periods (if he attends them), the trainer can be helpful in suggesting ideas and procedures, and illustrating by referring back to other experiences of workshop members. But it is quite important for him to vest complete authority for taking action in the team itself. They're the ones who have to live with the consequences, and attempting to persuade or sell a team on a proposed action usually produces reluctance, or sometimes subsequent mistakes if the action is carried out.

Teams usually work best when they are functional—the members normally have to work together anyway. Finding time for "extra" meetings is always difficult.

Variations: (1) The team may dry-run a proposed action in the training group to get needed practice.

(2) Teams may simply report *proposed* actions to each other in the training group, to gain added support and get criticism from a friendly source.

(3) A team may hold a public planning session. They proceed just as they normally would in planning and analyzing, but with other members of the training group watching as an audience. Later, discussion can often point up blind spots and provide new ideas. Since the audience has to *listen,* and also understands the existing relationships within the team observed, their suggestions often have considerable merit.

(4) A team may ask other members of the training group to visit them on the job during an action-taking phase, observe, and later analyze how the action went.

Notes:

Reporting sessions

Finally, it may be useful to comment on the problem of keeping the training group in contact with whatever training-relevant actions are being taken on the job. Assuming that a series of sessions is taking place, action-taking on the job should involve reporting back to the total training group. Training, after all, is aimed at certain consequences—better functioning in groups on the job—and it is important for trainer and members alike to have a clear idea of what the consequences are. Knowing how things have worked out on the job can lead to thoughtful redesigning of the next training session, and in turn to better job functioning.

EXAMPLE OF REPORTING SESSION

Training problem: How can faculty meetings be improved?

Procedure: Members of a team who have planned and carried out some experimental action report what they did. (For example, a junior high school team of grade level chairmen and the vice-principal explain what they did during the closing minutes of the regular faculty meeting to help the teachers get started in a process of self-study and improvement of future faculty meetings.)

The team members use as vivid and direct means of communication as possible. They play back a tape recording of the discussion, and interrupt it from time to time to comment on and explain what is happening. As added data, they also bring in the results of post-meeting reaction sheets.

As the other training group members listen, they ask for clarification, raise new questions, and help the team members identify new problems on which they would like help. ("What do you do when someone denies strongly that there is anything wrong with the meetings, when it's plain that they have been quite unproductive? That's something that really bothers us.") The reporting session thus leads to planning further training activities which will support further action-taking on the job.

Comment: Thoughtful planning of the reporting procedure makes it more likely that the listeners will be actively involved, and will be able to give (and receive) help. One side effect of such a session is that members also get training in how to report effectively. Saving some time for analyzing the effectiveness of the reporting method used (ex: oral account, tape recording, role playing, visuals) is a good idea.

Reports should focus both on the success experiences members had on the job and on the areas where further help is needed. A report focusing

[Reporting session cont'd]

only on positive things, or only on negative things, suggests that the reporting team has an ineffective relationship with the job organization, the training group, or both. For example, a "sweetness and light" report might be a signal that the team is bothered about its relation to some job authority figure who is also in the training group.

Sometimes this sort of problem can be worked on through subgroup activity, but the preferred treatment when job problems show up directly in the training group—as they inevitably do—is to examine them as explicitly as possible.

Almost all the activities described under "Studying Ongoing Group Processes" (pp. 101–23) can be adapted or used directly to study the effects of job relationships on behavior in the training group. For example, process observation or role analysis may deal with the effects of job status on the way one member, a high school principal whose teachers are in the group, behaves and is reacted to by others.

One caution: it's well to remember that the training program is finite in time, while the job goes on. The members of the training group cannot afford to, and should not, try to act as monitors of each other's every action on the job. An atmosphere of "sharing all" implies dependency and an unrealistic conception of the ability of the group to influence its members.[36]

As the end of the program approaches, there is ordinarily (and desirably) a gradual disengagement from the program. Teams and individuals share relatively less of what they are doing on the job and take, more and more, responsibility for their own actions. Usually the informal support function does continue to some extent. For example, members may have identified new confidants with whom they will share problems after the end of the program. Too, some training groups have occasional reunions or "booster shot" sessions. Hopefully, however, as suggested in Chapter IV, the training function is more and more built into the person, so that he can continue to learn informally on his own and with his job group, without frequent resort to explicitly-set-up training programs.

In a real sense, the reporting session is the crucial test of whether an experimental approach to learning better behavior has been internalized by members. Have members been able to move beyond mere talk to tough-minded planning, action, evaluation, and re-planning? This is the central question of training for better group behavior.

Variations: (1) Role playing can be used as a method of reporting what

---

[36] For other comments on interim work, see A. H. Passow *et al., op. cit.,* pp. 121–2, 61–73 (how team and individual problems were brought into a series of training sessions) and pp. 45–53 (analyzing back-home problems and planning action).

happened in an action situation (for example, the pressures from above and below on a central curriculum committee) for further diagnosis and planning.

(2) Teams can break up, and random "cross-team" groups can meet to talk informally about actions taken on the job.

(3) Brief reports can be made by each of several teams, with a reporting outline planned by the total training group. This is useful as a general check on where a team's work is at a particular point in time.

(4) An audience can be broken into sectors to listen for different things in a report (for example, clarity, points which need to be elaborated, things being overlooked, and the like).

Notes:

Summary Comment

This concludes the presentation of illustrative training activities. The chapter began with a discussion of criteria for selecting training activities, and went on to describe activities of three broad types. These involve the study of ongoing, spontaneously-happening processes in the training group itself, the deliberate planning of special learning situations, and the linking of the training program with the problems of the job situation.

Below appears a second index to the training activities of this chapter, broken down by type of activity.

The following chapter deals with the problem of training design— how training activities like the ones described above can be set up appropriately with a given training group.

INDEX TO TRAINING ACTIVITIES, BY TYPE OF ACTIVITY

[Cont'd p. 176]

NOTE. For cross references, and slight additional detail, see over-all book index.

CHAPTER VI

DESIGNING TRAINING ACTIVITIES

How are training activities designed? To readers who have not seen a training group in action, the welter of illustrative activities in the preceding chapter may seem overwhelming. Many of them look like complicated arrangements that cannot be duplicated without much toil and worry. But ability to duplicate is not the answer. The trainer's skill lies in his ability to assess the needs of the particular group he is working with and to help plan training activities honestly and systematically to fit those needs. In such planning, he may draw very closely from activities described in Chapter V, or strike out in new directions. The emphasis is always on helping the training group members solve the problems they face in improving their group behavior.

This chapter assumes that a planning committee, the training group as a whole, a subcommittee, the trainer, or any combination of these may plan specific training activities, carry them out, and evaluate results. The illustrative activities of Chapter V can serve planners as illustrations and sources of ideas—but not as models to be slavishly copied.[1]

Any activity described in Chapter V will have to be adapted, if only to a minor extent, to fit the needs of a particular training group (and, it might be said, the skills and style of a particular trainer). It is precisely for this reason that the activity descriptions above did not include detailed, step-by-step directions. Good training design is a matter of experimental adaptation, recombination, invention—not recipe following. The activities reported in Chapter V will be ineffective if they are applied "as is" without regard to the immediate training situation.

[1] The reader may also wish to refer for ideas to Appendix A, which contains an annotated bibliography of descriptive accounts of training sessions.

This chapter first deals with problems of designing training activities, then with problems of carrying them out effectively. The concluding section describes the use of certain training aids, including role playing, films, and tape recording, and gives a number of resource suggestions.

How to Design a Training Activity

The process of planning and carrying out training activities can be an exciting and productive experience for any group. The group experiences of many people have been restricted to following a rigid agenda or carrying on a rambling discussion. The sensation of branching out, of actively planning procedures that will help everyone in the group to learn, is an exciting one—exciting for the trainer if he plans alone, and incomparably more so if he shares the planning with the group. Once there is active motivation to learn and to share the responsibility for planning, high productivity is possible. A kind of vigorous social inventiveness often appears. More nearly than other groups, a training group controls its own destiny, and this is at once a sobering—sometimes upsetting—and zestful experience.

The discussion below is keyed primarily to the problems of designing specific training activities or sessions.[2] It includes suggestions on (1) identifying training problems, (2) selecting training methods, (3) producing a tentative design, and (4) testing the design against criteria of adequacy. Typical problems that show up when the final design is carried out are discussed in the section on "Operating the Training Design" (pp. 186–91).

Identifying training problems

A fundamental aspect of training design is being sure that clear, relevant, compelling training problems have been carefully identified. Any training activity will have little meaning unless the training group mem-

---

[2] The reader is referred to Chapter IV (pp. 85–87) for comments on general program design: assembling a series of activities into a meaningful psychological sequence; providing for alternation of training activities; maintaining the right degree of firmness in the over-all design; and providing for activities which bridge between the training group and the job.

bers have identified a shared problem about which they are curious, interested, concerned, puzzled, blocked, or dissatisfied. Even before the group has met, there is enormous importance in careful, explicit assessment of training problems (see Chapter IV, pp. 66–68, on planning for training).

A training problem shared by many members implies some underlying *needs*. These needs are more or less covert, and may or may not be different for each person. For example, a training problem might be: "How can a chairman handle conflict situations most effectively?" Member A's need in relation to this problem might be: "to feel less worried when conflict appears." Member B might share this need, and have another need: "to be able to see the signals that show conflict is building up." Member C might have as needs: "knowing the difference between healthy conflict and antagonism"; "finding out whether I provoke others too much when I argue."

Needs in this sense are private goals which members have in relation to the publicly-stated problem. Some needs will be shared by many members, others will be unique. Notice that any training activity designed to focus on a given problem will meet many different needs of individual members.

Needs and problems can be assessed by interviews, discussion, questionnaires, and observation. The trainer's task is to help group members express as many of their felt needs as is appropriate to getting clear statements of shared problems—always remembering that training is not psychotherapy.

The trainer has responsibility for sensitizing members to problems they may not see clearly or find difficult to state. But he should avoid trying to "master-mind" the training group by inferring or implying the existence of shared but unstated needs.

As planning proceeds, it is important to treat statements of a particular problem as tentative, and to check them with the group members or at least a subcommittee. That is, it is important to establish that the training problems are shared, and not of concern to a few members only. ("How many of us want to work on this problem of the chairman and his approach to conflict?")

A final step is phrasing the problem—and the implied or stated needs—in terms of desired outcomes. Outcomes are the changes in information, attitude, and behavior that are desired as a result of the training experience. In the example of "handling conflict" given above, the outcomes might be:

Information: Causes of conflict in groups, ways it builds up. Effects of conflict on group problem-solving (positive as well as negative).

Attitude: More acceptance of conflict, less tension when conflict appears.

Behavior: Ability to argue and disagree without causing antagonism.

Naming desired outcomes usually helps considerably in designing training activities. In the example given, a role-playing demonstration of conflict, followed by a short lecture analyzing what happened, and free discussion of implications might well produce the information and attitude outcomes given above. But skill in handling oneself (arguing without antagonism) was also specified as a desired outcome. An activity allowing for *practice* of behavior would also have to be included in the training design. That is, the actual behavior of arguing without causing antagonism can't be learned by demonstration or discussion—it must be tried out by the learner.

Clear identification of training outcomes may seem difficult at first, but it is basic to choosing appropriate training methods. Unless outcomes are specifically stated, training techniques may be selected at random or only because they're "interesting." The tendency to rush enthusiastically off into buzz groups, role playing, or other techniques without deciding *why* they are being used has probably accounted for more negative feeling about "group dynamics" than any other single factor. Slow down and think.

Selecting training methods

Once training problems and outcomes have become clear, the trainer and/or the planning group must make a decision as to the broad type of activity to be used. Which of the three general types of activity described in Chapter V is most likely to be appropriate?

In general, an activity involving the *study of ongoing group behavior* is appropriate if many training problems must be dealt with at once, or if the training problem is not clearly and sharply delimited (for example, "How to improve group decision-making?"). In effect, this type of activity merely sets a general procedure in motion (for example, intermittent process analysis) and members harvest the wide variety of learnings which may emerge.

On the other hand, if the training need appears to be narrowly defined and time is short, the decision may well be to set up a *planned situation*. This choice implies a more systematic, focused—and limited—approach to understanding a specific problem, such as the skill of summarizing two sides of a conflict.

Whether or not a *bridging activity* is chosen depends partly on time location in the over-all training program. Some bridging activity is useful at the beginning to help members link their job situations with training—but as indicated earlier, excessive job preoccupation at the beginning of training may often be a form of resistance. During the last third or so of a training program, however, a considerable amount of bridging activity is indicated if the training is to be of much help on the job.

Beyond choosing these broad types of activity, planners must choose specific methods, in terms of the desired training outcomes. Beginning trainers sometimes ask, "Is it more appropriate to use role playing or buzz groups in this particular session? This query must always be answered with another query: "What are you trying to accomplish in this session?" *Form follows function.* It is impossible to specify the value of any particular training method without reference to the training purposes involved.

Below are some guidelines indicating what training methods seem most appropriate to several types of training outcomes. These include change in the learner's information, attitude, behavioral skill, and action-taking on the job after training.

Information. The basic requirement for altering information (concepts, knowledge, facts) is that information be presented clearly, and that the learner have plenty of opportunity for questioning, clarification, and the like. In short, the presenter of the information must be able to get feedback on the success of his attempts to communicate. Otherwise it is unreasonable to expect accurate learning.[3]

Appropriate methods for communicating information include lecture (if followed by question period, open discussion, listing of questions on cards, and the like); symposia (in large meetings) with representatives from the audience present to question a speaker for clarification; films, TV, or tape recordings, with the opportunity for analysis by the training group.

[3] See H. J. Leavitt and R. A. H. Mueller, "Some effects of feedback on communication," *Human Relations*, 4:401–10, 1951.

[Training methods guidelines cont'd]

Attitude. If attitudes, feelings, opinions, and the like are the basic things which are to be changed, some research evidence suggests [4] that it is important to provide a situation of low threat, where a person can tentatively shift his attitudes without feeling defensive or threatened. In addition, other studies indicate [5] that most attitudes are socially anchored. That is, a person holds attitudes as a part of his membership in specific groups (such as a school staff) and more general reference groups (such as "effective English teachers"). The durability of a new attitude is probably mostly a function of whether the learner feels approved and rewarded by an individual or group important to him when he expresses the attitude, either covertly or overtly. In general, the success of appeals to emotion, fear, prestige, or credibility as a means of opinion change (as in some research on films and mass media) is variable.[6] A frequent finding is that the "sleeper effect" occurs. Initial opinion changes are not durable; opinions often revert to their original level after some time has passed.

If attitude change is the main desired outcome, it is probably appropriate to choose as a training method small open-end, "off the record" discussion groups where the person feels unthreatened. To the degree that these discussion groups are important or valuable to the person, attitude changes are more than likely to be durable.

Other training methods which are helpful for bringing about attitude change include pair interview situations, where each member listens carefully to the other member's description of his job attitudes and problems, and role playing. Role playing is especially helpful in attitude change because the learner actually experiences the new attitude, feels little threat, and is supported by other members of the training group.

The "inspirational" speaker often used in larger conferences is unlikely to bring about permanent attitude change in any intended direction (although he may be able to produce a temporary glow or negative counterreaction). If the speaker is unusually non-threatening, symbolizes an important reference group, and can help learners analyze their attitudes thoughtfully, then a talk by him may help in changing attitudes. Not many speakers meet these three criteria.

---

[4] For theory underlying this, see K. Lewin and P. Grabbe, "Conduct, knowledge, and acceptance of new values," in K. Lewin, *Resolving social conflicts* (Harper, 1948), pp. 65ff.; and C. R. Rogers, *Client-centered therapy* (Houghton Mifflin, 1951), pp. 517ff.

[5] For an interesting review, see D. Cartwright, "Achieving change in people: some applications of group dynamics theory," *Human Relations*, 4:381–92, November 1951.

[6] See C. I. Hovland, "Effects of the mass media of communication," in G. Lindzey, ed., *Handbook of social psychology* (Addison-Wesley, 1954), chap. 28, pp. 1062–103.

Behavioral skill: Change in actual ability to *do* something usually requires guided practice with *feedback,* a report of results of the learner's attempts at doing something. Many people believe that group-relevant skills, such as "keeping people on the topic" in a discussion, can be learned by talking about or reading about "techniques" for coping with the particular problem involved. The point of view expressed here is, always and forever, that skills must be learned through practice. It is possible to learn all *about* driving a car by reading a book, but driving a car can only be learned by doing, seeing results, and doing some more.

Methods using tape recording and playback are helpful in improving skills in group behavior, as is any method involving here-and-now analysis of the effectiveness of behavior which someone has just produced (ex: intermittent process analysis, use of group observer, coaching sessions, critiques of role playing, etc.).

Taking action on the job. Research indicates that actual follow-through on some action step (such as trying out post-meeting reaction sheets with a school faculty) is likely to depend on the person's commitment to a group decision about the action.[7] Other research evidence indicates that follow-through after training is higher when the learner feels supported and reinforced on the job by other members of a team with whom he has attended training.[8]

From this point of view, the best methods for influencing post-training action-taking are those which involve group discussion and group decision to undertake new things on the job. Individual planning sessions followed by reporting to the group (for support and reinforcement) are also appropriate, as are team planning sessions and many of the other activities cited in Chapter V under "Relating Training and Job Experiences."

It should be apparent by now that answers to questions like "Should I use role playing?" cannot be given directly. Role playing, with variations, may be used to bring about change in information, change in attitude, improvement in skill, or to help insure follow-through on the job. The important thing is to identify the type (more usually types) of outcomes desired, and then select training methods that meet the basic requirements suggested above.

[7] K. Lewin, "Studies in group decision," in D. Cartwright and A. F. Zander, *Group dynamics* (Row, Peterson, 1953), pp. 287–304. Also K. Lewin, "Group decision and social change," in Maccoby, Newcomb, and Hartley, *op. cit.,* pp. 197–211; also Bennett article, pp. 212–19.

[8] R. Lippitt, *Training in community relations* (Harper, 1949), pp. 212–20.

Producing a tentative training design

Once needs and outcomes have been identified and tentative methods selected, the trainer and planning committee (or training group as a whole) must assemble a series of methods (such as role playing, open discussion, coaching teams, or buzz groups) into a training design. "Design" is used here to mean a combination of training methods into an over-all plan for a session.

In studying ongoing group behavior, and in many bridging activities, such as those presented in section III of Chapter V, very little *specific* design-making may be involved. Planners need only to clarify the general method to be used (for example, process observation) and plan how to get it started with the group.

For planned situations (such as an experimental demonstration), however, the trainer and other planners should ordinarily work out a tentative timetable, on paper, resembling the first-session plans presented in Chapter IV. Otherwise it is difficult to be sure the desired phenomena will appear for study.

It is difficult to give general suggestions for design assembly, but the reader may be able to get hints from examining the many different activities reported in Chapter V, and the program design principles presented in Chapter IV (pp. 85-87). The important thing at this point is to be *tentative* about the design, so that it does not assume its final form prematurely. Getting the design up on a chalkboard or on newsprint, if more than one planner is present, is highly desirable. Often three or four different designs, each with variations, may be drawn up for consideration before a final one is produced.

During this process, creative imagination becomes highly important. Assuming that needs have been clearly identified, an almost infinite number of different learning activities can be planned. The two most frequent mistakes here are (1) excessive reliance on familiar methods of learning, such as discussion and lectures, and (2) getting enamored of a particular procedure, such as analysis of tape recordings, role playing, or case analysis, and trying to make it fit the expressed need rather than the other way around. *Form follows function.* When the trainer or a member knows of a particular training method which seems highly valuable to him, it is tempting to jump into using this procedure without regard to the training need at hand. Yield not to temptation.

Testing the design against criteria

Before the final design is decided on, it may be a good idea for planners to test the tentative design against the seven criteria of adequacy suggested in Chapter V (pp. 98–99). Unless the design measures up well on all seven criteria, it should be revamped until it meets each criterion to the planners' satisfaction.

An eighth criterion might be added—clarity. The training design finally selected should be planned in sufficient detail so that everyone who has responsibility for its operation knows what he is to do. For large meetings or complex training designs like some of those in Chapter V under "planned situations," a detailed training plan may be required. It should include a notation of each step of the design (for example, "discussion of role players' feelings"), who is responsible, and how long the step is to take.

For other kinds of designs, usually those involving the study of ongoing group behavior in one training group, and the simpler types of bridging activity, it is only important that the trainer and group members be aware of their general responsibilities. "Playing by ear" in such designs is not only permissible but desirable. Over-planning, particularly if it is done by the trainer or a subcommittee rather than the total group, can stifle real creativity and learning.

Under-planning, on the other hand, can be equally undesirable. It may result in superficial learning, lack of interest, vagueness, and unnecessary frustration, hostility, and anxiety on the part of the learners. Disinclination to do careful planning may be a symptom that the trainer and other planners (1) feel uncomfortable about their roles, or (2) have special needs to be liked by the training group, or (3) simply are not clear about what they hope the training sessions will accomplish. A device which helps one avoid the dangers of over- and under-planning is the "option point"—a point in the design where the trainer and group decide what to do when they get there. (For example, "Just after the initial report from the role players, we'll check to see whether it would be better to replay the scene immediately while it's hot, or go on to dig in for more generalizations and implications.")

Planners and the trainer should do sufficient planning to maintain their own security, to meet group needs without stifling people with structure, and to fit the immediate activity sensibly into a sequence of other activities. Planning which reduces the learning and initiative of group members, restricts spontaneity, or has the basic purpose of maintaining the power of the planning group is undesirable.

Operating the Training Design

Most training designs do not work out exactly as intended, even when the intent is broad and general, as in many of the activities listed in "Studying Ongoing Group Behavior" (Chapter V). Below are some comments on how to operate a training design and shift it with the group as the exigencies of the training situation require.

Checking the training problem

At the beginning of an activity, it is often important to check with the group members to find out whether the original concern for which the activity was proposed is still a real and important one. Everyone should understand the training problem (for example, handling conflict, or effective group problem-solving) in roughly the same way. If, since the design was first planned, personal needs have so changed that the problem is not now a problem to most of the members, then altering or abandoning the design is the best thing to do. Usually no more than a brief, matter-of-fact check on members' interest in the problem is necessary, and the trainer should be careful not to over-react to minority expressions of low interest.

Explaining the procedure

As the group moves into the design, it is usually important for the trainer to give a *brief* overview of the procedure being proposed, so that all group members have a common time perspective and understand what will be happening next. In some designs, the trainer may pause for members to indicate that they approve the procedure; in others he may move directly into the procedure, depending on the mandate previously given to the planning group by the total group, and on his usual role as trainer. Explanation of an unusual procedure may be needed so members can understand just how it will help with the training problem.

Setting up the situation

If the original plan was for the group members to participate in setting up part of the design (such as a role-playing situation), it should be clearly indicated who is responsible for aiding the group to do this (usually the trainer). If the group members do build a situation, it should be kept vivid and simple, but real enough to be challenging. Good situation-building is easier if the group have clearly in mind both the training problem and the proposed outcomes (information, skill. etc.). A situation built by a group is usually better tailored to a problem and has higher interest and involvement than one set up beforehand by the trainer. It takes time to build a good situation, in either case.

When role playing is new to a group, it is often easier for the trainer, instead of starting a long process of situation construction, to outline a simple situation, check for general interest, and ease the group into it. Sometimes demonstrating role playing is easier and quicker than talking about it. For example; "Suppose Joe was the superintendent, and I was the teacher. I'd say [turning to Joe]: 'Mr. Turner, I represent the teachers, and we've been a little concerned . . .'" Comments like these are also helpful in moving into role playing informally:

"Let's try that out."

"What would the chairman say? We'll be the committee."

"I'll be the teacher you're interviewing. Let's do it instead of talking about it."

"Could someone show us how a 'tough' principal would handle that?"

"Show us what you might do."

This informal "easing in" works best when roles and the situation are simple. In more complex situations, people need time to get warmed up and thoroughly briefed in their roles, so they can act spontaneously and not feel forced or uncomfortable.

Getting volunteers for roles is usually better than appointing them. For some exercises, a random procedure (counting off, person sitting closest to the door) can be used. Usually, the trainer should not say that any specific person should have a specific role. The risk in doing so is that a member may get forced into taking a role that is too close to his own real-life role or personally upsetting and threatening.

Whether or not role playing is to be involved in the action part of the training design, the entire group should have very clearly in mind the procedures to be followed. Ordinarily they should have all relevant information about the situation they are going through. The exception to this is when some group members are briefed with special information so that others' reactions to their behavior will be genuinely spontaneous. Private briefings, where each person has information only he knows, may also be used.

Usually the trainer should check with the entire group just before the action phase of a design to summarize what is being done and to see that everything which should be clear, is clear.

The action phase

Such a check on clarity also helps to insure that everyone moves into the action phase at the same time. In role playing, the trainer can watch for people "dropping out of role" (making remarks which indicate they are acting as their real selves and not as role players) and help them get back into role. This may mean supplying extra background information or—usually—just brief encouragement.

In general, however, the trainer should almost never intervene in an action situation once it is well under way, unless it is clear that serious misunderstandings of the training procedure are involved. Intervention in the middle of an action phase, ninety-nine times out of a hundred, only serves to restrict and confuse people. When group members are using a design to study their own ongoing behavior (such as intermittent process analysis), and the trainer feels very clearly that the procedure is not meeting the purpose it was built for, he may well intervene to ask whether the procedure should be revised. If his diagnosis is wrong, the group will let him know promptly that his advice is unwanted.

The action part of a training design should go on only as long as is necessary to get the basic material needed to help with the original training problem. The trainer or some specific member should take responsibility for starting the action phase and for stopping it. Very often a training design—especially one set up for the study of ongoing group behavior—may include in it a specified length of time for the action phase. ("We'll have the observer watch our discussion for 15 minutes, then report.")

Planned situations require judgment on the part of the trainer as to when to cut the action phase. A common mistake when role playing is used is to let the scene go on too long. Ten or twelve minutes is usually adequate to produce the phenomena desired (such as communication blocks, problem-solving steps, subgroups lining up against each other).

Guiding the analysis

Most training designs include an analysis period in which the immediately-preceding experience can be examined for its implications. The analysis should be guided by the basic training problem and desired outcomes for which the design was originally set up.

Evidence from the action phase—whether from observers or from the recollections of participants—should be made available to the entire group by reports, discussion, or listing on the chalkboard. This evidence can take many forms—feelings, reactions, perceptions, records of overt behavior—and is the basic data from which the group can begin to make generalizations. The trainer should help the evidence-sharing phase to move along smoothly, so that all relevant data are put out where people can hear and/or see them. If some members were "on the spot" during the action phase (for example, were trying out a difficult skill in a practice session), it is usually a good idea to get their reactions first.

During the analysis phase, it's important that the group distinguish two kinds of comments and reactions: (1) comments made *within* the framework of the situation which the group has just experienced ("I found myself sympathizing with the supervisor as Jane played her, in spite of myself") and (2) comments viewing the situation from the *outside* ("It seemed to me we were not very realistic in setting up the scene and Steve dropped out of his role a couple of times"). Both of these are useful reactions, but the first should be expressed immediately while direct generalizations from the experience are being made. The latter type of comment can be reserved for a critique period, or for the time when the next situation is being planned. It is often difficult to separate these two kinds of comments, but the trainer can help by pointing up the difference between them as they are made.

The generalizations that a group draws from a situation (again the chalkboard is a help) will vary with the purposes of the activity. Some possibilities are shown on the following page.

A list of reasons for the behaviors shown in the situation.

Suggestions on what to do when such a problem comes up again.

Questions, problems, or new ideas for trying out in the next training activity.

Better definition of the problem the group had been trying to solve.

Conclusion that a previous hypothesis the group had set up was correct, or had to be changed in light of the facts.

Explicit applications to job groups where the same kind of problem arises.

General learnings or insights about the nature of the problem.

Evaluating and replanning

As suggested in the criteria listed in Chapter V, it is very desirable to take time to critique the entire training activity with the group. Not all members of training groups are equally interested in training as a process, but a brief period of evaluation often proves decidedly helpful in further planning.

(In addition, where some members are especially interested in learning the skills of being a trainer, it may be well to set up a special "trainer development" group that meets outside regular training sessions. They can take plenty of time to criticize and analyze the process of constructing and carrying out effective training activities.)

Following an analysis period, the members of a training group often decide to revise and repeat the general method (such as process observation) which has just been employed. This is especially true where skill practice is the central feature. In Chapter V the variations suggested indicate how training activities can be easily revised to meet emerging needs.[9]

The trainer's role in operating the design

As the training design unfolds, the trainer's role is to *facilitate*. He must be sensitive to just how the learning environment is proceeding, rather than only to the content of what is being said or done. For example, if a group is doing a role-played interview between a principal and a teacher to examine effects of threat, the trainer should not become so absorbed in what the "principal" and "teacher" are saying to each

[9] The reader who wants to know more about how training activities look when they are carried out is reminded of the annotated reading suggestions in Appendix A.

other that he fails to notice that over half of the audience members seem bored. Or, if the analysis of the role playing seems to be confused or lagging, he should be sensitive to this too, rather than only to the things members are saying on the topic, "What I've learned about threat and defense." Just as the trainer is a procedural methodologist during the period of planning the design, so he is a procedural guardian (if only a timekeeper) as the training design proceeds. This is not the only role of the trainer (see Chapter VII), but it is an important one.

Some Useful Training Aids

This section is supplementary to the material on training design given above. It discusses the use of role playing, films, and tape recording as aids to learning better group behavior. These aids are essentially ways of presenting the training group members with behavior (other than their own immediate, real-life behavior) which can be discussed and analyzed. Each has been noted in passing as it was involved in a particular training activity. However, each aid is treated in some detail here to help planners get an over-all idea of its uses, values, and disadvantages. Other references are suggested which supply step-by-step help in how to use role playing, films, and tape recording. Here, the focus is on the most effective use of these aids in training programs.[10]

Role playing

Role playing[11] is essentially an action, *doing* technique. Any reader who has gotten this far knows that in role playing members react to each other spontaneously within the framework of a defined situation which is provisional, or "not for keeps." In this way, behaviors of people

[10] For a detailed review of training methods and techniques, see O. H. Golden, "Training techniques, a bibliographic review" (Industrial Relations Center, University of Chicago, September 1955). This pamphlet deals with conference method, case method, role playing, audio-visual aids, and a variety of other procedures used in small and large group meetings.

[11] This section does not deal with role playing exhaustively or on a how-to-do-it basis. For detailed suggestions, see such treatments as:

A. F. Klein, *Role playing in leadership training and group problem solving* (Association Press, 1956). (Comprehensive and practical treatment.)

G. and F. R. Shaftel, "Role playing the problem story, an approach to human relations in the classroom" (National Conference of Christians and Jews, 1952.) (Very helpful; gives transcript of session with 5th-graders.)   [Footnote cont'd]

can be examined with a minimum of threat, and their approach to the problem can be improved after discussion and analysis.

1. *Values of role playing.* There are a number of features of role playing which make it especially valuable for leadership training.

A bridge between talk and action. Role playing provides learners with the chance to get from theory to practice, as they see it. People can make a rapid, effective transition from the point where they intellectually *understand* a new kind of group behavior to the point where they actually try out this new behavior on the job. Inconsistencies between words and action are likely to decrease when role playing has been used as a training method.

A safe learning environment. In role playing, new behaviors can be tried out, without fear of punishment or failure. Since the person's "role" is being discussed and criticized, rather than his real-life behavior, he is more likely to feel free to experiment with new actions. Mistakes become fodder for improvement rather than threatening to be dangerous or costly errors.

To this extent, the "not-for-keeps" atmosphere is unlike real life. However, some research has suggested that reactions in role playing are far nearer real life than mere verbalization or pencil-and-paper questionnaire responses.[12] Role playing is sometimes criticized as "artificial" or "unreal." (When this is said in a training group, it may be a sign that members are needing to protect themselves from the threatening implications of a particular role-playing scene.) Perhaps it is more precise to say that role playing represents an "irreal" experience, one on a temporarily different level of reality.

G. Levit, "Learning through role playing," in *Adult Leadership,* 2:9–16, October 1953. (A complete "tool kit," describing methods of running role playing, plus case examples.)

C. E. Hendry, R. Lippitt, and A. F. Zander, "What is role playing?" in K. D. Benne and B. Muntyan, *Human relations in curriculum change* (Dryden, 1951), pp. 223–41. (Case examples, principles.)

C. Argyris, *Role playing in action* (New York State School of Industrial and Labor Relations, Cornell University). (Practical manual.)

G. Sharp, *Curriculum development as re-education of the teacher.* (Teachers College Bureau of Publications, 1951). (Appendix describes principles of role playing, and suggests applications.)

Business Information Bureau, Cleveland Public Library, "Role playing, or dramatization in training methods," *Business Information Sources,* 26:1–4, February 1955. (An annotated bibliography, dealing with role playing in industrial and other applications, the use of role reversal, leader role definition, psychodrama, and socio-drama.)

C. S. Schuman and O. Tarcov, "To clarify our problems: a guide to role playing" (Anti-Defamation League of B'nai B'rith, n.d.). (Suggestions for setting up and using role playing.)

[12] See E. F. Borgatta, "An analysis of three levels of response: an approach to some relationships among dimensions of personality," *Sociometry,* 14:267–316, 1951.

Concreteness. Role playing makes actual behavior available for study, analysis, and improvement. It is highly action-centered, and provides the group with a focused, common experience which they can talk about without falling into semantic traps. It furnishes immediately-available data on human relationships which are ordinarily rather difficult to collect.

Spontaneity and flexibility. Role playing gives people a chance to experiment with new ideas as whole, creative people, and to have fun doing it. It gives them the opportunity to unbend, and it can be an emotionally releasing and "re-creating" experience.

2. *Uses of role playing.* With the characteristics above, role playing can be especially helpful in training for better group behavior. It can be used at several stages of problem solving in a training group. Four different uses are discussed below.

Increasing insight into a human relations situation. Most human relations problems are made more acute because the parties to the situation cannot transcend their own private views of what's wrong. Failure to understand the perceptions and feelings of others almost inevitably leads to partial, distorted views and the deepening of problems. Role playing offers an excellent opportunity to "stand in another's shoes." Devices like role reversal, and a learner's deliberately taking a role of a person to whom he feels unsympathetic are excellent aids to deepening one's willingness to see a human situation from another's point of view.

Diagnosing situations. When members of a training group are faced with a problem situation, they frequently oversimplify the problem or attempt to jump immediately to solutions. Complex situations may be diagnosed rapidly and sketchily ("The trouble with the teachers is that they are too rigid to do teacher-pupil planning"). Sometimes the solutions to a problem are suggested even before the nature of the problem and the conditions for its solution are really defined (for the "diagnosis" above, "Why couldn't we show that film on cooperative planning," or "The supervisors should sit down and discuss cooperative planning methods with each teacher").

Role playing can aid problem diagnosis and definition in several ways. It can make a concrete situation available for study and analysis. Almost always after role playing, the complexity of human relations problems is dramatized—different members of the training group usually see the scene in varied ways. When a group re-plays a scene following coaching, or thorough analysis of the situation, this often shows vividly that careful

[Uses of role playing cont'd]

attention to "What's the trouble?" leads to better results than jumping to solutions. Role playing can slow people down, sober them, make them far less confident that human relations problems can be solved by word-magic.

Pre-testing problem solutions. When a problem situation has been diagnosed, perhaps by role playing as suggested above, there may be several possible approaches to resolving the difficulty. The validity of these solutions can be assessed before they are tried out on the job.

Re-playing a problem scene, with one or two members trying out a specific approach, is a useful way to test the adequacy of a diagnosis and solutions stemming from it. For example, given a situation where a group seems unable to come out with any decisions at all, one diagnosis might be that subgroup factions are covertly vying for control of the group, and this is blocking things.

The training group members could set up a role-playing situation with subgroup conflict, and one member at a time could individually plan and try out different solutions, such as urging more harmony, commenting directly on the conflict, suggesting a break, and so on. Each approach could be evaluated for its effect on group decision-making.

Practicing needed skills. Role playing is especially helpful after members of a training group have a very clear idea of what action is most likely to be effective in a situation, but are still unsure of their ability to carry it out. The use of role playing as a dry run can be very helpful in improving skills which are to be used in an actual future situation on the job (ex: building agenda in a staff meeting in a new way, coping with a dominating member, or giving a task to buzz groups in a large meeting clearly and concisely). Dry runs are essential when a really novel approach to a job problem is being considered, or when the consequences of failure are likely to be very negative.[13]

Films

1. *Films as a training medium.* Films can be useful in training for better group behavior, if they are carefully built into a supporting train-

[13] For other illustrations of uses of role playing at various stages of the problem-solving process, see the film *Role playing in human relations training* (National Training Laboratories). One scene, for example, shows how a "crusty old foreman" communicates his interviewing skill by role playing when he cannot do it in words. Other scenes deal with the uses of role playing discussed here and in Chapter V.

ing design. That is, a film can be used as a common experience—a slice of life which can be started, stopped, dissected, and used as a basis for practicing group skills. Passive exposure to films dealing with group situations is not likely to have a durable effect on later group behavior of learners, even if the film is one of the few designed to teach about group behavior and leadership. If a film is to do more than provide information, stimulate thinking, or alter superficial attitudes, it must be used *actively*. (For illustrations, see index for Chapter V, pp. 175-76, where four different uses of films are listed, and Chapter IV, pp. 76-77, 81, where the active use of films in opening sessions is described.)

2. *Advantages and disadvantages.* A film has the substantial advantage that members of a training group feel perfectly free to attack it, and impugn the motives of the actors with even greater feelings of freedom than when role playing is used. The fact that a film or film segment can be repeated precisely several times also makes it valuable for training purposes; sensitivity to what is actually going on in a group situation can be deepened considerably.

The major disadvantages of films from the point of view of training are inflexibility (the film content cannot be changed) and inaccessibility (it usually takes searching plus a week's mailing time before any given film is available for showing). In Chapter V, many of the activities described illustrate the flexible use of films and film excerpts; in the section below, some helpful training films and a list of film location sources are given.

The use of films [14] in training should naturally follow from some shared group concern. The purpose for which a film is to be used should be clear, and the film should of course be previewed by a subcommittee or the trainer to make sure that it can in fact help solve the training problem at hand. Physical and technical arrangements need to be handled competently.

3. *Selected training films.* Some educational films have considerable relevance to training for effective group behavior. They come from varied sources (industry, nursing, adult education, human relations training),

[14] For general material on film use, see such excellent and comprehensive helps as:

E. Dale, *Audio-visual methods in teaching* (Dryden, 1954).

W. A. Wittich and C. F. Schuller, *Audio-visual materials: their nature and use* (Harper, 1957).

P. R. Wendt, *Audio-visual instruction* (National Education Association, 1957). An excellent brief review of research relating to use of audio-visual devices.

and can be easily and productively used with a training group, even though not all of them were originally designed to focus on group behavior).[15] Several guides are helpful for locating films.[16]

[15] Some films of this sort are:

All I need is a conference (Henry Strauss & Co.). Technically excellent and exciting analysis of a problem-solving staff conference in industry.

Experimental studies in the social climate of groups (Iowa State University). Experiments on authoritarian, democratic and laissez-faire group atmospheres.

How to conduct a discussion (Encyclopedia Britannica Films). Principles of discussion leadership presented by illustrations.

Human relations and supervision (McGraw-Hill). Cases involving specific human relations problems.

Learning through cooperative planning (Teachers College, Columbia). Shows how an elementary school class plans a joint project.

Let's discuss it (Canadian National Film Board). Steps in organizing a group, principles of discussion leadership.

Let's talk about films (Canadian National Film Board). Shows formal, ineffective film discussion group, and more effective, group-centered discussion. Leader role examined.

Meeting in session (Teachers College, Columbia). An ineffective and a more effective meeting of a nursing staff. Can be analyzed from many directions; good for studying climate, group problem-solving, leadership functions.

Men at work (McGraw-Hill). Human relations problems in a production line situation; resistance to change.

Our invisible committees (National Training Laboratories, Washington). Shows how strong, conflicting loyalties and needs hamper good group work.

Production 5118 (Modern Talking Picture Co.). Incidents dramatizing communication problems between people; ending incomplete—good discussion-starter.

Room for discussion (Encyclopedia Britannica Films). Overview of value and importance of discussion in a democracy.

The inner man steps out (General Electric). The supervisor's role in accepting the workers' needs as persons.

The whole town's talking (Guthrie Center) (Iowa State College). Useful for large meeting situations. Shows unstaged town meeting debating the pros and cons of a new courthouse.

We plan together (Teachers College, Columbia). An eleventh grade group plans learning activities in its core class.

Working together (Encyclopedia Britannica Films). Labor-management conflict and solution in an industrial plant. Several small group situations.

[16] The most useful source is *Educational Film Guide*, F. A. Krahn, ed. (H. W. Wilson Co., 1953 and annual supplements). It describes over 11,000 films, with a title and subject index, and has a complete listing of film producers.

See also:

N. A. Fattu and B. Blain, *Selected films for teacher education: a bibliography* (Indiana University, 1950). Includes annotations.

A. Nichtenhauser *et al.*, *Films in psychiatry, psychology and mental health* (Health Education Council, Medical Audio-visual Institute, American Medical College, 1953).

J. J. Jehring, *A guide to audio-visual material in industrial and labor relations* (New York State School of Industrial and Labor Relations, Cornell University), Bulletin No. 22, August 1952.

S. Reid, A. Carpenter, and A. R. Daugherty, *A directory of 3300 16 mm. film libraries* (U. S. Department of Health, Education and Welfare, Office of Education, Washington).

4. *Other sources of films.* The relatively limited listing in footnote 15 actually has only seven films directly focused on group behavior as such. However, many films, including the other nine described in the footnote, contain within them one or several group situations which can be studied and analyzed for purposes other than that for which they were originally made. For example, portions of *We plan together* can be used to illuminate leadership problems. *All I need is a conference* can be used to improve group members' diagnostic abilities by stopping the film halfway through, and asking people to predict or diagnose what is the real trouble in the meeting, and what will happen next. An excerpt from a film such as *Maintaining classroom discipline* (McGraw-Hill) can be used as a starter for a role-playing scene between a principal and a teacher who is portrayed in the film. In one training group, a tense scene in a sheriff's office was excerpted from a western so that the training group could study the process of decision making.

Using films in this way assumes that the training group has agreed ahead of time on some training problems for study, and that someone has had the time to identify a profitable excerpt.[17]

Kinescopes of television shows are a frequently overlooked source of study material. One training group watched kinescopes of a televised seminar in an attempt to identify the teacher behavior and the student participation patterns involved. Many kinescopes are already available for educational use.[18]

[17] Excerpting of feature films is done by Teaching Film Custodians (a non-profit educational service affiliate of the motion picture industry). Excerpts are listed in *Films for classroom use* (1952, supplements 1954, 1956), available from Teaching Film Custodians. Sample excerpts:

"Due process of law denied," from *The oxbow incident* (20th Century-Fox). Shows variety of informal group situations leading up to vigilante execution of innocent men. Good for study of decision making, critiques of "groupthink."

"Executive interview," from *The high cost of loving* (MGM). An industrial executive puts a subordinate under stress to assess his merit for promotion. Good for studying threat and defense.

[18] For a comprehensive catalog of 777 kinescopes and TV films, see NET Film Service, *1958 Descriptive catalog* (Audio-visual Center, Indiana University). Samples:

Why do people misunderstand each other? (Talking Sense Series, WOI-TV). Problems of listening, and comprehending what people are really meaning with the words they use.

The gang (Searchlights on Delinquency Series, WTTW). Delinquency as a group phenomenon; shows gang activities, contrasts with team behavior.

Learning from discussion (The Great Ideas Series, Palmer Films). Discussion as a basic method of adult learning.

(If a kinescope does not appear in this catalog, it can sometimes be obtained for educational use by writing the station where the show originated.)

An occasional Hollywood feature movie focuses more or less directly on small group situations. Availability is a problem,[19] but exhibitors in large cities who specialize in re-runs can occasionally be persuaded to show to the public a film in which a training group is also actively interested.[20]

In general, locating films that are really appropriate at any particular point in a training group's life is difficult and takes much planning time. However, a few films, such as those listed above, seem to be useful and are often worth the time, especially in planning for a longer workshop or program series.

Tape recording

Next to a chalkboard or a newsprint pad, a tape recorder is probably the single most valuable piece of audio-visual equipment in leadership training programs.[21] Like a chalkboard and newsprint, it will retain faithfully all information fed to it. The information is extremely comprehensive; it is an impersonal, complete record of all audible behavior that takes place while the machine is operating. Tape recordings can thus be a permanent verbatim record, a kind of objective mirror of a particular session or activity. Immediate playback, with any number of precise repetitions, is possible.

[19] However, several companies, such as Brandon and United World Films, have been making available 16 mm. prints of Hollywood feature films. See *Educational Film Guide* for listings, which are becoming fairly extensive.

[20] Examples of such films are:

Twelve angry men (United Artists). A detailed, concrete, and powerful study of jury decision-making processes. Action is continuous and does not leave the jury room. Excellent for studying deviance, group decision-making, hostility, conflicting values, problem solving.

Executive suite (MGM). A study of what happens after a top executive dies. Helpful in studying influence and power in hierarchical organizations.

Lifeboat (20th Century-Fox). An analysis of the experience of castaways from a shipwreck. Good for conflict, subgroup structure, leadership.

Home of the brave (United Artists). A story of GI's during combat, one of them a Negro. Good for examining the individual's response to group rejection and acceptance.

Lost boundaries (Film Classics). The experience of a Negro family who had "passed" for white in their community. Useful for studying the effects of group membership.

All the king's men (Columbia). The rise and fall of a demagogue. Helpful in illuminating individual use and abuse of authority and the exercise of power.

[21] This discussion deals primarily with tape recording as a means for training in better group behavior. For more general discussions of tape recording, see D. Hodgson and H. J. Bullen, *How to use a tape recorder* (Hastings House, 1957), and R. and M. Marshall, *Your tape recorder* (Greenberg, 1955).

1. *Advantages.* The tape recorder has many values that make it a useful training tool. Recordings are ordinarily quite faithful, so that objective, factual checks can be made on misinterpretations and misunderstandings. Recordings are an unusually flexible training medium; they can be started and stopped, replayed, and listened to whenever and however the training group members desire.

Tape can be edited. Almost any desired audible stimulus (for example, a montage of difficult points in a meeting, alter-ego comments or clarifier comments inserted in the record of an actual session, dramatized episodes, soliloquies, etc.) can be produced for training use.

In addition, tape recordings can be used to gather data from a training activity in a relatively easy, unobtrusive, undisruptive fashion. Some training devices, such as the use of a group observer or clarifier, may alter the phenomena being examined. When a tape recording is played back, however, everyone in the group can be a process observer at the same time. Clarifying and observing skills can be practiced almost as well with a tape recording as with a live performance.

Tape recordings also have very high concreteness and specificity. Persons who have only vague notions about what their behavior in groups is like, or who do not see the difference between "giving opinion" and "giving information" can find out very rapidly and directly the answers to their training concerns.

Finally, using tape recording is for many people an especially interesting experience. Even today, when the tape recorder is part of the culture of most schools, some persons have never heard objectively how they themselves really sound to other people. They may be relatively unaware of their characteristic style of speech, way of interacting with others, method of attacking problems, and so on. Mirrors have fascination for most people over and beyond their functional uses.

2. *Disadvantages.* The characteristics of the tape recorder described above also mean that some difficulties may appear when the machine is used in training.

Trainers who have not used a tape recorder frequently may wonder whether it will inhibit or disturb people. As suggested in Chapter V, this does happen, but such effects are unlikely when the machine is seen as a useful instrument by the group, and its use is planned for by the entire group. There may be occasional initial self-consciousness—concern that the machine is preserving one's errors for posterity. But when group members decide to record their meetings regularly, it is unusual to notice any reference to the machine (except for functional comments like "turn the reel over") after the first two or three minutes of work of the first meeting. Objections to tape recording rarely arise when it is clear that the recordings will never be listened to without consent by anyone with power to reward or punish the training group members.

The tape recorder also limits its recall to audible behavior. This means that some important features of interaction are completely missing—facial expressions, glances, body movement, reference to printed or other visual material. People who usually spend most of their time in a meeting watching others may find themselves at a disadvantage in using tapes. Using tape recordings excessively may also tend to build in blind spots. Members may *listen* more and more to what is being said in a meeting, but cut down on their watching.

Tape recordings are also a *sequential* record. During playback, locating a particular episode in a meeting can use up a good deal of time. It is not possible to jump instantly to point B or to "What Bill said back there," as is possible with a non-sequential display, such as a chalkboard. When much location of episodes is planned, it is a good idea to use a machine equipped with a revolution counter or similar device. During recording, a person should sit beside the machine and keep a record of the counter reading when certain incidents are happening.

There are some technical problems, too, mostly of a minor nature. Unless the training group is blessed with a binaural (stereophonic) machine, a tape recorder hears undiscriminatingly, with only "one ear." Thus, the noise from a low-flying airplane, which no one heard during a low-voiced but intense discussion, can suddenly roar during playback to make hearing nearly impossible. Problems of fidelity, microphone placement, tape quality, and tape or machine breakage are always present, and the reader is referred to treatments like those suggested in footnote 21 on page 198.

3. *Methods of using a tape recorder in training.* Reference to the index at the end of Chapter V will help the reader locate over a dozen different ways of using a tape recorder to aid a training group in its work. Here it may be enough to comment on four broad types of tape recorder use.

Playback and critique. The most direct way of learning from a tape recording is simply to play back a segment of a group meeting, and stop it from time to time whenever members wish to comment on what has been happening. Many variations of this simple theme are possible, and they have been discussed in Chapter V.

This use is enormously helpful for deepening insight re "what leads to what" in group meetings, that is, the actual consequences of particular behaviors of specific persons. The playback and critique method is also excellent for resolving differences of perception, and for gaining, from an objective point of view, insight into what one's actual role in a group has been like.

Playback, with guided analysis. A tape recording may also be played back while group members use an observation sheet, respond to a checklist, fill out ratings, or jot down estimates of what they think was happening in the situation. These secondary sources of data can then be compared with the reactions of other group members, and with the tape recording itself in a second playback.

In general, this is a good way to improve the sensitivity of group members to what is going on. It also extends the members' skill in using particular observation or rating methods. For example, if the problem is to help people distinguish the difference between "making an action suggestion" and "setting procedural standards," repeated tape playback can accomplish in a few minutes what might take a half hour's abstract argument.

Playback as communication. Tape recordings are also a good means of communicating the essence of an interpersonal situation to which the hearers were not originally a party. This is a familiar use in regular classroom teaching. In training programs, the sessions of a committee meeting, for example, can be carried into the training group for analysis, diagnosis, and individual help. Dramatic presentations, describing the history of a group's development over a long series of meetings by means of edited critical incidents, are also possible.

Tape recordings can also communicate emotional material. One training workshop began its opening general session with a tape-recorded soliloquy by a typical member. An empty chair was placed at the front of the room, and the audience was encouraged to think themselves into the chair while they listened to the member describe some of her hopes, anxieties, and expectations for the training program just ahead. The directness, spontaneity, and immediacy of this presentation helped other members to express their feelings and real concerns for the workshop.

Playback and action continuation. As described in Chapter V, tape recordings can be used as a stimulus for practice behavior in the training group —either role playing or actual behavior. The use of a tape-recorded episode as a jump-off point seems to be an economical and plausible way to help people start trying out new behaviors (as contrasted with elaborate scene-setting, exhortations to "try it out," and the like).

4. *Methods of producing tape recordings.* The simplest method of obtaining tape recordings is to record an entire session, or all sessions, of the training group. This provides a complete record, but can swamp the group in tapes unless clear decisions are made about which material is most relevant to the group, and how it will be used in training. Observer notes can help in picking out useful material.

A second source of tape recordings is a selected-ahead-of-time portion of a group's meeting, or a planned training situation, such as a role-playing scene. A recording made this way is likely to be seen as highly functional, since it is being used as a specific method for examining a limited piece of interaction. Problems of editing and locating episodes are less likely to arise. A possible disadvantage when a pre-selected incident or part of a meeting is recorded is that the parties to the situation may be self-conscious, since the tape recorder may not have been a usual part of the group's activity.

A third type of tape recording is deliberately-constructed recordings (episodes strung together as in a photographic montage, special recordings involving narration or other background effects, material prepared from scripts,[22] and the like). Careful work by members outside the training group is needed in order to produce a recording that will be really helpful. The emphasis is on deliberateness, focus, effect, rather than on the capturing of spontaneity or the simple recording of data for later analysis.

Which of these three methods of tape recording is employed depends, of course, on the training problem and the desired outcomes.

Summary Comment

This chapter has focused on the process of constructing training activities, starting from accurately-assessed training problems. Once outcomes have been specified, appropriate training methods can be selected and combined into a workable, plausible design. Trainer and group can then move into the actual operation of the design, still maintaining flexi-

---

[22] As in S. M. Corey, P. M. Halverson, and E. Lowe, *Teachers prepare for discussion group leadership* (Teachers College Bureau of Publications, 1953), a pamphlet described in Chapter III, pp. 28–30.

bility as they proceed. Many specific suggestions were given about design operation; they tended to emphasize clarity, procedural facilitation by the trainer, and—always—the experimental approach. The final portion of the chapter has reviewed role playing, films, and tape recording as useful technical aids to the learning of better group behavior, noted some usual disadvantages and trouble spots, and made specific resource suggestions.

CHAPTER VII

TAKING THE TRAINER ROLE

The trainer is a person with special responsibility for helping individual and group members learn from their experiences. Being a trainer is as complicated and difficult as being a good teacher—or more so—and thorough discussion of the trainer role is outside the scope of this book. However, this chapter is aimed at helping the person who takes, or is considering taking, the trainer role in groups of the sort described throughout the book. Once again, the reader is asked to suspend any negative reactions he may have to the word "trainer" until he has looked at the discussion below of what the trainer does.

A wide variety of persons in a school system may fill the trainer role in a systematic training program—curriculum directors, teachers, principals, guidance workers, superintendents, supervisors, helping teachers. Their jobs require them to do some informal training every day. The teacher who evaluates committee work with her class, the guidance worker who visits a homeroom group, the superintendent who helps a curriculum council improve its methods of work, are acting informally as trainers, even though they may not see themselves in the role.

This book focuses, however, on training in explicitly-set-up programs, and this chapter discusses the aspects of the trainer role which make it special—different from the usual role of the superintendent, the guidance worker, or the teacher.

Naturally, the type of training program with which the trainer is working may range widely: a workshop, an evening PTA session on "Getting More Out of Committees," a social studies unit on "How Groups Work," an informal study group of high school faculty members.

Although many of the ideas on the trainer role presented below are drawn from intensive laboratory training settings (such as the sessions held at Bethel [1]), no assumption is made that the trainer in a local school setting must reach some *a priori* standard of sophistication, skill, or excellence. The ideas are thought to be basic enough to apply to the trainer role in general, regardless of the nature of the specific training situation at hand.[2]

The first section below describes the trainer's role in some detail. It is followed by a section on the background qualifications of an effective trainer. The final section—since few school systems include a person who has had systematic experience in the trainer role—suggests ways of learning the trainer role.[3]

The Trainer Role

The trainer's responsibility is to facilitate learning about better group behavior. He is basically a teacher—but he usually deals more in the analysis of here-and-now behavior than do most teachers. He is not precisely a member of the group—yet he must retain some membership in the group, or his efforts will be fruitless. He is certainly not a leader or a discussion chairman—yet his acts do influence the group in moving toward shared goals. Basically, the trainer facilitates and guides *learning*. When the training group gets bogged down, or becomes apathetic, or is full of fight, the trainer's job is *not* necessarily to help the group "get out of this mess," but to help them learn from the mess. Doing this may at times require that the trainer act differently from a teacher, a member, or a leader.

In brief, the trainer must act as a planner prior to a training activity, as a guide during the operation of the activity, and as an evaluator during the planning of new activities.

[1] See National Training Laboratory in Group Development, *Explorations in human relations training* (NEA, 1953).

[2] Aspects of the trainer's role have been discussed in earlier portions of the book. Chapter IV specifies in some detail the planning functions with which the trainer must help. The reader who examines the illustrative activities in Chapter V, and the accounts of training sessions referred to in Appendix A, will gain some feeling of how the trainer guides an activity as it unfolds. The comments in Chapter VI on designing training activities are also centrally relevant to the trainer's role.

[3] For convenience, the trainer is referred to as "he" throughout the chapter. Actually, "she" or "they"—when two trainers are working with the same group—are frequently appropriate in practice.

The trainer as planner

During the planning stages of a program—or a specific training activity—the trainer's role is primarily to help group members produce practical, promising plans for learning. He helps the planning group assess the needs and expectancies of participants in the training group as carefully as possible, and aids in the construction of learning experiences which fit these needs. The reader is referred to Chapter IV (pp. 61–71) for a review of the various decisions that must be made during the planning of an over-all program; many of these decisions must also be made during the planning of a particular training activity.

The major contribution of the trainer during planning is probably methodological. He can supply technical help to the planners. ("Perhaps if we used a coaching session to get at this business of how to handle irrelevancies, it would give us the practice people say they need at this point," or "Using a tape playback is an easy way to increase sensitivity to what's happening in a group.")

Beyond providing immediate technical help, the trainer also needs to be sensitive to how well the training process in general is going:

Are real dissatisfactions being worked on?

Is the training climate psychologically safe—does it allow people to unfreeze their old ways of doing things?

Are members getting an opportunity to practice new kinds of behaviors and learn how well they succeeded?

Are people getting a chance to *think* about what they are going through, and how it applies to their own future behavior on the job?

Is the training group developing as a group?

Does the situation support and aid each member's own private quest for improvement?

The trainer must keep concerns like these constantly in the forefront of his thinking and also help the group members pay attention to them from time to time. The conception of leadership presented in Chapter II assumes that leadership functions need not necessarily be centralized in one person, but may be shared through the group, even though there is an appointed chairman. Just so, training functions may be shared through the group, even though one person is designated as trainer. If learning is to become a self-operative process, each member of the training group must, in some part, come to take responsibility for guiding his own learning. The trainer role, like the chairman role, is thus a kind of "safety net"—the trainer will fill needed training functions in the group, but only if no one else does. If trainer and group see the trainer role as a supportive one, it helps to reduce the worries of the beginning trainer that he must be omniscient and omnipotent. Of this more below.

The trainer as guide: building group norms

During the actual operation of a training activity, the trainer's basic role is to help things keep moving so that people learn as much as possible. The trainer's behavior during training sessions helps to set group *norms,* that is, informal standards, ways of behaving that are highly valued by the members of a group. In a training group, certain norms are needed if training (as described in Chapter III) is to take place.[4] In job groups, these shared beliefs may or may not exist—but they are essential in a group set up to help people learn better group behavior. Below are suggested some of these training-relevant norms.

People are important. The trainer has a basic feeling of respect for the worth of persons. He does not interrupt, he listens, he rejects ideas but not people, he shows that he believes that persons are ends and all else is means. As he demonstrates his belief, he serves to some degree as a model for other group members, and the norm of basic respect for persons gradually bcomes established in the training group.

It's safe to try things out here. The trainer also indicates by his actions that things are "off the record" in this group, that trying something new is not only permissible but desirable. He permits and invites discussion of his own behavior. He does not criticize anyone for expressing any feeling or idea. Gradually, willingness to experiment becomes a group norm too.

Feelings are important. The trainer takes expressions of feeling seriously. When people say they feel mad, sad, bad, glad, he helps the group see that these are basic data from which to work. Feelings of group members tell us how well progress on the task is going—whether people are interested and involved, whether the goal is clear, how well a particular leader's

---

[4] This view has been discussed most completely by J. R. Gibb in "A norm-centered view of T-group training," in *Theories of T-group training,* L. P. Bradford and J. R. Gibb, eds. (National Training Laboratories, in preparation). "T-group" is shorthand for a training group which makes an intensive study of its own ongoing processes.

approach is working. Frank expression of feeling is essential if the group members are to understand the processes going on.

Things are not taken personally. The trainer responds objectively to expressions of feeling. Feelings are facts, his behavior says to the group. If Joe gets mad at me, that tells us something about what has been happening. From this we can learn about what leads to what in a group. Antagonism or syrupy smoothings-over have no place in what the trainer does. Too, when he encourages analysis of process, using a tape recorder, a process observer, or post-meeting reaction sheets, the trainer is in effect saying, "We can look at ourselves objectively and learn from this." As the group moves along, members come to share a work-centered kind of objectivity.

We learn from doing things and analyzing them. From the start, the trainer indicates by his actions that he sees learning as beginning with concrete experience. He does not lecture the group, and he does not encourage windy discussions of "leadership" or "how to handle the blocker." He helps the group members examine their own experience. He helps them set up trials of particular approaches to problems. He helps the group members think about what they have done. More and more as the training group proceeds, the members act as if they too shared this basic norm—that provisional trials, carefully analyzed, are the major road to learning.

What's happening here and now is the important thing. The trainer does not usually encourage the group members to talk about the past, other groups, back-home experiences, things they have read, or what might happen in the future. Mostly, he talks directly to what is going on in the training group as it is happening right now, right here. By what he says and does, he dramatizes his belief that the problem is not someone else's behavior, but our own behavior as it is unfolding every minute in front of our own eyes.

We plan together. Finally, the trainer shows the group members that he believes the training group is basically a shared, planful enterprise. He does not spring things on the group. He does not attempt to pull his rank on others. He does not take a laissez-faire attitude; he invites cooperative planning. He refuses to take sole responsibility for the success of the training group.

The trainer communicates his belief in these norms for effective training group operation by everything he does. As the training group proceeds, members have successful experiences with analyzing how the group works, with discussing the here-and-now, with trying out new behaviors, with reacting objectively instead of antagonistically, with learning from doing rather than from being told, and so on. The trainer's norms become more and more built into the group situation—more and more a part of an over-all training climate. Once this climate is established, the group can become a strikingly effective, self-operative learning situation for all its members. Even more basically, as suggested in Chapter III, members' acceptance of these norms will aid them in continued independent learning after the training program is over.

It is far more important that the trainer accept these norms in his own set of personal values than it is that he be especially proficient in the specific methods and techniques of training. This is not said as exhortation, but simply as a fact of life which the trainer must face. For example, the new trainer who is basically contemptuous of people and pretends a respect he does not feel will get only coolness or outright resentment from group members. Good trainers can be aggressive or docile, outgoing or reserved, jovial or serious—but the trainer's personality must almost certainly include some commitment to norms like those above.

Of course, no trainer exemplifies these norms to the nth degree. The trainer's belief in these norms is revised and deepened as he experiences many different training group situations. As he works, for example, he understands more clearly what it means to be objective, or he copes more effectively with his own propensity for lecturing instead of helping people learn from their own experience.

The trainer as guide: specific behaviors

As the trainer encourages the development of norms like those suggested above, he must also supply certain functions in the training group during a training activity, or see that they are supplied. Below are described six functions which a trainer may fill from time to time as a training program proceeds: providing methodological help, guiding analysis, giving support, encouraging group growth, controlling group movement, and maintaining his own membership in the group.[5] The

[5] For another discussion of trainer functions, see H. A. Thelen, *The dynamics of groups at work* (University of Chicago Press, 1954), pp. 169–78, "How the trainer operates."

basic skill of the trainer lies in being able to decide when a particular function is needed—and when it is not. Whatever his specific behavior (including the behavior of keeping quiet), the trainer always has one basic purpose—helping to set conditions for effective learning.

Below, as each function is described, typical behaviors are given, and brief comments are made on problems the new trainer usually faces.

1. *Providing methodological help.* The trainer must be able to help the group invent, construct, or adapt learning activities to help the members learn what they want to learn. The activities in Chapter V and the suggestions for designing activities in Chapter VI give some ideas on the skills involved. Someone has called this the "learning technician" role.

Typical behaviors would be: suggesting the use of a particular device such as alter ego comments; pointing out the need for briefing role players in a special way; suggesting three or four methods of role analysis when it is clear the group wishes to do this; acting as timekeeper.

The problem for beginning trainers here is often one of insecurity, of concern about not having a big enough "arsenal" of methodological ideas. Given some skill at cooperative planning with a group, and willingness to assess needs and outcomes carefully, as outlined in Chapter VI, methodological sophistication can come quickly. It's important that the trainer feel secure enough to suggest trying out training methods which he himself has not experienced.

2. *Guiding analysis.* Here the trainer comments on, generalizes from, raises questions about, and in general helps the group members think explicitly about the experiences they have been going through. This has sometimes been called the "making visible" function, but it involves more than merely pointing up group phenomena. It also includes the guidance of thoughtful discussion (see pp. 189–90 of Chapter VI).

Typical analysis behaviors are: making interpretations about what is happening in the group; asking why something has been going on; introducing a social science concept into the discussion; asking for implications of the preceding experience; pointing out something that has just been happening and inviting analysis of it; inviting people to formulate their learnings from an experience. Most good teachers can supply the analysis function well.

The trainer may also find himself helping to analyze the nature of the training group itself, interpreting the training method being used, or explaining the rationale behind training (as described in Chapter III) as another form of analysis.

People who are learning the trainer role often feel concerned because they do not have sufficient background in formal knowledge of groups and group behavior. This is a legitimate concern, and should be remedied by reading and study.

Being able to relate formal, on-paper concepts to the living, breathing reality of the training group is something else again. This probably can be best learned by practice. In general, the trainer who has a seeking, inquiring attitude about the understanding of group behavior usually has little difficulty in evoking enthusiastic and productive thinking on the part of other group members. It's usually the brilliant, scholarly trainer who ends up by doing group members' thinking about groups for them, just as many teachers do not really encourage thinking in the classroom but only try to lead students to a predetermined "correct" answer.

3. *Giving support.* As a training activity goes forward, it is important for group members to have emotional support as they work and learn. A training group experience, in effect, requires that members expose their own behavior to analysis, and that they be willing to try things out provisionally to see what happens. Members need support to do these things. At the beginning of a training group's work, support may have to come mostly from the trainer. As the group works, support comes more and more from other group members, through the development of norms like "It's safe to try things out here."

Typical support behaviors are: acting to reduce excessive conflict between members; behaving in a warm or friendly fashion; encouraging members as they try out difficult things; relieving group tension.

New trainers are likely to overemphasize the need for support in a training group. Excessive trainer support may result in dependence, or in a sweetness-and-light atmosphere. The trainer needs to be encouraging enough to permit the group to grow and learn, without promoting emotional stickiness or overdependence on him.

Beginning trainers sometimes get tense when groups they are working with get into conflict, seem apathetic, or are unable to move ahead and make decisions. This is natural, but when group members are tense or bothered about the way things are going, it is important that the trainer not become over-anxious and bothered too. He must be free enough to be able to see how to help members learn from the tense situation they are going through. From this point of view, he must avoid being seduced into acting like a group member. The new trainer who rushes in to support a group at every evidence of tension will find that he is not helping people to learn.

Foresight is important, however; the "don't start what you can't finish" rule applies here. If the trainer cannot foresee, or believes he cannot cope with, the consequences of an activity, he should not invite the group to begin it.

Training is not psychotherapy. Still, events in a training group often have considerable emotional impact for individual members. The trainer needs to be reasonably alert to situations which are placing particular members under stress (for example, Jane's behavior in a role-playing scene was unintentionally close to Jane's real-life role, and the following discussion is beginning to make her feel very uncomfortable). The trainer must protect the integrity of persons when other group members do not seem to be doing so.

Training is usually best served if the trainer's interventions and comments are about the group situation as a whole. If he gets into the habit of constantly protecting Jane from critical remarks by others of the group, or if he and Jane regularly have long talks after the training sessions, the trainer is likely to intensify the very problems which led him to provide extra support in the first place. He certainly must be psychologically accessible to members who want to talk about the group and their reactions to it, but he should almost always invite such members to bring their reactions to the training group for discussion and comment. When members seek out the trainer for special help, it is usually a symptom that the trainer and group are not doing a very good job of cooperative planning of helpful training activities.

4. *Encouraging group growth.* As the trainer suggests training methods, helps the group think, and supplies emotional support, he also needs to encourage the group members to join him in taking responsibility for these matters. For example, rather than set up roles for role players himself, he suggests that the group do so. He does not always give the first interpretation of what has been happening—he invites analysis by the group. He need not be the first to praise a shy member who has tried something difficult—he keeps quiet long enough so other group members can do so.

Other typical behaviors here include: turning questions back to the group as a whole; pointing out successful decisions made and responsibilities assumed by the group; encouraging the group to make plans without the trainer's participation. Giving different members in turn the chance to practice service roles (chairman, recorder, observer, etc.) also spreads responsibility and aids group growth.

The trainer's basic job, in a phrase, is to work himself out of a job. The new trainer may have difficulty in this area at first. He may be so pre-occupied with helping the group analyze experiences, construct new ones, and so on, that he may not notice that many other members of the group also have training skills which the group needs and should be using. The opposite (and more usual) mistake is to abdicate one's training responsibilities by withdrawing completely, or trying to act like "just another group member."

5. *Controlling group movement.* The entire question of how the trainer influences what the training group does is an interesting and perplexing one. Undeniably, the trainer exerts some control on the group through the timing of his suggestions, the particular methods he proposes for learning, the points at which he chooses to remain silent, and so on. Most trainers ordinarily refrain from chairman-like acts, such as testing for a decision or "keeping people on the topic." Usually, it is not the trainer's responsibility to help the group accomplish any particular discussion task.[6] For example, suppose that a training group was struggling over which of three agenda items should be tackled next. Ordinarily the trainer would not attempt to aid the group to choose among the three agenda alternatives, but would devote his attention to helping the group analyze why it was so difficult to choose among them, what the implications were, and so on.

Even if the trainer refrains from overt control behavior, however, the members of the training group usually have widely varied feelings about how much he *should* be controlling the group. As suggested in Chapter IV (pp. 89–90), training groups sometimes become divided into factions—those who wish the trainer to exert more control over what is happening, and those who resent his comments and wish he would remain silent or leave. The analysis of these different feelings of dependence and counter-dependence can often be extremely fruitful in understanding how people feel about the problem of leadership.

New trainers often err by over-controlling (ex: setting up enormously detailed procedures of which one is sole guardian) or under-controlling (ex: remaining completely passive, without helping the group analyze the chaos which usually results from such "trainer abdication"). Learning the right amount and kind of control behavior is a matter for practice and reflection.

6. *Maintaining membership in the group.* Obviously, the trainer must be seen as having some membership in the training group, or his comments and suggestions will have very little impact. He needs to say enough to

---

[6] This statement must naturally be qualified according to the setting of the training group. In the classroom, a teacher who is acting as trainer may well choose to supply more control than is suggested here.

[Trainer functions cont'd]

indicate that he values membership in the training group. The beginning trainer who tries to remain emotionally aloof from the other members, or who demands special status, is in trouble; the group may well isolate him, and he will be unable to help.

But as suggested above, the trainer cannot afford to be *only* "a member of the group." He cannot give up his responsibility for helping learning procedures proceed fruitfully and well. He has an authority of expertness, in a sense, which he cannot and must not try to give up.

If he acts only like a member of the group (ex: by supporting a goal suggested by another member, entering actively into group discussion aside from process analysis, or arguing with what another member is saying) he may well lose his ability to be helpful to the group. Thelen has remarked: "The trainer must not get into the position of being a protagonist in and a commentator on the battle at one and the same time." [7]

This point is emphasized here because most new trainers' natural tendency is to be anxiously friendly, over-warm, "just another member of the group." Genuine warmth and membership are important—even essential to good learning—but the other five functions described above are just as important. As the training group proceeds and members take more and more responsibility for its success, the trainer will find it easier to assert his own membership.

Nothing said here, incidentally, should be construed to mean that the trainer should be a "zombie," as one member put it. He has feelings and he should express them as a person. Since the trainer does have special responsibilities, however, he should be reasonably sure that his being spontaneous at any given point will help, not make things more difficult.

The reader new to training will almost surely feel that this discussion of trainer functions is excessively honeycombed with statements of "On the other hand . . ." It *is* very difficult to suggest precise rules; the trainer must diagnose the immediate situation, and supply needed functions to the best of his ability. For this reason, practice and analysis of the trainer role are essential; of this more below in the section on "Learning the Trainer Role."

The trainer as evaluator

Just as the trainer helps in planning and in guiding training activities, so must he aid in evaluation and re-planning. The topic of evaluation

[7] *Op. cit.,* p. 176.

is discussed at length in the next chapter. Here it is sufficient to say that the trainer must be open to continuous and thoughtful analysis by the training group of such matters as: the effectiveness of his own role; the value of the activities he has helped to plan; and trouble spots in the activities which need to be reduced or eliminated through new planning. Without such session-by-session evaluation, even the best of trainers will do a poor job.

The Effective Trainer

As indicated earlier, persons in almost any professional job in a school system can plausibly serve in the trainer role. Below are suggested some general characteristics of effective trainers. For a person considering taking the trainer role, this list of characteristics can be treated as guideposts for planning. The more intensive or formal the program is, the more importance these guideposts assume. They are listed in approximate order of priority.

1. *Openness to change.* Because the trainer role is not simple, and requires "sensitive use of the self," as one trainer put it, the prospective trainer must be willing to look at himself, question things he does and has always taken for granted. The person whose views of himself are unchangeable will have considerable difficulty in working as a trainer.

2. *Reasonable "comfortableness."* To do a good job as a trainer, one must be secure enough to try out new things. Training—like teaching, or any form of human interaction—inevitably gets one off base, and into puzzling situations for which there are no ready-made answers. An effective trainer needs to like himself as a person, be comfortable with others, be reasonably able to cope with new situations without getting upset. "Reasonably" is the key word here.

3. *Desire to help.* The effective trainer needs to have genuine motivation for helping people learn. The person who tries out the trainer role *only* because it is "interesting," or because it gives him feelings of power over others, or because a superior told him to, is unlikely to get very far before things freeze up or the group becomes apathetic. The beginning trainer may wonder whether he is really aware of his motivations for wanting to help people. Psychotherapy is not being suggested—only a thoughtful self-appraisal of one's reasons for wishing to try out the trainer role. (See Chapter IV, p. 50, for more on this.)

4. *Being seen as helpful.* The trainer must be seen by the members of the training group as being potentially (and actually) able to help them learn. This seems obvious, but is easily overlooked. Without acceptance of one's trainership by group members, little learning is possible.[8]

Most persons markedly lacking in the other characteristics listed here will also tend to be seen by potential members of the training group as being unable to provide training assistance. This boils down to: "Do people in the group think I am competent to help?"

5. *Role flexibility.* It helps if the trainer is a person who can do different kinds of things in group situations without too much difficulty. He need not be a super-member or an unusually skilled individual, but he ought to be able to handle himself with a minimum of strain in group situations. Tennis coaches need not, and probably should not, be Wimbledon finalists, but they do need to know how to play the game fairly well.

6. *Sensitivity to groups.* A good trainer *notices* things in group situations. He picks up what is going on, can see objectively and accurately what is happening. If he has not learned this sensitivity, it will be difficult for him to help members develop it.

7. *Formal and practical knowledge about groups.* It helps if the trainer knows something about group dynamics as an area of social psychology, and is comfortable with concepts in this area. Background experience with many different kinds of groups is also useful.

8. *Understanding of the training process.* A good trainer has a reasonably clear picture of how people can learn in the inductive, experience-centered way that is described in this book.

9. *Methodological knowledge.* For effectiveness, the trainer needs to have a good repertoire of methods for learning, like those in Chapter V.

What an array! The reader is reminded once more that these criteria for effectiveness in taking the trainer role are presented in approximate order of importance. Complete, detailed understanding of specific training methods, for example, is far less important than a reasonable degree of openness to change, or role flexibility.

Again, these are open-end criteria. Even an accomplished trainer could show improvement on all of them. The person who is experimenting with the trainer role for the first time can use these criteria as guideposts to evaluate and improve his performance as he proceeds.

---

[8] Compare I. Knickerbocker's position that the leader is one who group members believe can aid them in reaching their goals; see Chapter II of this book.

Learning the Trainer Role

Most school people already have some of the skills and abilities described above. The trainer role is not so different from the role of teacher, group member, or leader that assuming it requires a lot of brand-new behaviors and attitudes. The reader who has been examining himself against the norms, behaviors, and general characteristics discussed above may well have discovered that acting like a trainer is at least plausible for him.

Yet no good purpose is served by pretending that being an effective trainer does not take skill. How is this skill learned? It will come as no surprise that the preferred answer is: try it out, analyze, and try again. Learning to be a trainer, like learning to be an effective member or leader of a group, is an experience-centered process. Below are suggested ways of learning the trainer role, focused mainly around the last five criteria suggested in the section above. No attempt is made to cope with the problem of "being seen as helpful," which is mostly a matter of role expectations unique to one's own organizational situation. Little advice is given on the first three criteria listed since they are primarily personally oriented, and relatively indeterminate. They are suggested mainly as "flags"; the person who is particularly rigid, tense, insecure, or without a genuine desire for helping others is simply not a good bet as a trainer. Making substantial improvement on these criteria may require considerable personal reorientation.

Prior to the training program

Before a person begins working actively as a trainer, there are a number of experiences useful in helping him prepare for the trainer role. Which learning experience a prospective trainer chooses must depend first of all on what the training activity is going to be like, and then on a careful assessment of whether his abilities are sufficient for the task. If this assessment suggests that one needs more formal knowledge of group dynamics, it usually can be gained through reading and by attending classes in colleges or universities. Courses in group dynamics and human relations are now offered quite widely. Too, at least a dozen university centers use training procedures like those described in this book rather than a formal course pattern.

Formal knowledge must usually be deepened by applying concepts concretely in a thoughtful analysis of one's own day-to-day group experience. If, in staff meetings, one has listened only to *what* was being said, it can be extremely illuminating to note *who* is saying things to *whom,* and to relate this in one's thinking to concepts of influence, communication, and prestige.

Understanding of the training process, and some methodological sophistication, can be gotten from a book like the present one in conjunction with the references which have been cited along the way.[9] The printed word, however, must be supplemented with direct experience. The prospective trainer who has experienced role playing as a participant has a far clearer idea of exactly how it works than does anyone who has only read about it. Reading and watching are not enough.

For this reason, participating in human relations training workshops [10] is perhaps the most helpful thing a prospective trainer can do to bring about improvement with respect to many of the criteria above, especially role flexibility and sensitivity to forces at work in groups. In some cases, participation in a "lab" can also provide the person with added insight into how he measures up on the criteria of openness to change, personal comfortableness, and desire to help others.

Some school systems (for example, Seattle, Baltimore, and Prince George's County, Md.) have found it extremely profitable to send one

[9] See especially the references suggested in Appendix B for purchase by school systems.

[10] An increasing number of two- and three-day workshops are being held during the year at universities and in conjunction with the work of the National Training Laboratories. In addition, intensive two- and three-week human relations training laboratories are held during the summer at many different locations; for example, some recent ones are:

National Training Laboratory in Group Development, Bethel, Maine.

Pacific Northwest Laboratory in Group Development, Seattle, Washington, Public Schools Administrative and Service Center.

Workshop in Community Human Relations, University of Chicago.

Workshop in the Improvement of Human Relations, Boston University Human Relations Center (Osgood Hill, North Andover, Mass.).

The Human Relations Training Laboratory, Southern Methodist University, Dallas, Texas.

Intermountain Laboratory in Group Development, University of Utah, Salt Lake City, Utah.

Advanced Laboratory in Human Relations, sponsored by Western Training Laboratory in Group Development, University of California Extension, Los Angeles, California.

These training laboratories have been in operation from four to twelve years, and provide an intensive training environment, using the methods described in this book. Further information can be had by writing the sponsoring organizations involved. A list of these and other summer training opportunities usually appears in the April and May issues of the magazine *Adult Leadership.*

or two staff members a year to training laboratories. In this way, the pool of persons with training skills grows rapidly, and many different types of activities can be tried out.[11]

Many universities and colleges now have one or more staff members who are especially interested in training of the sort described in this book. Such persons may be found in departments of education, psychology, sociology, speech, business, nursing or public health; they can supply materials and serve as consultants during the planning stages of a training program. Or they may move beyond this and work as trainers, with local people playing a training-associate role. The outside trainer serves as a coach and helper to insiders who are trying out the trainer role for the first time.[12]

Many of the training laboratories mentioned above also have an attached "trainer development" program designed specifically to help former laboratory participants expand their skills as trainers. Such trainers-in-training may be available to help with the planning and operation of local training programs. Persons from one's own local area who have attended laboratories as regular participants may be able to help too. Names of former laboratory or "trainer development" participants can usually be obtained by writing National Training Laboratories, or the nearest regional training laboratory.

This wide range of outside resources is suggested here for reference purposes. It is important to emphasize, however, that use of such outside resources is certainly not essential to a good training program. The basic requirement is that training be competently planned and carried out in a way that is sensitive to the actual day-to-day needs of people in the school system concerned. Local persons, drawing on outside resources where needed, can usually design and carry out a training program superior to one that most outsiders can construct—because local persons can build a program around the real problems of real people in a continuing fashion.

---

[11] See, for example, D. Nylen and W. Dick, "A program of group study and human relations training" (mimeographed), Administrative and Service Center, Seattle Public Schools, Washington.

[12] National Training Laboratories now supplies coordination for the work of seventy-six training consultants in all parts of the country. For information write National Training Laboratories, 1201 Sixteenth St., N.W., Washington 6, D. C. and ask whether a member of NTL Associates or another consultant is available in your local area.

During the training program

Once a local program has gotten under way, what can local trainers do to improve their skills?

Persons who spend most of their time doing training for better group behavior frequently remark that they feel they are learning more than anyone else in the group. Any teacher knows that the way really to understand an unfamiliar subject is to teach it to others. A great deal can be learned about the trainer role by trying it out with a local school group. There are several means of helping insure that good learning will take place.

1. *Regular evaluation and critique periods* as a part of the training program can be very helpful. At the end of each training activity, there can normally be a period of five or ten minutes when the training experience itself—including the role of the trainer—is evaluated and criticized. This helps to sharpen trainer skills *and* improve the quality of the next activity. The reactions of other members of the training group are a very important resource for learning.

The main idea is that one is neither tensely infallible nor falsely humble about helping others. The "let's try it out and see what happens" approach makes things go more easily, and helps the entire group take an experimental view of their activities. New trainers naturally have doubts about evaluating training activities with their groups; they wonder whether admitting fallibility may confuse the group, be resented, or be seen as weakness. These consequences rarely materialize. The trainer who sees himself as a resource person helping the group as best he can, and who trusts the training group to grow and develop in spite of his mistakes, is most likely to do an effective job.

All this says once again that an experimental approach to training is essential for good learning. Group members will probably not want to experiment with their behavior unless the trainer shows his willingness to try new things out himself.

2. *Tape recording* of training sessions is another useful aid to learning the trainer role. Sitting down alone or with other trainers after the activity and questioning oneself ("Now why didn't I step in there and comment on what was happening?") is usually profitable. All of the values of tape recording described in Chapter VI apply as well to trainers as to members.

3. *Discussion with other trainers* is another helpful approach. One need not go it alone. Many training groups involve two persons in the trainer role, both concerned with the kinds of functions described above. Nearly everyone has blind spots. Co-trainers can supplement each other's skills during the training activities, and are in an excellent position to point out to each other ways in which their behavior can be improved in the next session.

In any training program involving more than a dozen people, there will usually be several different groups. Even if trainers have not been in the same training activity together, they stand to gain a great deal from getting together to discuss "why that role-playing scene didn't click," or "how you handled the problem of getting started in the training group." Even in training laboratories like the ones mentioned above, where highly skilled and sophisticated staff members are filling the trainer roles, there is a great deal of informal discussion constantly going on between trainers outside the sessions on problems they are facing in their groups. The essence of the trainer role—like the teacher role—is its almost infinite challenge.

4. *Diaries* kept by the trainer(s), and by group members, can be unusually valuable as an aid to learning the trainer role.[13] Trainer diaries are helpful in supplying perspective, especially if entries are written immediately after sessions with the help of notes taken during the session. Group member diaries are especially good for showing how the same training group event (for example, the arbitrary behavior of a self-appointed chairman) is seen in a wide variety of different ways by members. It should be made crystal clear at the outset who will read diaries (the trainer only? any interested member? all members?) and why they are being kept in the first place (to help the trainer learn? to supply the group with more data on what is happening? as an evaluation method?).

Following the training program

Assuming that a training program includes constant opportunity for practice and improvement in trainer skills, there are several follow-up activities which can deepen one's understanding of the trainer role.

[13] See references by I. R. Weschler and J. Reisel, and R. Lippitt in Appendix A for examples.

1. *Writing a report* of the training activity is often a good way to order and conceptualize one's learnings. Having to describe the events of a training group to an audience of interested school people who were not present at the training program itself is an excellent exercise. It forces one to be specific, and to move beyond vague noises like "Well, we were looking at the group process."

2. *The experience of making plans* for a new training program or activity can also help sharpen one's understanding of the trainer role and training process, especially if the re-planning involves new persons not previously involved.

3. Finally, if a continuing training program does materialize, setting up a *trainer development* group can be growth producing. Such a group includes persons who are all practicing and learning the trainer role. They can use tape recording, role playing, observation—the full range of experiences described in this book—to aid their own development as trainers. A trainer development group helps to insure that the training function becomes built into the school system's in-service education program.

Summary Comment

This chapter began by suggesting that the trainer's role is basically that of facilitator of learning, and as such is complex but learnable. During planning stages, the trainer serves as a technician, suggesting useful methods. As training activities proceed, he embodies his belief in certain important ways of behaving in the training group, and these gradually become group norms which guide further group learning. The trainer's central task is to assess the learning situation, decide which of several specific training functions is needed at any given point, and see that it is supplied either by him or by some group member. A list of characteristics of the effective trainer was proposed; it emphasized reasonable personal adequacy and a cluster of skills that might be termed "practical sophistication" about groups and about training. Some ways of growing into the trainer role by practice and analysis prior, during, and after the training activity were suggested.

CHAPTER VIII

EVALUATING TRAINING

This chapter deals with the problem of finding out how well training purposes and outcomes are being achieved. Training, like any educational endeavor, requires the expenditure of time, energy, and money. People who have to make such expenditures need to know whether their investment has been worth the effort.

The chapter begins with a general discussion of the evaluation process, and outlines some of the special problems inherent in evaluating training for better group behavior. Short-term evaluation for purposes of ongoing planning is explored briefly, and research designs for long-term or over-all assessment are also analyzed. Finally, some useful types of instruments are discussed in terms of their appropriateness for assessing the results of training.[1]

The Evaluation Process

Evaluation is a process of trying to find out whether certain actions have led to desired consequences. Ordinarily, one must (1) specify the desired consequences or outcomes of the action; (2) devise ways of measuring the degree to which the goals have been achieved; (3) carry out the action; (4) collect the desired information; and (5) make analysis

[1] Naturally, this chapter cannot deal thoroughly with problems of evaluating the impact of educational experiences. The reader is encouraged to explore such useful treatments as J. W. Wrightstone, J. Justman, and I. Robbins, *Evaluation in modern education* (American Book Co., 1956), and R. L. Thorndike and E. Hagen, *Measurement and evaluation in psychology and education* (Wiley, 1955).

and interpretation of it before going on to plan the next relevant activity.[2] Teachers do this all the time; they set up purposes, make lesson plans, devise tests, and examine the results for evidence of the learning they hoped for in the first place. Any person, in fact, is engaged in informal, continuous evaluation of the effectiveness of his own activities as he goes about them.

The view expressed in this chapter is that local school people who are conducting training programs will benefit if their approach is less casual and haphazard, and increasingly more systematic and thoughtful at each of the steps outlined above. The discussion assumes that the persons who are responsible for the planning and operating of a training program are the ones who are in the best position to improve it through evaluation.[3]

Let us examine each step in the evaluation process in somewhat more detail.

Defining goals

The idea dies hard—as evidenced in the format of this book—that evaluation is something you do at the end of an activity. It should be clear, however, that the first step in the evaluation process is the early, clear identification of outcomes which the training program is being set up to produce. Planners must accomplish this step anyway (regardless of evaluation plans), as they are setting up the training program (Chapter IV, p. 61) and during the planning for specific activities (Chapter VI, pp. 178–80). Planners must go beyond identifying broad aims. They must examine very clearly the job difficulties which training is expected to resolve. Ultimately, they must face up to the issue of "What will a person who participates in this program *do* differently afterward?" Planners need to take general learning outcomes like "sensitivity," "diagnostic ability," "behavioral skill" (Chapter II, pp. 23–26) and define them as operationally as possible: "What would a person *do* who was

[2] For a discussion of steps in evaluation as applied in social work, see D. G. French, *An approach to measuring results in social work* (Columbia University Press, 1952), pp. 44–73.
[3] This point of view is discussed more fully in S. M. Corey, *Action research to improve school practices* (Teachers College Bureau of Publications, 1953).

For an overview of problems of research and evaluation, the reader may also wish to turn to *Research for curriculum improvement*, 1957 Yearbook, Association for Supervision and Curriculum Development (Washington, The Association, 1957).

more sensitive than before to forces in groups?"[4] or, "How would you tell if a person had really begun to take a self-training approach?" (Chapter IV, pp. 94–95). Until training outcomes are defined in some agreed-on fashion, neither the training itself nor the evaluation of it can proceed effectively.

Naturally, the process of defining outcomes is necessarily filled with all kinds of value judgments. Are these training outcomes worthy, acceptable, significant, congruent with other important values (such as respect for persons)? What, really, is a "good" leadership act? (Chapter II, pp. 18–19.) Value conflicts and agreements need to be made as explicit as possible, or planners may end up trying to evaluate nothing, or everything, instead of the outcomes that really count.

Planning ways of measuring change

Once outcomes have been identified, planners must begin specifying just how they will measure change in terms of these outcomes. Here are a number of subquestions, classified into five broad areas:

The targets of change. Are we looking at change in terms of the individual and his knowledge, beliefs, attitudes, behaviors? Or are we looking at the effectiveness of committees and groups of which he is a member? Or are we looking at broader factors—the general state of morale in his school or school system? Or at a combination of these?

Evaluation of change. Is change to be evaluated in terms of a pass-fail criterion, or the degree to which the learner fulfills his own capacities, or the achievement of standardized, "normal" scores, or the meeting of a socially desirable standard—or what?[5]

Instruments to be used. Shall we employ questionnaires, ratings, interviews, observation, oral evaluation, sociometric devices? Do the instruments measure what we want to measure? (For example, does this rating scale give us an accurate, stable idea of chairmen's ability to keep groups working productively on their tasks?)

[4] See pages 242–43 for a measuring instrument which answered this question with "He would notice, and could list if asked, many helping and hindering behaviors of others in a group situation."

[5] For further discussion of this particular problem (and associated problems) in the evaluation of a learning experience, see V. E. Herrick, "The evaluation of change in programs of in-service education," Chap. 13 in *In-service education,* 1957 Yearbook, National Society for the Study of Education (University of Chicago Press, 1957), pp. 311–38.

Design for data collection. Are we to use the instruments both before and after training? Will a control group be used? In what sequence will particular measuring methods be used?

Plan for data analysis. Will results be added up and averaged, or are we going to analyze the data person by person? Will we try to relate the results of several different instruments? Precisely how will the questionnaire replies be tabulated and compared? Exactly what will we do with the interview tapes?

All the questions named here must be coped with in some way, preferably before the training activity begins. Otherwise laments like "If we only had gotten some reaction from the principals *before* the workshop, we might have some idea of what it has accomplished!" are likely to arise. Planning for evaluation must be an integral part of planning for the training activity. This integration is not urged academically; data collection is a very important and practical part of the training enterprise.[6] Without good information on a program as it goes forward, it is difficult to make sensible training decisions.

Part of many people's resistance to "research" may stem from the mistaken belief that in order to be acceptable evaluation must be bristling with correlations, tests of significance, and random samples of a thousand persons.[7] The position taken here is that *any* evaluation attempts which move in the direction of more systematic and thoughtful assessment of what is happening in a training program are all to the good.

Collecting data

Before, during, and after the training experience, information will be collected via the measuring instruments which planners have selected, adapted, or devised for their own purposes. An over-all data-collection

[6] For many helpful suggestions, see R. Beckhard, *How to plan and conduct workshops and conferences* (Association Press, 1956), particularly Chapter II, "Fact-finding and evaluation," pp. 19–28. The author describes many different kinds of information needed by planners (for example, audience expectations, degree to which subject matter is getting across, perceived usefulness of the meeting), and devices for getting information (such as questionnaires, interviews, "roving reporters," and informal bull sessions).

[7] See, for some interesting ideas on this problem, R. Mooney, "The researcher himself," in Association for Supervision and Curriculum Development, 1957 Yearbook, pp. 154–86. Mooney makes a distinction between the "consumer's" viewpoint toward research, which stresses formal, logical completeness, "scientific objectivity," and quantification, and the "producer's" view, which stresses the meaning of research as something a puzzled human being does in trying to find answers to problems important to him as a person.

plan is needed. It should specify, for example, when members are to fill out a particular questionnaire, just who will be interviewed and how the results will be fed into the planning, how many sessions will be tape-recorded for information purposes, which job associates will be talked to about their impressions of the persons who attended the program, which student committees will be observed by the teacher for evidence of the effects of classroom training. The data-collection plan will naturally change somewhat as the training program develops, but without a clear statement of what information is needed, and how and when it will be collected, evaluation is difficult, to say the least.

An important and often overlooked aspect of data collection is the simple keeping of records of the training activities as they proceed. Descriptive accounts are usually much needed in planning for later programs, and in reporting the program to people who did not attend. Record keeping may involve no more than putting session plans into a file folder. For more detail, note taking or tape recording may be used.

New trainers are sometimes concerned that getting evaluation data will hinder training or cause negative attitudes. The author's experience with data collection before, during, and after training is that group members feel best about data collection when (1) they see the specific instruments as being reasonably clear and sensible; (2) they feel that the evaluation is an integral part of the training program, and feeds right into its improvement; (3) they understand that there is a well-thought-out plan for data collection and analysis. These three perceptions are more likely to occur if group members have had a hand in planning the evaluation instead of being passive "subjects."

Analyzing and interpreting

As data are collected, planners need to summarize them and draw implications for the training—both as it is proceeding and in terms of future activities. This is not the place for a thorough discussion of data analysis and interpretation; the reader is referred elsewhere for help in qualitative and quantitative methods.[8]

[8] See V. E. Herrick and C. W. Harris, "Handling data," Chap. V, pp. 83–118, in Association for Supervision and Curriculum Development, 1957 Yearbook, *op. cit.*, and "Analysis and interpretation," M. Jahoda, M. Deutsch, and S. W. Cook, *op. cit.*, pp. 251–304; also C. S. Bebell, "Getting meaning from research," Chap. VI, pp. 119–51, Association for Supervision and Curriculum Development, 1957 Yearbook, *op. cit.*

Ordinarily, data "do not speak for themselves." The planners' main problem is to extract meaning from the data, pull out generalizations and relationships—hopefully, perhaps, principles—which can serve as useful guides to further planning.

Some Special Problems of Training Evaluation

Any teacher who has really tried to find out what difference his teaching is making knows this in his bones:·evaluating any educational activity is a complex, difficult job. Evaluating training is no exception.

One special difficulty is that the outcomes of training for better group behavior are fairly complex and—initially at least—not very clear to planners. What, precisely, is meant by "diagnostic ability"? What kinds of attitude change can we expect from people after they experience a series of role-played episodes? Can one ever really define what it is that makes for effective group membership, or specify what skills a student council chairman needs?

And when one moves to measurement problems, there are even more difficulties. Group behavior in a school system has—like all behavior—multiple causes. It is very difficult to set up a measuring design to cancel out all of the chance factors that *could* intervene to help persons improve their group work, even in the absence of a training activity. Also, most of the relevant instruments which have been devised by professional researchers are difficult and technical to apply, or of uncertain validity and reliability. They are also widely scattered in the literature. This means that planners, more often than not, have to devise their own instruments.

Building brand-new instruments can help make evaluation directly responsive to the needs of the immediate situation, but planners may well have the nagging worry that the particular measuring devices they are using are not all they might be. (Is our questionnaire stable—or are the changes we found with it just chance shifts of opinion? Can we really count on what the teachers say about the effectiveness of their principal's behavior since the workshop?)

Evaluation of training is further complicated by the fact that important and salient aspects of people's behavior are being looked at. This can prove to be threatening to members in a training program, or at least bothersome.

And even where individuals do not feel threatened, and participate actively in data collection, problems of "wishful thinking" may appear. Individuals who have spent a great deal of time and energy in a training program—either as trainers or as participants—may respond to ratings, questionnaires, or interviews in a positively-biased way ("If I've spent this much time on it, it *must* have been good").[9]

In the face of all these problems, what are planners to do? The counsel here is one of patience with imperfection. It is totally impossible to get firm and complete answers to all the questions which planners have about the effects of training. The problem then becomes: How can we *improve* the information we get about what training is accomplishing? Matter-of-fact attempts to get practical information are far more likely to be helpful to the success of a training program than mistakenly abstract ventures into what someone thinks is "rigorous research." Practical, simple, steadily improving methods of evaluation, actually carried out, are preferable to grandly-conceived designs which fall apart or never materialize.[10]

Short-term evaluation

Much of the data collection in training programs is information-gathering for immediate planning purposes. This has been called "steering" research, since the information is used to decide which way to move next with the program. In Chapter IV (pp. 84–85) and Chapter V (pp. 111–13) various short-term evaluation methods have been described. Whether post-meeting reaction sheets, group interviews, or general evaluation sessions are used, the basic aim is to find out how well the training is going, and to get this information fed back into the planning process. Some useful methods of gathering data for immediate planning are also discussed in this chapter's final section (pp. 235 ff.). Here it is sufficient to re-emphasize the importance of steering from data, rather than from *a priori* assertions, vague impressions, or pet theories.

[9] For an interesting discussion of problems of evaluating training, see I. R. Weschler, R. Tannenbaum, and J. H. Zenger, "Yardsticks for human relations training" (Adult Education Association, 1957). The discussion focuses on "sensitivity training," a somewhat more personally-oriented approach than the group-relevant one being taken in this book, but the discussion of evaluation problems is very relevant.

[10] For more comments on practical evaluation, see L. D. Korb, *Training the supervisor* (United States Government Printing Office, 1956), Chap. 7, "How to measure results," pp. 94–106.

Assessment research

Ordinarily, steering research is insufficient for planners who are concerned with operating a training program. They want to find out whether the program as a whole has influenced participants in the ways hoped for. What, really, was the impact of that week-end workshop on the members of the Central Curriculum Committee? Are PTA meetings going any more smoothly after that clinic? How productive are class discussions now, after the students in English 10-B listened to those tape recordings? Do grade-level chairmen seem to be more comfortable and less dependent on the supervisors as a result of last year's study group?

Assessment research is long-term evaluation. It is basically concerned with change in people, over a period of time. Planners are ordinarily interested in such questions as these:

Has any detectable change taken place?

How much change has occurred?

Was the change actually caused by the training program?

How durable does this change seem to be? Are people maintaining it, or are they "backsliding"?

What is the *direction* of the change, in relation to what planners and members think is good or correct?

Assuming that more than one kind of change has been measured, how are the changes interrelated?

Are there any factors which seem to help explain *why* the changes have occurred?

How much change has taken place during the training program itself, as contrasted with change measured later on the job? [11]

Research designs

How do we get answers to questions like those above? In order to assess change in persons, measurements at different points in time are required. Below are suggested five alternative data-collection designs which can be used for assessment purposes. The time dimension goes from left to right.

[11] For further comment on dimensions of change, see Herrick, *op. cit.*, pp. 314–18.

DESIGN 1: POST-TEST ONLY

Experimental Group:	Train	Measure

In this design, sometimes called the case study, data are gathered from members of the experimental group (those persons who are attending the training program) after the training is over. The data may be collected by post-training evaluation sheets, interviews on "what you learned from the training," or other devices.

Note that this design has some severe limitations. There is no way of insuring that the results found in the measurement are really attributable to the training experience at all. Maybe people would have given the same response even if they had never attended training. Also, no precise measure of change is possible, since there are no data to indicate the members' status before training began. Yet this design is used with great frequency by nearly everyone in education (as in a class with final exam at the end of the course).

The data gathered with this design can be improved if the experimental group members are asked to recall what they believe they have learned, or how much they have changed.[12]

Another useful way to buttress this design is to ask each member of the experimental group to describe exactly how he believes his job behavior has changed since the training experience—and simultaneously to ask some of his on-the-job associates to list any changes they have noticed in his behavior. By comparing the responses of each experimental group member and his job associates, and discarding all those which do not show correspondence, a fairly tough-minded measure of change can be developed.[13]

Associates and training group members may also be asked whether they would attribute the changes to the training program, although the answers obtained should be regarded cautiously.

[12] One study found that such perceived-change (sometimes called post-only) measures had fair validity, but showed more change than a questionnaire given before and after training. The post-only questionnaire is especially helpful when one has not anticipated before training that a particular kind of change should be measured. See H. Baumgartel, "An analysis of the validity of perceived change measures" (Institute for Social Research, University of Michigan, 1954, mimeo.).

[13] For a straightforward account of how this worked out in practice see P. C. Buchanan, "Evaluating the results of supervisory training," *Personnel,* 33:362–70, 1957, and P. C. Buchanan, "Testing the validity of an evaluation program," *Personnel,* 34:78–81, 1957.

DESIGN 2: PRE-TEST AND POST-TEST

Experimental Group:	Measure	Train	Measure

This approach gets rid of some of the obvious disadvantages of Design 1. Change from pre- to post-test can be found by subtracting the difference between scores on the measuring instrument for each person in the experimental group. If the average change is not zero, it is plausible to assume that some change has taken place in the participants.

However, notice that it is impossible to state with any certainty that the change did in fact result from the training itself. Maybe the participants would have changed even without attending the training program. They may have changed spontaneously, or as a result of some other event (ex: a salary rise, a new principal, the onset of spring fever), or simply because they have gotten more "test-wise" or sophisticated about the measuring instrument being used. So Design 2, while certainly more helpful than Design 1, still leaves something to be desired.

DESIGN 3: PRE-TEST AND POST-TEST, PLUS CONTROL GROUP

Experimental Group:	Measure	Train	Measure
Control Group:	Measure		Measure

This design, the traditional control group design, adds a group of persons who do not attend the training program. They, too, are given pre- and post-measures. If the change shown in the experimental group does not appear in the control group, then one can infer with reasonable certainty that the training experience caused the change.

Notice, however, that some important assumptions are involved. For example, before training begins, the experimental group and the control group should be quite comparable in interest, capability, and performance on the measures used. This is usually difficult to be sure of, since the persons who come to a training program are often more highly motivated than those who do not.

One way to deal with this problem is to supply training for only half the number of people who wish it, and to postpone the training experience of the other half, who become the control group. Whether or not a person came to training would be randomly decided (coin-flipping, etc.).

Another practical way of getting a control group for a training program is to ask each prospective participant to identify one other person on the job to whom he is roughly similar, and ask these matched persons to serve as a control group. A third method is simply to take a random sample of persons in the school system who are not attending the training program.

When intact groups, such as classes or school staffs, are attending training, the control groups should also be intact classes or staffs. With intact groups, it is even more important to match the groups carefully, or to choose them on a genuinely random basis.

By and large, it seems fair to say that very few studies of training in the general literature have involved the use of control groups. This holds true for most program evaluation designs in local school systems too. There is every indication, however, that if we are to move beyond impressions and hunches in assessing the genuine effects of training experiences, the increased use of control groups is essential.

Design 4: Post-test only, plus Control Group

Experimental Group:	Train	Measure
Control Group:		Measure

One weakness of Design 3 is that the pre-test measure before the training experience may have sensitized people to the questionnaire itself. Thus at post-test time a "practice effect" occurs—individuals have simply learned better how to respond to the instrument. Another type of "fake" change may occur because taking the questionnaire caused people to be more alert and responsive to the training than would otherwise have been the case.

One way of getting around these problems is to use only a post-test measure, with an experimental and control group as in Design 4. If there are differences between experimental and control groups after training, then one can assume that the changes came genuinely from training and not from exposure to the questionnaire or interview that was used, *if* one important condition has been met: *The experimental group and the control group must have been originally picked on a random-sample basis,* as described under Design 3. Otherwise, some real pre-training differences (in motivation, level of skill) may exist to cloud the results.

If random assignment to training is not possible for practical reasons within the local school system, then Design 4 should not be used, because it would permit only slightly more certainty than Design 1.

Design 5: Own-control Group

Experimental Group:	Measure	Measure	Train	Measure

In many school systems, finding a control group may prove to be difficult. Design 5 gets around this problem quite neatly by having the participants serve as their own control group.[14]

In this design, the persons who will attend training are measured some time before the training experience, measured again after the lapse of some time, attend the training program, and then are measured a third time, after an interval comparable to that between the first two measures has elapsed. If changes between measurements 2 and 3 are greater than those between measurements 1 and 2, then the inference is that the training has caused these changes.

With this design, it is of course very important to be sure that the instrument is not subject to serious practice effects. This can be done by locating a random sample of other persons in the system who will respond to the instrument at two different times. Like Design 4, this design has much to recommend it, but is rarely used.

Some additional comments on design are worth making. First, any single one of these designs can be augmented by repeating measurements after a considerable interval. Suppose, for example, that a questionnaire is given to an experimental and a control group before a workshop, and then shortly after its completion. It may well be profitable to re-administer the questionnaire six or eight months later to detect whether the changes earlier noted between pre- and post-test have disappeared, stayed the same, or grown larger.

Second, the reader should note that designs for long-term evaluation of training activities need not—and should not—be independent of data gathered for steering purposes. For example, a pre-test using a questionnaire on attitudes toward working in groups can serve (1) as an aid in planning the opening session, and (2) as a preliminary measure for assessment purposes. The same measure repeated after training would help show how attitudes toward groups had shifted because of the train-

[14] This design was suggested by P. C. Buchanan (Republic Aviation Corp.), and is described more fully in a forthcoming book (written with H. A. Shepard) on training for organizational effectiveness.

ing program. Most measurement devices can be made to do double duty in this way. (Exception: in some cases the results of an instrument should not be reported to participants until the post-test has been completed, because to do so would alter the responses.)

This discussion of design problems clearly implies a need for the construction of an over-all evaluation plan, in which the uses of instruments for steering and assessment purposes are clearly defined and put on paper.

Clearly, careful assessment of training effects takes time and thought. One must plan a design which is feasible and will increase one's confidence in the solidity of the findings.[15] It is perhaps worth re-emphasizing, however, that no design is better than the measurements that go into it. If a questionnaire does not really get at important and relevant aspects of group behavior, then no matter how carefully it is administered and tabulated, the results will not be useful at all. More fundamental than general research design is the process of carefully identifying desired training outcomes, and planning thoughtful, practical ways of measuring them. It is to the latter problem that we now turn.

Data Collection Methods

The position taken in this discussion of evaluation is that actual behavior in the job situation is the ultimate criterion of effectiveness in any training program of the sort described in this book. Changes in attitude, different perceptions of group work, increased ability to diagnose group situations—all these are important, but they are secondary to the basic question: *Can this person now behave any more effectively in group situations than before?*

How to answer this question? Someone has remarked that if you wish to get information about a person's behavior, there are only two main alternatives. You can *observe* him directly, or you can ask him (or a third party) to give you a *report* of his behavior. Such a report may be given orally, as in interviewing, or it may consist of pencil marks on

---

[15] The reader who has found this discussion of research designs interesting may wish to move on to D. T. Campbell's article, "Factors relevant to the validity of experiments in social settings," *Psychological Bulletin*, 54:297–312, 1957. This article is technical, but quite fascinating in examining research designs, including most of those described above.

Another helpful reference on research design is T. Hillway, *Introduction to research* (Houghton Mifflin, 1956). Pages 153–74 discuss and illustrate what is involved in designing experiments.

paper. The sections below discuss the advantages and disadvantages of each of these three broad methods of gathering data: observation, interviewing, paper-and-pencil techniques. Examples of more specific techniques are given, applicable to the assessment of change both in the job situation and during the training program itself.[16]

Observation

Watching and recording the actual performance of training group members after they have returned to the job situation is the most direct, hard-headed—and probably most widely used—method of measuring change. Curiously, professional researchers have spent far more time on paper-and-pencil tests for predicting behavior than they have in refining methods of examining actual behavior. Most school system personnel, however, are inclined to be quite concrete; they judge the effectiveness of a program by whether or not the participants *do* anything differently afterward.

Unfortunately, in most attempts to observe behavior on the job, observations are made unsystematically, and are not recorded carefully. All the usual limitations of biased, selective perception, of "seeing what we want to see," apply.

Observation must be guided and supported by some sort of paper-and-pencil recording method, such as an anecdotal account, a checklist, or a a series of ratings. Needless to say, the data emerging from observation are only as good as the recording procedures. A good observation-and-recording method is reliable; several persons using the method will get the same results as they watch a situation. But such agreement takes practice and checking.[17] Here are some possible observation techniques usable on the job:

[16] The reader with interest in systematic inquiry may profit from examining books such as L. Festinger and D. Katz, *Research methods in the behavioral sciences* (Dryden, 1953); M. Jahoda, M. Deutsch, and S. Cook, *Research methods in social relations*, 2 vols. (Dryden, 1951); and G. Lindzey (ed.), *Handbook of social psychology*, (Addison-Wesley, 1954). These books have technical, comprehensive chapters on such matters as: observation of group behavior, sociometrics, attitude measurement, interviewing, and questionnaires. Specific references to these chapters are noted where relevant in the following pages.

[17] For technical suggestions on the observation of group behavior, see R. W. Heyns and A. F. Zander, "Observation of group behavior," pp. 381–418 in Festinger and Katz, *op. cit.*; A. F. Zander, "Systematic observation of small face-to-face groups," pp. 515–38, and "Data collection: observational method," pp. 130–50 in Jahoda, Deutsch, and Cook, *op. cit.* See also the material in Chapter V, pp. 107–08, on use of a group observer.

1. Function checklists like those mentioned in Chapter V, p. 130 (useful to discover whether people fill more different functions after training than before).

2. Standardized observation methods like Bales' categories,[18] Gropper's conference checklist,[19] and Withall's climate index.[20]

3. Specially-made observation guides aimed at specific behaviors (ex: amount of participation, summarizing, question-asking).

4. Informal observation of the training group member by others as he works in different group settings. Job associates (or other students, when training is done in the classroom) use a simple recording form to jot down short responses to one or two questions like these:

> Please describe some things this person did which helped the group as it worked.
>
> Please describe some things this person did which hindered the group as it worked.
>
> Please give a thumbnail sketch (2–3 sentences) describing what this person did in this meeting.
>
> In your opinion, has this person changed his behavior in working groups in any way since November (time when training program was held)? If yes, please describe.

As suggested earlier, this approach can be quite helpful if the training group member's views of how he has changed are compared with the observations of others. Using several job associates as informal observers cuts down bias unique to one observer or one group setting.

Checking actual performance by means of observation is probably the most tough-minded way available for measuring change. This is particularly true when those observing the participant are job associates or other students who have not attended the training program. They are not likely to be very much impressed by his verbalizations of "how much I've learned," and in any event may not be sensitive to small changes in behavior. Often, after training, a person has to change his

---

[18] R. F. Bales, *Interaction process analysis* (Addison-Wesley, 1950).

[19] G. L. Gropper, *The critical requirements of conference behavior,* (The Maynard Foundation, 1956). This instrument was developed by using the "critical incident" method described more fully in J. C. Flanagan, "The critical incident technique," *Psychological Bulletin,* 51:327–58, 1954. Essentially, one looks for specific events and behaviors which appear to be markedly important for the success or failure of an activity, such as a staff meeting.

[20] J. Withall, "An objective measurement of a teacher's classroom interaction," *Journal of Educational Psychology,* 47:203–12, 1956.

behavior quite drastically before he "crashes through" the barrier of usual role expectations which job associates hold ("Same old Joe, no matter how many workshops he goes to"). Actually, Joe may be trying some new things that go unnoticed, and observation by job associates may be an *overly* tough-minded, insensitive method of data collection. The participant's observation and report of his own behavior should not be left out of the picture.

During the training program itself, observation can be extremely fruitful. Since procedures there can be specially planned, it is possible to set up standardized situations or performance tests for assessing participants' skills of working in groups. This kind of standardization is usually very difficult on the job—the demands of immediate tasks ordinarily outweigh training needs.

If, however, behavior is observed for evaluation purposes in the training session, it is very important to note that certain assumptions are involved: (1) the training session is reasonably like the job situations in which most people are working; (2) a person who behaves in a certain way in a training group will behave in a reasonably similar way on the job. Needless to say, these assumptions are not always met (the model student in the classroom may be a terror on the playground). But the existence of a skill during a training group assessment period is probably a necessary—if not a sufficient—condition for performance of this skill on the job. The person who lacks the skill to help a training group stay on the topic or define its goal probably cannot produce these behaviors on the job either. The person who demonstrates his skill in the training group *may* be able to use these skills on the job.

There are several different ways of getting data by observation of performance in training groups.

1. Members can be given a standardized discussion task, such as agreeing on a group rank-ordering of ten statements about what a "good teacher" is like. The resulting discussion can be watched with the aid of a checklist or other observation guide.

2. Following such a discussion task, members can:
   a. Rate each other's performance.
   b. Make sociometric choices (ex: "Which persons contributed most to the solution of the problem?").
   c. Fill out the same checklist used by observers.

3. Training exercises like those in Chapter V can be adapted for measure-

ment purposes. For example, a conflict scene is tape-recorded and played back to the training group. The members are asked to continue the scene so as to reduce the conflict. Adequacy of conflict-reducing behavior can be judged by ratings, sociometric choices, or observation as in methods 1 and 2 above.

4. Situational problems can be role-played to test members' skills. Those having objective, preferred solutions are especially useful.[21]

When systematic mutual observation is to be carried on in the training session it is important that members actively help in planning the activity, otherwise it will serve neither training nor evaluation goals. Words like "adequacy," "judge," "rate," can be unusually threatening unless everybody has helped to set up the evaluation method.

It may be valuable to point out here that as a training group proceeds through a number of sessions, the members ordinarily come to know each other quite well—perhaps more so than in usual job relationships. If, for example, they give sociometric judgments of one another's behavior in the group situation, these are built on a broad base of observations made over a period of close and objective acquaintance. So if estimates of performance in a training group situation disagree with job-situation data, one should not assume too hastily that the training group estimate is at fault.

Interviewing

Next to actual observation on the job, interviewing probably provides more complete and practical data than any other method. A great deal of information can be obtained about the consequences of training by interviewing participants or their job associates, either singly or in groups. Interviews can elicit systematic responses to a pre-planned set of questions, and are also vastly more flexible than any pre-structured questionnaire. The person being interviewed may come up with information that never occurred to the interviewer in the first place. And most people are flattered and interested to have their opinion asked about something, and enjoy being listened to.

Using an interview for data collection requires devising some kind of systematic interview guide. As with observation, an adequate record-

[21] See N. R. F. Maier, A. R. Solem, and A. A. Maier, *Supervisory and executive development* (Wiley, 1957) for a series of problems usable for this purpose.

ing method is essential if data are not to be lost, since even a good interviewer's notes may miss up to 50 per cent of what is said. If the decision is to tape-record the interview and then transcribe it, bulk is a problem (a 15-minute interview may run to five or six typewritten pages) and the data are difficult to analyze. The use of guide questions under which interviewee responses are jotted is helpful when the full, complete flavor of the reaction to some specific question ("Do you think there should be another workshop like this one?") is needed.

Here are some sample questions from an interview guide the author devised when he and other trainers and planners of a 10-session workshop series began worrying about how well things were really going. An outside interviewer used it with one-sixth of the workshop members. The positive and negative feelings expressed proved extremely useful in planning.

A top sheet (not shown) gave detailed directions to the interviewer for introducing himself, explaining the purpose of the interview, creating rapport, and conducting the interview itself. On the interview guide, the questions were spaced to permit note-taking under each question.

INTERVIEW GUIDE

1. *General reactions* (use as a warm-up question)
   People's feelings tend to vary a lot about workshops. How have you felt personally about this year's workshop, in general? (Probe: What have been some of your reactions? How's the workshop going?)

2. *Others' feelings.* How do you think most of the other people in the workshop feel about the way it is going?

3. *Changes on the job.* Can you describe things you have done differently here, on the job, or in the community as a result of this workshop? (Get specific examples)

   . . . .

6. *Over-all changes and learnings.* In general, what would you say you've gotten out of the workshop so far?
   (Note: Open this out as a general question. Reflect and encourage. When all material seems to be out, then summarize items below which have been covered, and probe on the ones which have not been covered.)
   a. Are there any techniques or skills you've learned?
   b. Are there any new ways you've learned of doing things in a group?

c. Are there any new ideas or concepts that you've learned?

d. Do you have any new attitudes toward groups and group work, or toward other people in groups?

e. Has your picture of the way you see yourself in groups changed?

. . . .

8. *Salient experiences.* Now, getting back to the workshop itself. Do you recall any experiences at the workshop which really stand out for you?

9. *Workshop design.* How do you feel in general about the way the workshop is set up? (Probe: Afternoon sessions, evening sessions, steering committee, writing logs, post-meeting reaction sheets, etc.)

. . . .

11. *Improvements.* If it were up to you to plan this workshop, what changes would you suggest for the remaining five sessions? (Follow-up) Why?

12. *Future of the workshop. a.* If you heard there was to be a workshop next year, would you recommend it to a friend? (Follow-up) Can you say why?

b. Would you come yourself? (Follow-up) Can you say why?

These questions do not exhaust the possibilities. Before or after training, participants or their job associates may also be interviewed to determine such things as these:

How the participant usually works in groups.

What his major strengths and weaknesses in group work are.

The problems the participant feels he would like to work on in the training program.

Feelings, attitudes, perceptions, and understandings as they are seen by the participant.

Expectancies for training.

What factors help or hinder the job applications of learnings gained during training.

The group interview, either on the job or during training itself, is an often-overlooked tool. Given a good series of guide questions, an interviewer can get a large amount of information from a small group, with less net time expended than would be the case with a series of individual interviews.[22] Of course, an individual's responses in a group

[22] For added comments on this point, see H. A. Thelen, *The dynamics of groups at work* (University of Chicago Press, 1954), pp. 215-16.

interview are influenced by what others in the interview group have said, but this is not always a disadvantage.

Finally, interviewing approaches should always be practiced, if different interviewers are to get comparable results.[23]

Paper-and-pencil techniques

A wide variety of paper-and-pencil techniques is available for use in evaluating training. Most such devices are self-administering, and can be mailed to respondents or distributed quickly in a meeting. The same, standard questions or items can be presented to all the members of a training group at one time. The data are recorded directly by the respondent; no intervening third person is required. If anonymity or confidentiality is desired, it is far easier to assure it with questionnaires than with observations or interviews.

But pencil-and-paper tests are not observation of behavior, and are not oral reports of behavior. The basic problem is making sure that the marks someone makes on paper have a clear relation to what he actually does in a group situation.[24]

Below, five different kinds of paper-and-pencil devices are discussed, each with specific examples helpful in training evaluation.

1. *Open-end devices.* There is much to be said for instruments which do not pre-structure or tie down the answer of the respondent in a specific way.

Data from devices of this sort are usually quite rich and correspondingly difficult to analyze, except on an intuitive, general-impression basis. They can be very helpful, however, when getting the full qualitative flavor of respondents' reactions is more important than being highly systematic and precise.

[23] For technical material on interviewing, see E. E. Maccoby and N. Maccoby, "The interview: a tool of social science," pp. 449–87 in Lindzey, *op. cit.;* C. F. Cannell and R. L. Kahn, "The collection of data by interviewing," pp. 327–80 in Festinger and Katz, *op. cit.;* R. L. Kahn and C. F. Cannell, *The dynamics of interviewing* (Wiley, 1957); and P. B. Sheatsley, "The art of interviewing, and a guide to interviewer selection and training," pp. 463–92 in Jahoda, Deutsch, and Cook, *op. cit.* Also "Data collection: the questionnaire and interview approach," pp. 151–208, *Ibid.*

[24] The reader is reminded that even intelligence tests—perhaps the best standardized and most widely used of paper-and-pencil devices—can predict at most only about half of the variation in, say, school marks. In the field of social behavior, a good test (say, a well-standardized sociometric) can account for perhaps 25 per cent of the behavior it is designed to predict. "Predictable man" is a long way off.

EXAMPLES:

a. The Planning for Learning questionnaire (Chapter IV, p. 66) can be given as a pre-test, and then re-administered some time after training with questions revised along the line of "Things I think I understand better about groups." The data are vivid, though hard to treat, and can supply very practical evidence of the consequences of a training program—as seen from the participant's point of view.

The author used this approach in a one-day training session for chairmen, recorders, and consultants in a subsequent conference. Some initially desired learnings, such as "how to set group goals," did show up as net learnings afterward. Other initially-felt needs, such as "how to handle disruptive members," were not mentioned in the post-test, and may have been dealt with by the training, or simply did not show up in the conference itself. Finally, a great many learnings appeared which the person had not anticipated before the training session ("I feel more willing to trust the group members to work and take responsibility").

b. Open-end analysis of a group situation is another useful technique. Participants are asked to write down the helping and hindering things they notice in a role-playing scene, tape recording, or film. The total number of a person's responses is a crude measure of his sensitivity to forces in groups. When this device has been used by the author at the beginning and end of training programs, positive changes in "sensitivity" have almost always been evident.

Participants can also be asked to diagnose the reasons for the behavior in the scene, and to suggest appropriate action, although such material is much more difficult to score.

c. Asking participants and their job associates to describe changes in their existing job behavior, using an open-end form, has already been described above (p. 237).

2. *Questionnaires.* It is possible to construct an almost interminable number of questionnaires relevant to the purposes of training. Each question ordinarily has several fixed alternative responses, from which the respondent chooses the most appropriate answer or answers. Alternatives may be standard for all questions ("Always, Frequently, Sometimes, Never"), or especially tailored for different questions. Thus results from different respondents can be easily and systematically compared. The data are consequently less rich, but more stable than those gained from less-structured devices like those described in section 1 above.

Many questionnaires have been carefully standardized by being administered to large numbers of respondents, and are published for general use. Unfortunately, few such questionnaires are easily applicable to the problems of group training in the local school situation.[25] The reader is therefore encouraged to construct his own questionnaires.

EXAMPLES:

a. A post-only questionnaire may ask training group members to check their beliefs about how much they have changed in regard to various attitudes, skills, and the use of specific techniques on the job.[26]

b. During training, post-meeting reaction sheets (see Chapter V, pp. 111–13) are a form of questionnaire combining fixed-alternative questions, open-end questions, and ratings (see below). Post-meeting reaction sheets are decidedly helpful in supplying steering data for planning. They allow every member of the training group to have a complete say in response to the questionnaire (as contrasted with a group interview situation or an oral evaluation session where everyone may not get a chance to speak).

c. Post-meeting reaction sheets can be built item by item with members of the training group at the meeting rather than made ahead of time.

d. Finally, questionnaires can be administered either to members of the training group or to job associates (or other students, when training is carried on in the classroom). Associates may be instructed to react to the questionnaire in terms of their estimate of change or growth in the participant, in the way they believe the participant himself would answer, or in terms of their own behavior (if they are used as a control group).

3. *Ratings.* Ratings usually involve checking the amount or degree of some factor (such as skill in group behavior, satisfaction with a training activity, contribution as a group member) in response to fixed-alternative descriptions or along a scale with marked positions. Ratings are very widely used as measures of performance in the armed forces and industry.

There are substantial problems in constructing a rating scale which is a psychologically and statistically meaningful measuring instrument (that is, is not a rubber ruler where the inches are longer or shorter at different

[25] Those who doubt this assertion are invited to refer to O. K. Buros (ed.) *Fourth Mental Measurements Yearbook* (Gryphon Press, 1953), which reviews 830 published tests.

[26] See A. H. Passow, M. B. Miles, S. M. Corey, and D. C. Draper, *Training curriculum leaders for cooperative research* (Teachers College Bureau of Publications, 1955), pp. 140–46, for a sample questionnaire of this sort. A second questionnaire in the same book (pp. 147–55) was designed to get at a number of predictive factors, such as feelings about the training group, back-home team relationships, and the nature of own job problems. These factors would help explain *why* people showed high or low change on the basic questionnaire.

times, or a distorted ruler where some inches are longer than other inches).[27] However, teachers use informal rating methods all the time (letter grades), and descriptive ratings may be fairly easy to set up if the results are interpreted with some caution. Note also that ratings often carry judgmental overtones and may cause negative feelings—in raters as well as those rated.

EXAMPLES:[28]

a. Ratings (see comments under Questionnaires) can be administered to trainers, participants, or their associates, with a variety of directions for responding.

b. Ratings may be presented in a variety of ways. For example, the alternatives for choice may be fixed, as in this example:

How effective is this person in his work with others in groups, in your judgment?

———Extremely effective
———Quite effective
———Reasonably effective
———Not very effective
———Not effective at all

or the rater may be asked to check his estimate somewhere along a line with a few positions labelled:

How do you personally feel about your own skills of working with groups on the job? (Check along line)

Very dissatisfied	Neither satisfied nor dissatisfied	Very satisfied

c. It helps to provide more stable ratings if the rater is given a rather thorough description of what he is rating. This device has seemed helpful in some of the author's research: The respondent is first asked to write down the things he hopes to learn by attending the training program, as on the open-end device "Planning for learning" (p. 66). Then he is asked to turn the page over and fill out this rating:

[27] See Thorndike and Hagen, *op. cit.,* pp. 337–66; and Wrightstone, Justman, and Robbins, *op. cit.,* pp. 156–58 and 163–70, for examples and thorough treatments of how to make sound rating scales.

[28] For samples of ratings of leader behavior, see R. M. Stogdill and A. E. Coons, *Leader behavior: its description and measurement* (Bureau of Business Research, The Ohio State University, 1957), especially pp. 29, 57, 87–88.

RATING SCALE

People differ as to how they feel about a workshop like this, and what they hope to get out of it. In answering below, please be as accurate as you can in assessing *your own real feelings.*

Please read the two statements below (Statement A and Statement B).

Statement A	Statement B
I did write some things on the other side, but I do not have any particular feeling about them one way or the other. I feel pretty matter-of-fact about them.	Thinking about the things I wrote on the other side, I feel very strongly about them. There aren't many things I feel more acutely.

Now decide which one comes closer to describing how you personally feel. Check the answer that fits you best—there are no right or wrong answers.

I feel much more like A than B.	I feel somewhat more like A than B.	I feel slightly more like A than B.	I feel slightly more like B than A.	I feel somewhat more like B than A.	I feel much more like B than A.

Another device for adding stability asks the rater to anchor certain points on the scale. Here is another rating scale, with directions the author has used in asking for ratings from trainers.

TRAINER RATINGS

We wish to have an over-all rating of the effectiveness of the members of your training group. In order to have a careful and discriminating rating, we ask your thoughtful attention to the following procedure.

Please think back over the participants you have had in your various training groups. Most likely, some were outstanding in terms of their sensitivity, diagnostic ability, and action skills, while some seemed to be relatively ineffective in the group. Most were average. On the nine-point Index Scale below, please fill in at least the first name of one of the best all-round participants you have ever worked with at point 8. Fill in the name of one of the least effective participants you have known at point 2. Then try to recall the name of one of the participants who was not more or less effective than most, and write his name at point 5.

INDEX SCALE Over-all effectiveness as a group member	(name)			(name)			(name)	
	↑			↑			↑	
1	2	3	4	5	6	7	8	9

We do not ask you to use the extremes of the scale for your effective and ineffective participants because it is unlikely that any one person will stand at the top or the bottom of any training group in all respects.

Now, please use the attached sheets to rate each member of the training group you are now working with. Go through and make all five ratings for one person before proceeding to the next participant. Use the same Index Scale all the way through to anchor your ratings (that is, compare the participant to be rated with the names you entered in the Index Scale, and circle the number on each one of the five separate scales that seems most appropriate for the participant you are rating.)

Participant: _____

1. **Sensitivity**   (low) 1 2 3 4 5 6 7 8 9 (high)

Is alert to happenings in the group, has ability to pick up things, notice accurately what is going on.

2. **Diagnostic ability**   1 2 3 4 5 6 7 8 9

Is able to understand *why* things happened as they did, has ability to explain group difficulties, as a basis for corrective or supportive action.

3. **Behavioral skill—task**   1 2 3 4 5 6 7 8 9

Helps the group to make progress on the task.

4. **Behavioral skill—maintenance**   1 2 3 4 5 6 7 8 9

Helps to maintain a good working relationship in the group.

5. **Over-all effectiveness as a group member**   1 2 3 4 5 6 7 8 9

A rater who has observed all members of a group may be asked to sort out the names of all group members into categories, as a way of assigning ratings. This requires some careful person-to-person comparison and may add some stability to the rating. For an example, see the next page.

Member rankings

Think of the members of the group as to their relative *effectiveness in helping the group get work done.* Write their names in the appropriate column below. Each column should have only the number of names given in it.

Least effective (1)	Next least (2)	Average effectiveness in this group (6)	Next most (2)	Most effective (1)

A variant of this procedure asks for a top-to-bottom ranking of group members. Note that these methods give judgments relative to other group members, not absolute estimates of the qualities of any given member.

4. *Sociometrics.* Sociometric or nomination techniques ask the respondent to name other persons in the group who fall in certain categories ("I would like to be with this person on a committee"). There is a fair-sized literature indicating that such methods are especially useful for evaluating performance in group situations.[29]

When they are used during training, sociometric methods require group members to pull together in their minds many specific events in the training group, and to come up with an over-all judgment about the behavior of specific other persons, as it has occurred in the group. Thus sociometric judgments may be quite stable and accurate.

Sociometrics have been widely used in the classroom but have focused mainly on acceptance and rejection (who likes whom). However, in using sociometrics as a measurement device for training evaluation—with adults or students—the acceptance-rejection dimension is threatening, and far less appropriate than are other group-relevant dimensions of the sort described below in example *a.*

[29] For a summary, see J. S. Mouton, R. R. Blake, and B. Fruchter, "The reliability of sociometric responses," *Sociometry,* 18:7–40, 1955; and "The validity of sociometric responses," *Sociometry,* 18:181–206, 1955.

For technical material on sociometrics, see C. H. Proctor and C. P. Loomis, "Analysis of sociometric data," pp. 561–87 in Jahoda, Deutsch, and Cook, *op. cit.;* and G. Lindzey and E. F. Borgatta, "Sociometric measurement," pp. 405–48 in Lindzey, *op. cit.*

Two cautions: (1) Planners should not confuse the increased acquaintance and mutual liking that usually develop during training with change in actual adequacy of performance. (2) Data from sociometrics should be treated confidentially, or threat and resistance are likely to ensue. The only exception to this rule occurs when training group members have decided to use relationship charting as an aid to learning (as in Chapter V, 117-19).

EXAMPLES:

a. The nomination technique can be used. Each group member is asked to respond to questions like these:

Who are the one or two members of the training group most effective in helping the group with its task? Least effective?

Which members are the most sensitive to forces in the group? Least sensitive?

Who most frequently plays these roles: summarizer? encourager? opinion giver? clarifier? standard setter? Who least frequently plays these roles?

Who in your training group would you most like to have as chairman of a committee you are working on?

Who in your training group has helped you learn the most about groups?

The usual method of scoring an item like, "Who helps the group most with its task?" is to add up the number of mentions each person receives from the remainder of the group. (This assumes that each member has been asked for a standard number of nominations rather than as many or as few names as he wishes.) Unless the data are to be used to examine things about the group as a whole, like cohesiveness or friendship groupings, graphic plotting methods (sociograms) need not be employed.

b. Sociometric devices can also be set up as rating scales, as rankings, and as "Guess Who" devices (the group member is asked to match behavior descriptions—"Doesn't say much," "Helps the group move ahead"— with names of other members).[30]

c. Sociometric data can be gathered from members of job groups before and after the training program. If one member of the job group attended training, any changes in the sociometric score he received from others would presumably reflect the effects of what he learned.

d. During training, sociometric data can be gathered following a situational test of the sort described under methods of observation (pp. 238-39).

---

[30] See Wrightstone, Justman, and Robbins, *op. cit.*, pp. 200-01, for other examples; also pp. 206-14 for suggestions on constructing and giving sociometric tests. Another useful reference is M. L. Northway and L. Weld, *Sociometric testing: a guide for teachers* (University of Toronto Press, 1957).

5. *Projective methods.* It is possible to gather pencil-and-paper data by methods which present an ambiguous or indeterminate stimulus and ask the respondent to react. Since the stimulus (such as a picture, incomplete sentence, or single word) does not ask for a specific, determined answer, the person's reactions are presumably indicative of his own unique approach to the particular problem being studied. Making infer-ences about *behavior* from data gathered with projective instruments is a risky business—considerable uncertainty is involved. There are several projective approaches, however, that bear some promise in the evaluation of training experiences.

EXAMPLES:

a. The sentence completion technique can provide useful, informal data for planners. The respondent may be asked to finish incomplete sentences like the following:

> The trouble with most groups is
> When I am in a group I
> Most leaders seem to

Data from instruments of this sort are difficult to interpret in more than general-impression terms, but pre- and post-test responses to items like the above can easily be categorized (for example, in terms of favorableness-unfavorableness to group work). Results can be of some help in inter-preting the effects of a training program.[31]

b. Planners may also wish to experiment with using pictures as a way of evoking responses. For example, showing participants a picture of a group situation, and asking them to explain "what has been happening in the situation, what is going on now, and what is likely to happen in the future," can be quite illuminative of people's attitudes toward working in groups. There is some evidence that if the training group as a whole is given the task of agreeing on a story about what is happening in the picture, the result tends to reflect characteristics of the training group as a

---

[31] For an account of a technically well-developed sentence-completion device, see H. A. Thelen's account of the Reactions to Group Situations Test, reported in *Methods for studying work and emotionality in groups* (Human Dynamics Laboratory, University of Chicago, 1954), and in D. Stock and H. A. Thelen, *Emotional dynamics and group culture* (National Training Laboratories, 1958).

For technical advice on sentence-completion techniques, see H. Nash, "Incomplete sen-tences in personality research," *Educational and Psychological Measurement,* 18:569–81, 1958; and A. Dole and F. M. Fletcher, Jr., "Some principles in the construction of incomplete sentences," *Educational and Psychological Measurement,* 15:101–10, 1955.

whole.[32] If individuals are asked to write their own stories, the results will presumably tend to reflect more personal attitudes toward group participation.

c. Word association techniques may also be used to supply data for training evaluation. For example, at the first session of a training group, members may be asked to write down the first word that jumps into their minds when the trainer pronounces a series of words, such as "group," "leader," "consensus," etc. The results can be analyzed for positive connotations ("productive," "helpful," "comfortable," "respect") or negative connotations ("waste," "uniformity," "antagonism," "superficial"). Associations to the same stimulus words near the end of training can be analyzed in the same way, and compared with the pre-test responses.

Note that all three projective methods suggested above are focused on group-relevant matters. The planner who is interested in projective devices will do well to stay on the group level, and should be extremely cautious about making inferences from data gathered by any projective method.

Summary Comment

Some general points may bear repeating. Evaluation of training is best seen as a continuous process engaged in by the people who are responsible for setting up and carrying out training activities. Absolute standards of rigor in evaluation are undesirable, but it is important to make evaluation procedures more and more systematic. Evaluation is needed for immediate steering purposes, and for longer-term assessment purposes. Many instruments can be used to contribute to both ends. The basic step in evaluation planning is clear specification of the learning outcomes which the training is being set up to produce. After that come instrumentation, data collection, analysis and interpretation, and new program planning.

This chapter has stressed evaluation for the improvement of local training activities. Beyond this immediate aim, careful evaluation of

---

[32] See W. E. Henry and H. Guetzkow, "Group projection sketches for the study of small groups," *Journal of Social Psychology*, 33:77–102, 1951; also M. Horwitz and D. Cartwright, "A projective method for the diagnosis of group properties," *Human Relations*, 6:397–410, 1953. The measuring device used is a series of five large pictures of individual and group situations which are used as described above. A rating method, and an over-all judgment method are given for producing scores from the responses to the test.

local programs can make a much-needed broader contribution. Human relations training as a field of inquiry is little more than a decade old. We need far more information about its consequences than we now have, even though many persons in different parts of the country have been working intensively in the sort of programs described here. Reports of local training programs, if given broader circulation, can aid immeasurably in the improvement of group life in today's schools. That improvement is essential if the American school is to realize our hopes for it.

APPENDIX A

Published Accounts of Training Sessions

THE person who wants to know more about how training proceeds can usually profit from studying a description of what happened in a particular training meeting.

Most of the twenty-nine references below are relatively accessible. Some include protocols (direct transcriptions of sessions) and others do not, but the emphasis in all is to analyze the dynamics of training by presenting a concrete case study. Brief annotations follow each reference. Some of the accounts have been presented earlier in the book but are mentioned here again for reference purposes.

M. Barron and G. Krulee. "Case study of a basic skill training group." *Journal of Social Issues,* 4, 2:15–30, 1948.

This is a fairly thorough account of the development of a 15-session, three-week training group held at the National Training Laboratory in Group Development at Bethel, Maine. The nature of the group's activities is described, and occasional snatches of interaction are presented and analyzed. An accompanying article discusses the personality of the trainer who worked with the group.

K. D. Benne and B. Muntyan. *Human relations in curriculum change.* Dryden, 1951.

This collection of readings supplies accounts of many different sorts of training sessions. Usually these are accompanied by analysis or commentary on what is happening in the session. The sessions described here include:

"Training consultants and groups to work together," by L. P. Bradford, pp. 210–16, describes a role-played session designed to increase members' skills in and understandings of the role of the consultant. Two sessions are described, one with some protocol detail. (The same material is presented in "The use of psychodrama for group consultants," same author, *Sociatry,* 1, 2:192–97, June 1947.)

"Diagnosing group difficulties," by L. P. Bradford, K. D. Benne, and R. Lippitt, pp. 145–52, gives a protocol of a group meeting on the job, then analyzes it just as members of a training group might. (The same material is presented in "The promise of group dynamics for education," same authors, *NEA Journal,* 37, 6:35–52, September 1948.)

"Complacency shock and retraining," by L. P. Bradford and P. Sheats, pp. 202–07, describes part of the second session during a summer school workshop for school principals and superintendents. The account shows how a principal is aided to deepen his perception of the feelings of teachers by listening in on a role-played conversation in the "teachers' room." (This material is presented more fully in "Complacency shock as a prerequisite to training," same authors, in *Sociatry,* 2:1 and 2:38–48, April–August 1948.)

"What is role playing?" by C. E. Hendry, R. Lippitt, and A. Zander, gives actual transcriptions of a role-playing scene in a sociology course. The protocol includes the phase of setting up the scene, the scene itself, and some final analysis. The protocol is presented in a two-column approach, with the transcript on the left and the analytic comments on the right. The protocol is followed by some general discussion of methods used in the development of a role-playing situation. (This material is presented by the same authors in "Reality practice as educational method," *Psychodrama Monographs,* No. 9, Beacon House, New York, 1944.)

"Group self-evaluation," by D. H. Jenkins, pp. 161–72, discusses the role of the group observer in giving feedback and gives (pp. 163–65) a brief protocol showing how the observer reported on what had been going on in a meeting. (This material is reported more fully in Jenkins' article, "Feedback and group self-evaluation," *Journal of Social Issues,* 4, 2:50–60, Spring 1948.)

"Changing the administrator's perception," by R. Lippitt, pp. 269–82, describes a session involving role playing with a clarifier. The session was originally presented to some government administrators as a demonstration of a new type of training program. (The same material is presented in "Administrator perception and administrative approval," *Sociatry,* 1, 2:209–19, June 1947.)

"Introducing the group idea to people," by R. Lippitt, L. P. Bradford, and K. D. Benne, pp. 192–202, describes an opening general session for a two-week workshop (reported in R. Lippitt, *Training in community relations,* see below). On pp. 194–201, an edited recording of a role-playing scene is presented, including the introductory remarks of a trainer who served as a clarifier during the scene itself. Some audience participation is also included, plus final summarizing comments by the trainer. (This material is also presented in "Socio-dramatic clarification of leader and group roles as a starting point for effective group functioning," same authors, *Sociatry,* 1, 1:82–91, March 1947.)

In general, the Benne and Muntyan collection accounts are quite helpful, especially in indicating how role playing, when followed by a discussion, works out in an actual setting.

L. P. Bradford, G. L. Lippitt, and J. R. Gibb. "Human relations training in three days." *Adult Leadership,* 4, 10:11–26, April 1956.

> The sequence of activities in a three-day human relations training institute is presented in some detail, using a fictionalized case study approach. General sessions, groups working in planned situations, and "diagnostic groups" (training groups studying their own ongoing processes) are described.

S. M. Corey. *Action research to improve school practices.* Teachers College Bureau of Publications, 1953.

> Chapter VI, "Action research as a way to learn," describes the activities carried on during a one-semester seminar group which met to study the human relations problems of action research consultants. On pp. 113–18, there is an account of a sensitivity training session similar to the session on sensitivity to threat described in Chapter V, pp. 148–49 of the present book. The account is general rather than detailed. Other sections of the chapter deal with methods of assessing needs in a training group, evaluating sessions, and evaluating the training program as a whole.

S. M. Corey, P. M. Halverson, and E. Lowe. *Teachers prepare for discussion group leadership.* Teachers College Bureau of Publications, 1953.

> This describes a half-day training session for discussion group leaders for a reading conference held in a school system. (See Chapter III of the present book, pp. 28–30, for a general account.) The script used for the tape recording is also presented.

S. M. Corey. "An experiment in leadership training." *Educational Administration and Leadership,* 37:321–28, October 1951.

> A general descriptive account of a role-playing scene set up to study the problem of how a leader can behave most effectively when a group attempts to reject his solution to a problem.

J. D. Grambs and J. Axelrod. "Time out for training." *Adult Leadership,* 2:17–20, June 1953.

> This is a relatively detailed account of the third and fourth sessions in a sequence of meetings held with the staff of a community center. The meeting includes six staff members, a director, and an outside consultant. The material is presented with considerable flavor of the actual meeting and dramatizes very well the emotional problems involved in training with a small staff group.

The Human Relations Training Laboratory. *Proceedings.* Second, 1956; Third, 1957. The Human Relations Training Laboratory, Southern Methodist University.

> These are proceedings of a series of two-week training laboratories held in the Southwest. They include detailed content from general sessions, skill

practice group procedures, and detailed anecdotal accounts of training groups engaged in the study of ongoing group processes.

A. F. Klein, *Role playing in leadership training and group problem solving.* Association Press, 1956.

This thorough and helpful book includes several examples of role-playing sessions, including: the setup and action phases (pp. 21–29); a protocol of how a group planned a role-playing situation (pp. 29–33); a protocol of how a role-playing situation arose naturally during the course of a discussion in a training group (pp. 33–35). Also included are a protocol showing how a trainer can warm up an audience and role-playing participants by a public interview (pp. 80–83); and multiple role playing of all audience members in a large meeting (pp. 97–101). There are many other examples, both hypothetical and real, spread through the book.

G. Levit. "Learning through role playing." *Adult Leadership,* 2, 5:9–16, October 1953.

This article presents a detailed case example of a role-playing session, including identification of the group problem, establishing a situation, casting characters, briefing and warming up actors and observers, the actual action, cutting, analyzing the action, deriving generalizations and planning for re-practice, internalizing new insights, re-practice, summary, and evaluation. During the action and analysis phases, detailed transcripts are presented, and analytic comments are added in a column at the side.

R. Lippitt. *Training in community relations: a research exploration toward new group skills.* Harper, 1949.

A thorough account of a two-week workshop for intergroup relations workers, with careful evaluation data included. Accounts of training sessions include: a complete transcript of an opening general session demonstration with clarifier (pp. 81–88); brief excerpts from a training group session in which members are identifying problems they wish to work on (pp. 91–93); a bridging activity in which a back-home episode is role-played (pp. 102–04); a transcript showing role reversal and soliloquizing as training methods (pp. 105–08); a segment of a training group showing trainer comments and group self-evaluation (pp. 111–12); a general session in which trainers and members of different training groups describe and analyze what has been happening in their groups (pp. 114–17); analysis of a role-playing scene of a back-home problem (pp. 123–24) and the construction of several follow-up practice scenes (pp. 124–26); more role playing as a bridging activity (pp. 126–27); analysis of a chairman's role (pp. 128–29); practice in interpreting the workshop to others back home (pp. 123–33).

On pp. 136–55 is presented a synthesized "diary" of a delegate to the workshop (actually constructed from observations and records), indicating the sequence of activities and how a typical member might have reacted to them.

M. B. Miles and S. M. Corey. "The first cooperative curriculum research institute." Appendix B in *Research for curriculum improvement,* 1957 Yearbook, Association for Supervision and Curriculum Development. The Association, 1957.

> This is a description of a one-week training institute which focused on human relations skills and research techniques for curriculum workers. It includes accounts of general sessions (pp. 316–21); a training group which met for twelve hours (pp. 321–25), and several special interest groups on particular topics (pp. 325–28). The accounts are rather general, but give some picture of how the activities of a week-long institute or workshop experience fit together in an over-all sequence. A schedule of the week is given on p. 310.

National Training Laboratory in Group Development. *Reports of Summer Laboratory Sessions.* First (1947), Bulletin No. 1; Second (1948), Bulletin No. 3; Ninth (1955), Bulletin No. 6; Tenth (1956), Bulletin No. 7; Eleventh (1957), Bulletin No. 8; Twelfth (1958), Bulletin No. 9. National Training Laboratories.

> These are proceedings of the three-week laboratories held at Bethel. They give detailed content from general sessions, and detailed methods used in skill practice sessions, as well as general information about the Laboratory.

National Training Laboratory in Group Development. *Explorations in human relations training; an assessment of experience, 1947–53.* National Training Laboratories, 1954.

> A thorough account is given here of the summer training sessions held at Bethel, Maine. Pp. 4–9 present a fictionalized account of a visitor's experience during one day, including his reactions to the general climate of the conference, a theory session on "hidden agenda," a training group engaged in the study of ongoing group behavior, a skill practice session, a consultation session, an off-the-record group in which members evaluated their experiences during the day, and a general session on initiating social action.
>
> On pp. 36–44 are presented detailed procedures used in two skill practice sessions (decision making in groups, and working with feelings of like-dislike in groups).

A. H. Passow, M. B. Miles, S. M. Corey, and D. C. Draper. *Training curriculum leaders for cooperative research.* Teachers College Bureau of Publications, 1955.

> This collection describes the procedures used during a series of ten two-day meetings with public school personnel. The training sessions were aimed at improving human relations and action research skills. The accounts of specific sessions include a sequence of two days' activities in one of the conferences (pp. 18–21); intermittent process analysis during agenda building (pp. 23–25); analysis of the chairman's role (pp. 26–31); a study exercise on "hidden agenda"

(pp. 31–36); a perception check exercise (pp. 36–38); an experimental tryout of methods of orienting absent members (pp. 38–40); many different kinds of bridging activities, including team planning sessions, team reports, and analysis of one member's back-home problems (pp. 45–53); and an informal evaluation session of one of the two-day conferences (pp. 56–57).

H. A. Thelen. *The dynamics of groups at work*. The University of Chicago Press, 1954.

Chapter V on "Training for group participation: the laboratory method" has a detailed account of the history of one training group over ten weekly three-hour meetings (pp. 140–65,) plus analysis (pp. 165–69). The account is sequential and anecdotal, interspersed with thoughtful analytic comments on what seemed to be happening in the group. This is perhaps the best available account of how a skilled trainer can work with a training group, building training activities as needs emerge. The trainer in the account has considerable background in the study of small groups, and much training experience. The reader who is a prospective trainer in school groups should not expect that his groups should or will approximate the account presented here, but can learn much from it about sequence and flow of training activities, and the general stance of the trainer in relation to the group.

I. R. Weschler and J. Reisel. *Inside a sensitivity training group*. Human Relations Research Group, Institute of Industrial Relations, and Graduate School of Business Administration, University of California, 1958.

Thirty sessions of a sensitivity training group are described by means of (1) trainer recollections and comments; (2) excerpts from group members' diaries; (3) observations from a psychologist who attended sessions and interviewed the trainer afterward. The approach taken emphasizes personality primarily, rather than group functioning, and may be profitably compared with the Thelen reference above.

APPENDIX B

A Selected Library of Resources

WHICH of the hundred-and-sixty-odd references listed in this book would be most useful as a core library for a school system conducting training programs of the sort described in this book? Below are described 13 books, 15 pamphlets and reports, and 17 back issues of magazines and journals which provide a good background of resources. The total cost is about $85 (depending on discounts). Where less money than this is available, the annotations below may help the reader in choosing materials best suited to his immediate situation. Some of the materials can be purchased more cheaply in bulk.

Adult Education Association of the U. S. A. Leadership Pamphlet series. 743 No. Wabash, Chicago 11, Illinois.

These are short treatments of specific problem areas like those named below. The content is drawn from previous issues of *Adult Leadership*, with some new material added. Most relevant pamphlets are:

1. How to lead discussions.
4. Understanding how groups work.
5. How to teach adults.
6. How to use role playing and other tools for learning.
7. Supervision and consultation.
8. Training group leaders.
9. Conducting workshops and institutes.
11. Conferences that work.
14. Better boards and committees.
15. Streamlining parliamentary procedure.

Adult Leadership. Adult Education Association of the U. S. A. 743 No. Wabash, Chicago 11, Illinois.

Many back issues of this magazine were specifically designed to aid training programs of the sort described in this book. (See Bibliography for mention of specific articles). As with the pamphlets named above, the treatment is highly concrete and practical. The most helpful and relevant issues (topic named is sometimes an issue topic, sometimes a "Workshop" or subsection of the issue) are:

Vol. 1, No. 2, June 1952. Spotlight on leadership.
Vol. 1, No. 7, December 1952. Improving large meetings.
Vol. 1, No. 8, January 1953. Spotlight on member roles.
Vol. 2, No. 1, May 1953. Conferences that work.
Vol. 1, No. 11, April 1953. Evaluating program and performance.
Vol. 2, No. 2, June 1953. Leadership training.
Vol. 2, No. 4, September 1953. Committees, boards, and officers.
Vol. 1, No. 10, March 1953. Leading discussions.
Vol. 2, No. 5, October 1953. Social inventions for learning.
Vol. 2, No. 7, December 1953. The dynamics of work groups.
Vol. 3, No. 2, June 1954. The single-shot meeting.
Vol. 3, No. 3, September 1954. The larger organization.
Vol. 3, No. 10, April 1955. Effective consultation.
Vol. 4, No. 10, April 1956. Human relations training in three days.
Vol. 4, No. 7, January 1956. Workshops and institutes.
Vol. 5, No. 3, September 1956. Effective committees and work groups.

(Two collections, entitled *Leader's Digest,* vols. 1 and 2, also include much of the material from vols. 1 and 2 of the magazine.)

R. Beckhard. *How to plan and conduct workshops and conferences.* Association Press, 1956.

Brief, practical, clear discussion of what is involved in setting up, staging, and evaluating any short workshop or conference.

K. D. Benne and B. Muntyan, eds. *Human relations in curriculum change.* Dryden Press, 1951.

A compendium of readings drawn from many different sources. Sections on theory and concepts, training, use of group methods, democratic ethics, problem-solving. See annotations in Appendix A.

D. Cartwright and A. Zander, eds. *Group dynamics.* Row, Peterson and Co., 1953.

A collection of 35 research reports, organized into sections on general approaches to the study of groups, cohesiveness, standards, goals, structural properties, and leadership. Introductory chapters for each section especially helpful.

S. M. Corey, P. M. Halverson, and E. Lowe. *Teachers prepare for discussion group leadership.* Teachers College Bureau of Publications, 1953.

Straightforward account of how tape-recorded episodes were used to train leaders for a one-day conference in a school system. Script for episodes included. (See pp. 28–30 in present book for more detail.)

J. R. Gibb and L. M. Gibb. *Applied group dynamics*. National Training Laboratories, 1955.

A laboratory manual designed to be used as a resource guide by small training groups in programs of the sort described in the present book. Contains a wide range of materials on features of groups, observation methods, roles of members, leadership. Many suggested activities.

P. Hare, E. F. Borgatta, and R. F. Bales. *Small groups*. Alfred A. Knopf, 1955.

A collection of 55 research reports dealing with small groups. Includes general theoretical statements, studies of the individual in social situations, and studies of groups as systems of social interaction. An annotated bibliography includes 584 core studies of small groups done during the period 1900–54. An excellent resource.

L. E. Hock. *Using committees in the classroom*. Rinehart and Co., 1958.

Practical suggestions for the teacher who wishes to use small groups as a regular part of classroom activity.

A. F. Klein. *Role playing in leadership training and group problem solving*. Association Press, 1956.

Specific suggestions on setting up and carrying out role playing. See annotation in Appendix A.

M. Knowles and H. Knowles. *How to develop better leaders*. Association Press, 1955.

Concise, concrete ideas on leadership development, including the workshop approach and on-the-job activities. Specific methods and resources reviewed.

R. Lippitt. *Training in community relations: A research exploration toward new group skills*. Harper and Brothers, 1949.

A report of a two-week workshop for intergroup relations workers, with evaluation data included. This workshop was the immediate forerunner of the summer sessions at the National Training Laboratory in Group Development at Bethel, Maine, and was the source of many training procedures later used there. See annotation in Appendix A.

M. B. Miles. *Learning to work in groups*. Teachers College Bureau of Publications, 1959.

National Training Laboratory in Group Development. *Explorations in human relations training; an assessment of experience, 1947–53*. National Training Laboratories, 1954.

Account of the NTLGD summer training sessions, including a typical day at Bethel, review of research findings, over-all rationale of training approaches used, unsolved problems. See annotation in Appendix A.

W. W. Reeder. "Some methods and tools to increase interest, participation and teaching effectiveness." Cornell Extension Bulletin 907. Cornell University, 1954.

> Describes a variety of specific tools, such as small and large group discussion, panel, question-answer period, role playing, lecture, symposium, forum; gives suggestions for assembling these into effective meeting designs.

Review of Educational Research, 33:289–308, 1953. American Educational Research Association, 1201 Sixteenth St., N. W., Washington 6, D. C. (Includes K. D. Benne and G. Levit, "The nature of groups; and helping groups improve their operation," and M. Horwitz, "The conceptual status of group dynamics.")

> Both articles review research and theory relating to small groups; the first also outlines ways of improving group functioning (training, changing group composition, size, or task).

M. G. Ross and C. E. Hendry. *New understandings of leadership.* Association Press, 1957.

> Clear overview of leadership theory, review of research findings on leader qualities, leader activities, and group influences on the leader. Final section discusses implications and outlines a tentative leadership development program.

R. Strang. *Group work in education.* Harper and Brothers, 1958.

> Thorough discussion of use of small groups in all parts of the school program. Many references; unusually detailed and specific.

H. A. Thelen. *The dynamics of groups at work.* University of Chicago Press, 1954.

> The first section is a thoughtful examination of group functioning in many different settings—community action groups, classroom teaching, in-service training, administration, training programs, and large meetings. The second section presents conceptual material serving to unify and explain the earlier applications, dealing with a wide range of ideas (ex: membership in groups, group control systems, leadership, the group in the community, work and emotionality). See annotation in Appendix A.

R. L. Thorndike and E. Hagen. *Measurement and evaluation in psychology and education.* John Wiley and Sons, 1955.

> Thorough, helpful treatment of the entire range of technical and practical problems involved in evaluation and measurement.

BIBLIOGRAPHY

ALL books, articles, pamphlets, and duplicated materials mentioned in the text and footnotes are listed here alphabetically by author. Films are not included; to locate specific films see pp. 195–98. A list of film producers responsible for the films named in the text appears after this bibliography.

Adult Education Association of the U. S. A. "Designing the training group." *Training group leaders.* Chicago: The Association, 1956.

Adult leadership. (Contributors: A. V. Atkins *et al.*) "Workshop on the single-shot meeting." 3, 2:11–26, June 1954.

Adult leadership. (Issue Committee: F. Anderson *et al.*) "Conferences that work." 2, 1:2–24, May 1953.

Adult leadership. (Issue Committee: R. Beckhard *et al.*) "Improving large meetings." 1, 7:2–29, December 1952.

Adult leadership. (Issue Committee: R. R. Blake *et al.*) "Spotlight on member roles." 1, 8, January 1953.

Adult leadership. (Issue Committee: R. R. Blake *et al.*) "Tool Kit: Training in member roles." 1, 8:17–23, January 1953.

Adult leadership. (Issue Committee: S. M. Corey *et al.*) "Evaluating program and performance." 1, 11:1–23, April 1953.

Adult leadership. (Issue Committee: R. Canter *et al.*) "Can leadership training be liberal education?" 2, 2:1, June 1953.

Adult leadership. (Issue Committee: R. Canter *et al.*) "Improving the processes of leadership training." 2, 2:11–16, June 1953.

Adult leadership. "Resources: summer taining opportunities." April and May issues, current year.

Adult leadership. (Workshop Committee: L. P. Bradford *et al.*) "The dynamics of work groups." 2, 7:8–27, 1953.

Adult leadership. (Workshop Committee: L. P. Bradford, J. R. Gibb and G. L. Lippitt) "Human relations training in three days." 4, 10:11–26, April 1956.

Adult leadership. (Workshop Committee: M. R. Goodson, J. Jackson and G. Jensen) "Workshop on the larger organization." 3:13–29, September 1954.

Adult leadership. (Workshop Committee: N. McKeever *et al.*) "Workshop: effective consultation." 3, 10:13–26, April 1955.

Allport, G. W. and Odbert, H. S. "Trait names: a psycho-lexical study." *Psychological Monographs*, Vol. 47, No. 1, No. 211. Princeton, N. J.: Psychological Review Co., 1936.

Andrews, K. R. *The case method of teaching; human relations and administration.* Cambridge: Harvard University Press, 1953.

Argyris, C. *Role playing in action.* Ithaca: New York State School of Industrial and Labor Relations, Cornell University, n.d.

Association for Supervision and Curriculum Development. *Research for curriculum improvement.* 1957 Yearbook. Washington, D. C.: The Association, 1957.

Bales, R. F. *Interaction process analysis.* Cambridge: Addison-Wesley, 1950.

Baumgartel, H. "An analysis of the validity of perceived change measures." Ann Arbor: Institute for Social Research, University of Michigan, 1954 (mimeo).

Barron, M. K. and Krulee, G. "Case study of a basic skill training group." *Journal of Social Issues*, 4, 2, 25:28, Spring 1948.

Bebell, C. S. "Getting meaning from research." *Research for curriculum improvement.* 1957 Yearbook, Association for Supervision and Curriculum Development. Washington, D. C.: The Association, 1957.

Beckhard, R. *How to plan and conduct workshops and conferences.* New York: Association Press, 1956.

Benne, K. D. and Levit, G. "The nature of groups; helping groups improve their operation." *Review of Educational Research*, 33:289-308, 1953.

Benne, K. D. and Muntyan, B., eds. *Human relations in curriculum change.* New York: Dryden Press, 1951.

Benne, K. D. and Sheats, P. "Functional roles of group members." *Journal of Social Issues*, 4, 2:41-49, 1948.

Bennis, W. G. and Shepard, H. A. "A theory of group development." *Human Relations*, 9:415-37, 1956.

Bird, C. *Social psychology.* New York: D. Appleton-Century Co., 1940.

Bond, B. W. *Group discussion-decision.* Minneapolis: Minnesota State Department of Health, 1956.

Borgatta, E. F. "An analysis of three levels of response: an approach to some relationships among dimensions of personality." *Sociometry*, 14:267-316, 1951.

Bradford, L. P. "Training consultants and groups to work together." *Human relations in curriculum change*, K. D. Benne and B. Muntyan, eds. New York: Dryden Press, 1957.

Buchanan, P. C. "Evaluating the results of supervisory training." *Personnel*, 33:362-70, 1957.

Buchanan, P. C. "Testing the validity of an evaluation program." *Personnel*, 34:78-81, 1957.

Buros, O. K., ed. *Fourth Mental Measurements Yearbook.* Highland Park, N. J.: Gryphon Press, 1953.

Business Information Bureau, Cleveland Public Library. "Role playing, or dramatization in training methods." *Business Information Sources*, 26:1-4, February 1955.

Cabot, H. and Kahl, J. A. *Human relations: concepts and cases in concrete social science.* Cambridge: Harvard University Press, 1953.

Campbell, D. T. "Factors relevant to the validity of experiments in social settings." *Psychological Bulletin,* 54:297–312, 1957.

Cannell, C. F. and Kahn, R. L. "The collection of data by interviewing." *Research methods in the behavioral sciences,* L. Festinger and D. Katz, eds. New York: Dryden Press, 1953.

Cartwright, D. "Achieving change in people: some applications of group dynamics theory." *Human Relations,* 4:381–92, 1951.

Cartwright, D. and Zander, A., eds. *Group dynamics.* Evanston: Row, Peterson and Co., 1953.

Clark, T. C. and Miles, M. B. "Human relations training for school administrators." *Journal of Social Issues,* 10, 2:25–39, 1954.

Corey, S. M. *Action research to improve school practices.* New York: Bureau of Publications, Teachers College, Columbia, 1953.

Corey, S. M. "An experiment in leadership training." *Educational Administration and Leadership,* 37:321–28, October 1951.

Corey, S. M. and Halverson, P. M. "The educational leader's ideas about his interpersonal relations." *Bulletin, National Association of Secondary School Principals,* 36:57–63, 1952.

Corey, S. M., Halverson, P. M., and Lowe, E. *Teachers prepare for discussion group leadership.* New York: Bureau of Publications, Teachers College, Columbia, 1953.

Cunningham, R. *Understanding group behavior of boys and girls.* New York: Bureau of Publications, Teachers College, Columbia, 1951.

Dale, E. *Audio-visual methods in teaching.* New York: Dryden Press, 1954.

Dole, A. and Fletcher, F. M., Jr. "Some principles in the construction of incomplete sentences." *Educational and Psychological Measurement,* 15:101–10, 1955.

Doll, R. C., Halverson, P. M., Lawrence, R. E. and Lowe, E. "An experiment in training teachers for discussion group leadership." *Educational Leadership,* 10–112–17, November 1952.

Doll, R. C., Passow, A. H., and Corey, S. M. *Organizing for curriculum improvement.* New York: Bureau of Publications, Teachers College, Columbia, 1953.

Educational Film Guide. F. A. Krahn, ed. New York: H. W. Wilson Co., 1953. Annual supplements.

Fattu, N. A. and Blain, B. *Selected films for teacher education: a bibliography.* Bloomington: Indiana University, 1950.

Festinger, L. and Katz, D. *Research methods in the behavioral sciences.* New York: Dryden Press, 1953.

Films for classroom use. New York: Teaching Film Custodians, 1952. Supplements 1954, 1956.

Flanagan, J. C. "The critical incident technique." *Psychological Bulletin,* 51:327–58, 1954.

Flanders, N. and associates. *Teaching with groups.* Minneapolis: Burgess Publishing Co., 1954.

Foshay, A. W. "Action research as imaginative hindsight." *Educational Research Bulletin,* 34:169–71, October 12, 1955.

French, D. G. *An approach to measuring results in social work.* New York: Columbia University Press, 1952.

French, W. *Behavioral goals of general education in high school.* New York: Russell Sage Foundation, 1957.

Gibb, J. R. "A norm-centered view of T-group training." *Theories of T-group training,* L. P. Bradford and J. R. Gibb, eds. Washington, D. C.: National Training Laboratories; in preparation.

Gibb, J. R. and Gibb, L. M. *Applied group dynamics.* Washington, D. C.: National Training Laboratories, 1955.

Golden, O. H. "Training techniques, a bibliographic review." Chicago: Industrial Relations Center, University of Chicago, September 1955.

Grambs, J. D. and Axelrod J. "Time out for training." *Adult Leadership,* 2:17–20, June 1953.

Griffiths, D. E. *Human relations in school administration.* New York: Appleton-Century-Crofts, 1956.

Gropper, G. L. *The critical requirements of conference behavior.* Pittsburgh, The Maynard Foundation, 1956.

Hamburg, M. *Case studies in elementary school administration.* New York: Bureau of Publications, Teachers College, Columbia, 1957.

Hare, P., Borgatta, E. F. and Bales, R. F. *Small groups.* New York: Alfred A. Knopf, 1955.

Hendry, C. E., Lippitt, R. and Zander, A. F. "What is role playing?" *Human relations in curriculum change,* K. D. Benne and B. Muntyan, eds. New York: Dryden Press, 1951.

Henry, W. E. and Guetzkow, H. "Group projection sketches for the study of small groups." *Journal of Social Psychology,* 33:77–102, 1951.

Herrick, V. E. "The evaluation of change in programs of in-service education." *In-service education.* 1957 Yearbook, National Society for the Study of Education. Chicago: University of Chicago Press, 1957.

Herrick, V. E. and Harris, C. W. "Handling data." *Research for curriculum improvement.* 1957 Yearbook, Association for Supervision and Curriculum Development. Washington, D. C.: The Association, 1957.

Heyns, R. W. and Zander, A. F. "Observation of group behavior." *Research methods in the behavioral sciences,* L. Festinger and D. Katz, eds. New York: Dryden Press, 1953.

Hillway, T. *Introduction to research.* Boston: Houghton Mifflin Co., 1956.

Hock, L. E. *Using committees in the classroom.* New York: Rinehart and Co., 1958.

Hodgson, D. and Bullen, H. J. *How to use a tape recorder.* New York: Hastings House, 1957.

Horace Mann-Lincoln Institute Staff. *How to construct a sociogram.* New York: Bureau of Publications, Teachers College, Columbia, Ninth edition, 1957.

Horwitz, M. "The conceptual status of group dynamics." *Review of Educational Research,* 33:309–28, 1953.

Horwitz, M. and Cartwright, D. "A projective method for the diagnosis of group properties." *Human Relations,* 6:397–410, 1953.

Hovland, C. I. "Effects of the mass media of communication." *Handbook of social psychology,* G. Lindzey, ed. Cambridge: Addison-Wesley, 1954.

Human Relations Training Laboratory, The. *Proceedings.* Second, 1956; Third, 1957. Dallas: The Human Relations Training Laboratory, Southern Methodist University.

Jahoda, M., Deutsch, M., and Cook, S. W., eds. *Research methods in social relations,* vol. 1, "Basic processes"; vol. 2, "Selected techniques." New York: Dryden Press, 1951.

Jehring, J. J. *A guide to audio-visual material in industrial and labor relations.* Bulletin No. 22. Ithaca: New York School of Industrial and Labor Relations, Cornell University, August 1952.

Jenkins, D. H. "Feedback and group self-evaluation." *Journal of Social Issues,* 4:50–60, Spring 1948.

Jenkins, D. H. "Force field analysis applied to a school situation." *Human relations in curriculum change,* K. D. Benne and B. Muntyan, eds. New York: Dryden Press, 1951.

Jenkins, W. O. "A review of leadership studies with particular reference to military problems." *Psychological Bulletin,* 44:54–79, 1947.

Jensen, G. "The school as a social system." *Educational Research Bulletin,* 33:38–46, February 10, 1954.

Kahn, R. L. and Cannell, C. F. *The dynamics of interviewing.* New York: John Wiley and Sons, 1957.

Klein, A. F. *Role playing in leadership training and group problem solving.* New York: Association Press, 1956.

Knickerbocker, I. "Leadership: a conception and some implications." *Journal of Social Issues,* 4, 3:23–40, 1948.

Knowles, M. S. and Knowles, H. F. *How to develop better leaders.* New York: Association Press, 1955.

Korb, L. D. *Training the supervisor.* United States Civil Service Commission, Personnel Methods Series No. 4. Washington, D. C.: Superintendent of Documents, U. S. Government Printing Office, 1956.

Leavitt, H. J. and Mueller, R. A. H. "Some effects of feedback on communication." *Human Relations,* 4:401–10, 1951.

Lerner, H. and Kelman, H. C., eds. "Group methods in psychotherapy, social work and adult education." *Journal of Social Issues,* 8, 2, 1952 (entire issue).

Lesser, S. O. and Peter, H. W. "Training foreign nationals in the United States." UNESCO, *Some applications of behavioural research,* R. Likert and S. P. Hayes, eds. Paris: UNESCO, 1957.

Levit, G. "Learning through role playing." *Adult Leadership,* 2, 5:9–16, October 1953.

Lewin, K. "Group decision and social change." *Readings in social psychology,* E. E. Maccoby, T. M. Newcomb, and E. L. Hartley, eds. New York: Henry Holt and Co., 1958.

Lewin, K. *Resolving social conflicts.* New York: Harper and Brothers, 1948.

Lewin, K. "Studies in group decision." *Group dynamics,* D. Cartwright and A. Zander, eds. Evanston: Row, Peterson and Co., 1953.

Lewin, K. and Grabbe, P. "Conduct, knowledge, and acceptance of new values." *Resolving social conflicts.* New York: Harper and Brothers, 1948.

Lindzey, G., ed. *Handbook of social psychology.* Cambridge: Addison-Wesley, 1954.

Lindzey, G. and Borgatta, E. F. "Sociometric measurement." *Handbook of social psychology,* G. Lindzey, ed. Cambridge: Addison-Wesley, 1954.

Lippitt, G. L. "How to get results from a group." *Office Executive,* January 1955, pp. 13-15.

Lippitt, R. *Training in community relations: A research exploration toward new group skills.* New York: Harper and Brothers, 1949.

Lippitt, R., Watson, J., Kallen, D. and Zipf, S. *Evaluation of a human relations laboratory program.* National Training Laboratories, Monograph No. 3. New York: New York University Press, 1959.

Lloyd-Jones, E., Barry, R. *et al. Case studies in human relationships in secondary school.* New York: Bureau of Publications, Teachers College, Columbia, 1956.

Maccoby, E. E. and Jacoby, N. "The interview: a tool of social science." *Handbook of social psychology,* G. Lindzey, ed. Cambridge: Addison-Wesley, 1954.

Mackenzie, G. N., Corey, S. M. and associates. *Instructional leadership.* New York: Bureau of Publications, Teachers College, Columbia, 1954.

Maier, N. R. F. *Principles of human relations.* New York: John Wiley and Sons, 1952.

Maier, N. R. F., Solem, A. R. and Maier, A. A. *Supervisory and executive development: A manual for role playing.* New York: John Wiley and Sons, 1957.

Mann, J. "Experimental evaluations of role playing." *Psychological Bulletin,* 53:227-34, 1956.

Marshall, R. and Marshall, M. *Your tape recorder.* New York: Greenberg, Publisher, 1955.

Miel, A. *Cooperative procedures in learning.* New York: Bureau of Publications, Teachers College, Columbia, 1952.

Miel, A. "How to use experts and consultants." *Human relations in curriculum change,* K. D. Benne and B. Muntyan, eds. New York: Dryden Press, 1951.

Miles, M. B. "Human relations in cooperative research." *Research for curriculum improvement.* 1957 Yearbook, Association for Supervision and Curriculum Development. Washington, D. C.: The Association, 1957.

Miles, M. B. "Human relations training: how a group grows." *Teachers College Record,* 55:90-96, November 1953.

Miles, M. B. "The Leadership Training Project." *Progress Report,* Horace Mann-Lincoln Institute of School Experimentation, Teachers College, Columbia, 1958.

Miles, M. B. "Your professional meetings." *Nursing Outlook,* 2:469-71, 1954.

Miles, M. B. and Corey, S. M. "The first cooperative curriculum research institute." *Research for curriculum improvement.* 1957 Yearbook, Association for Supervision and Curriculum Development. Washington, D. C.: The Association, 1957.

Miles, M. B. and Passow, A. H. "Training in the skills needed for in-service education programs." *Fifty-sixth Yearbook,* National Society for the Study of Education. Chicago: University of Chicago Press, 1957.

Mooney, R. "The researcher himself." *Research for curriculum improvement.* 1957 Yearbook, Association for Supervision and Curriculum Development. Washington, D. C.: The Association, 1957.

Morris, G. *Practical guidance methods for principals and teachers.* New York: Harper and Brothers, 1952.

Mouton, J. S., Blake, R. R. and Fruchter, B. "The reliability of sociometric responses." *Sociometry,* 18:7–40, 1955.

Mouton, J. S., Blake, R. R. and Fruchter, B. "The validity of sociometric responses." *Sociometry,* 18:181–206, 1955.

Nash, H. "Incomplete sentences in personality research." *Educational and Psychological Measurement,* 18:569–81, 1958.

National Training Laboratory in Group Development. *Reports of Summer Laboratory Sessions:* First, 1947, Bull. No. 1; Second, 1948, Bull. No. 3; Ninth, 1955, Bull. No. 6; Tenth, 1956, Bull. No. 7; Eleventh, 1957, Bull. No. 8; Twelfth, 1958, Bull. No. 9. Washington, D. C.: National Education Association.

National Training Laboratory in Group Development. *Explorations in human relations training; an assessment of experience 1947–53.* Washington, D. C.: National Education Association, 1953.

National Training Laboratory in Group Development. "Leadership and participation in large group meetings." Bulletin No. 4. Washington, D. C.: National Education Association, 1951.

National Training Laboratory in Group Development. NTLGD Delegate Take-home Packet, Summer Session 1954. Washington, D. C.: National Training Laboratories, 1954.

N E T Film Service. *1958 Descriptive Catalog.* Bloomington: Audio-visual Center, Indiana University.

Nichtenhauser, A. *et al. Films in psychiatry, psychology, and mental health.* New York: Health Education Council, Medical Audio-visual Institute, American Medical College, 1953.

Northway, M. L. and Weld, L. *Sociometric testing; a guide for teachers.* Toronto: University of Toronto Press, 1957.

Nylen, D. and Dick, W. "A program of group study and human relations training." Seattle: Administrative and Service Center, Seattle Public Schools, n.d. (mimeographed).

Osborn, A. F. *Applied imagination.* New York: Charles Scribner's Sons, 1953.

Passow, A. H., Miles, M. B., Corey, S. M. and Draper, D. C. *Training curriculum leaders for cooperative research.* New York: Bureau of Publications, Teachers College, Columbia, 1955.

Proctor, C. H. and Loomis, C. P. "Analysis of sociometric data." *Research methods in social relations,* M. Jahoda, M. Deutsch and S. W. Cook, eds. vol. 2. New York: Dryden Press, 1951.

Reeder, W. W. "Some methods and tools to increase interest, participation and teaching effectiveness." Cornell Extension Bulletin 907. Ithaca: Cornell University, 1954.

Reid, S., Carpenter, A. and Daugherty, A. R. *A directory of 3300 16 mm. film libraries.* Washington, D. C.: United States Department of Health, Education and Welfare, Office of Education, 1956.

Riesman, D. *Individualism reconsidered.* Glencoe, Ill.: Free Press, 1954.

Riesman, D. *The lonely crowd.* New Haven: Yale University Press, 1950.

Rogers, C. R. *Client-centered therapy.* Boston: Houghton Mifflin Co., 1951.

Ross, M. G. and Hendry, C. E. *New understandings of leadership.* New York: Association Press, 1957.

Schuman, C. S. and Tarcov, O. "To clarify our problems: a guide to role-playing." New York: Anti-Defamation League of B'nai B'rith, n.d.

Shachter, S. "Deviation, rejection and communication." *Group dynamics,* D. Cartwright and A. Zander, eds. Evanston: Row, Peterson and Co., 1953.

Shaftel, G. and Shaftel, F. R. "Role playing the problem story, an approach to human relations in the classroom." New York: National Conference of Christians and Jews, 1952.

Sharp, G. *Curriculum development as re-education of the teacher.* New York: Bureau of Publications, Teachers College, Columbia, 1951.

Sheatsley, P. B. "The art of interviewing, and a guide to interviewer selection and training." *Research methods in social relations,* M. Jahoda, M. Deutsch and S. W. Cook, eds. 2 vols. New York: Dryden Press, 1951.

Stock, D. and Thelen, H. A. *Emotional dynamics and group culture.* Washington, D. C.: National Training Laboratories, 1958.

Stogdill, R. M. "Personal factors associated with leadership: a survey of the literature." *Journal of Psychology,* 25:37–71, 1948.

Stogdill, R. M. and Coons, A. E. *Leader behavior: its description and measurement.* Columbus: Bureau of Business Research, Ohio State University, 1957.

Strang, R. *Group work in education.* New York: Harper and Brothers, 1958.

Thelen, H. A. *Methods for studying work and emotionality in groups.* Chicago: Human Dynamics Laboratory, University of Chicago, 1954.

Thelen, H. A. "Resistance to change of teaching methods." *Progressive Education,* 26:208–14, May 1949.

Thelen, H. A. *The dynamics of groups at work.* Chicago: University of Chicago Press, 1954.

Thelen, H. A. and Dickerman, W. "Stereotypes and the growth of groups." *Educational Leadership,* 6:309–16, February 1949.

Thorndike, R. L. and Hagen, E. *Measurement and evaluation in psychology and education.* New York: John Wiley and Sons, 1955.

Torrance, E. P. "Perception of group functioning as a predictor of group performance." *Journal of Social Psychology,* 42:271–82, 1955.

University of Illinois Lay-Professional Conferences on Education. "The service roles which groups require." *Human relations in curriculum change,* K. D. Benne and B. Muntyan, eds. New York: Dryden Press, 1951.

Watson, J. and Lippitt, R. L. *Learning across cultures*. Ann Arbor: Research Center for Group Dynamics, Institute for Social Research, University of Michigan, 1955.

Wendt, P. R. *Audio-visual instruction*. Washington, D. C.: National Education Association, 1957.

Weschler, I. R. and Reisel, J. "Inside a sensitivity training group." Los Angeles: Human Relations Research Group, Institute of Industrial Relations, Graduate School of Business Administration, University of California, 1958 (mimeo.).

Weschler, I. R., Tannenbaum, R. and Zenger, J. H. "Yardsticks for human relations training." Chicago: Adult Education Association, 1957.

Wittich, W. A. and Schuller, C. F. *Audio-visual materials: their nature and use*. New York: Harper and Brothers, 1957.

Withall, J. "An objective measurement of a teacher's classroom interaction." *Journal of Educational Psychology*, 47:203–12, 1956.

Wrightstone, J. W., Justman, J. and Robbins, I. *Evaluation in modern education*. New York: American Book Co., 1956.

Whyte, W. H. *The organization man*. New York: Simon and Schuster, 1956.

Zander, A. F. "Systematic observation of small face-to-face groups"; and "Data collection: Observational methods." *Research methods in social relations*, M. Jahoda, M. Deutsch and S. Cook, eds. 2 vols. New York: Dryden Press, 1951.

Film producers

This list gives the producers of the films listed in the text. There are over three thousand film libraries in the United States (see reference by Reid *et al.* in the bibliography above), and films can usually be readily obtained through them by reference to the *Educational Film Guide* (see bibliography above).

Brandon Films, Inc., 200 West 57th Street, New York 19, New York.

Bureau of Publications, Teachers College, Columbia University, 525 West 120th Street, New York 27, New York.

Encyclopaedia Britannica Films, 1150 Wilmette Avenue, Wilmette, Illinois.

General Electric Co., 1 River Road, Schenectady 5, New York.

Henry Strauss and Co., 31 West 53rd Street, New York 19, New York.

Iowa State College, Film Production Unit, Alice Norton House, Ames, Iowa.

McGraw-Hill Book Co., Text-Film Department, 330 West 42nd Street, New York 36, New York.

Modern Talking Picture Service Inc., 3 East 54th Street, New York 22, New York.

National Film Board of Canada, Canada House, 680 Fifth Avenue, New York 19, New York.

National Training Laboratories, 1201 Sixteenth Street, N. W., Washington 6, D. C.

State University of Iowa, Bureau of Audio-Visual Instruction, Iowa City, Iowa.

Teaching Film Custodians, Inc., 25 West 43rd Street, New York 36, New York.

United World Films, 1445 Park Avenue, New York 29, New York.

INDEX